Poverty, Economic Reform & Income Distribution in Latin America

Critical Perspectives on
Latin America's Economy and Society

Series Editor
James Dietz, California State University–Fullerton

Editorial Board
Victor Bulmer-Thomas, Institute for Latin American Studies,
University of London

Gary Gereffi, Department of Sociology,
Duke University

Osvaldo Sunkel, CEPAL,
Santiago, Chile

Janet Tanski, Department of Economics,
New Mexico State University

Poverty, Economic Reform & Income Distribution in Latin America

edited by
Albert Berry

LYNNE
RIENNER
PUBLISHERS

BOULDER
LONDON

Published in the United States of America in 1998 by
Lynne Rienner Publishers, Inc.
1800 30th Street, Boulder, Colorado 80301

and in the United Kingdom by
Lynne Rienner Publishers, Inc.
3 Henrietta Street, Covent Garden, London WC2E 8LU

Librar y of Congr ess Cataloging-in-Publication Data
Poverty, economic reform, and income distribution in Latin America /
  edited by Albert Berry.
    p. cm. — (Critical perspectives on Latin America's economy
  and society)
    Includes bibliographical references (p.) and index.
  ✓ISBN 1-55587-746-X (hardcover).
    1. Income distribution—Latin America. 2. Poverty—Latin America.
3. Structural adjustment (Economic policy)—Latin America.
4. Manpower policy—Latin America. 5. Latin America—Economic
policy. I. Berry, R. Albert. II. Series.
HC130.I5P67   1997
339.'098—dc21   97-22276
                                                        CIP

British Cataloguing in Publication Data
A Cataloguing in Publication record for this book
is available from the British Library.

Printed and bound in the United States of America

    The paper used in this publication meets the requirements
∞ of the American National Standard for Permanence of
    Paper for Printed Library Materials Z39.48-1984.

    5 4 3 2

Contents

v

Illustrations

Tables

Figures

Boxes

Introduction

Albert Berry

The last two decades have been traumatic ones for the countries of Latin America and the Caribbean (LAC). Virtually all have confronted major economic crises and the related social and political strains. For many, the international debt crisis of the early 1980s triggered their own economic crises. In a few, the timing was different for reasons related to the country's own experience. The regional crisis of the early 1980s was associated with the high overhang of debt from the heavy borrowing of the 1970s, the abrupt increase in real interest rates, and the cessation of capital inflows. Then came the struggle for economic recovery, a struggle that eventually brought a major shift toward more market-friendly policies. Only now, in most countries, has a degree of economic and policy stability returned; with it comes the anxious wait to see whether the region will regain or perhaps surpass the growth performance of the 1945–1980 period.

In most LAC countries the early 1990s have been an important test period fueled by high expectations, at least on the part of the proponents of the new policies. Though regional per capita income is still nearly 10% below that of 1980, the regional growth rate has returned to the 3–4% range, hardly dramatic but enough to increase per capita incomes by about 6% from 1990 to 1994 (CEPALC, 1994: 11). A few strong performers (especially Chile) have created the hope that others should be able to follow. Some of the optimism is based simply on the better growth performance of the early 1990s; some on the dramatic return of capital inflows—both flight capital that had previously left and new foreign capital flows (Culpeper, 1993); some on the entry of Mexico and the planned entry of Chile into the North American Free Trade Agreement (NAFTA) and the expectation that other Latin American countries will benefit either from entry into a trading bloc or from closer integration in an already existing bloc; and some on the widespread belief that the currently more market-friendly economic policies have been a change for the better vis-à-vis the policies of the precrisis period.

How well founded are these hopes? Will a return to healthy growth bring a quick reduction of poverty and a gradual decline in the historically high levels of inequality characterizing this part of the world?[1] What policies will be most important in achieving growth with rapid poverty alleviation? Are the market-friendly economic reforms currently being widely adopted in the region promising for both growth and improved distribution?

The optimism about Latin America's growth prospects does not, for the most part, extend to these other facets of economic performance. The focus on the need to downsize both public sector employment and that of many private firms to improve their international competitiveness suggests a looming employment problem that might be expected to bring with it an increase in inequality. Any significant increase in inequality has to be especially unwelcome in Latin America, already well known for its unparalleled concentration of income. Any further deterioration on that score creates visions of political instability as well as continuing welfare loss and poverty. Chile, the first test case for the effects of the new policies cum context, has suffered one of the most extreme increases in inequality ever recorded statistically (see Chapters 1 and 4). In many countries, stable employment has become less the norm than before as temporary and part-time work rises as a share of all jobs.

How serious are such worries? The obvious and simple answer is that no one knows with much confidence. The corollary is that these concerns deserve careful empirical attention and analysis while the new model of development being installed in the region is still subject to modification. Such attention, although certainly not wholly absent, has been limited in the region for at least fifteen years, a legacy of the economic crisis itself that understandably shifted the spotlight to issues of growth and macroeconomic stability and away from issues of the labor market and income distribution.

This book is designed to contribute to the available literature and analysis of the effects of crisis, recovery, and policy change on income distribution and other labor-market outcomes in Latin America. Its immediate raison d'être is the accumulating evidence that the market-friendly policy shift has been systematically associated with an abrupt and significant deterioration in income distribution. The pivotal question is whether this association is a causal one. If so, it is urgent to ascertain which components of the typical policy package are most responsible for this outcome, in the hope that they are not the ones most important to strong growth performance under the new economic strategy. If not, it is nevertheless crucial to understand the source of this worsening and to plan remedial steps. The urgency of dealing with the region's unnecessary poverty—unnecessary because average incomes are generally high enough to imply that there would be little poverty if the income share of the bottom few deciles were not so low—has been heightened by the economic crisis of the 1980s and the sharp declines in per capita income suffered in many countries.

The book focuses on the effects of trade liberalization and increasing economic integration along with those of labor market reform. Until their respective crises, most LAC countries had, with varying degrees of intensity, pursued import-substituting industrialization (ISI) strategies of development put in place or fleshed out in the early postwar years. By the time the 1980s crises arrived, opinion among economists—in the industrial countries, the international institutions, and the developing countries themselves—had, again in varying degree, begun to shift against this strategy. Some felt that for countries like those of LAC, ISI had already made such contributions as it could make; others felt that ISI had been a mistake from the start and that free trade would have served these countries better all along (Corbo, 1988). In fact, several of the countries of the region had much earlier begun shifting toward more outward-oriented policies, with Brazil and Colombia undertaking clear moves in that direction by the late 1960s. In any case, when the crises were upon them, LAC countries found that their restricted policy space, perhaps combined with a lack of opportunity to consider policy alternatives, led to widespread adoption of the by-then-conventional economic policy prescription: trade and foreign investment liberalization; labor market reforms to reduce the degree of regulations and constraints on business; privatization and downsizing of the public sector; financial sector reforms; and tax reforms designed to simplify the systems, to reduce the apparent progressivity built into income taxes, and to replace direct with indirect taxes.

The most-discussed and perhaps the most important of these policy changes has been the liberalization of trade and foreign investment, which increases the integration of the less-developed countries (LDCs) into the world economy. Although many analysts feel that such integration will foster better growth performance in the LDCs, predictions as to the employment and distributional impact of market-oriented reform packages in general and trade liberalization in particular have varied widely and on balance have been less positive. The popular view that freer markets generally increase inequality has been countered by the view that trade liberalization should have the opposite effect, based on the simple Heckscher-Ohlin theory that the freeing of trade should shift factor demand in favor of unskilled labor and of agriculture in the LDCs and thereby improve the distribution of income (e.g., Krueger, 1988). The main reason that the balance has shifted toward pessimism on this front, however, is not the predictions of the theory, which are in any case ambiguous, but the empirical evidence on the aftermaths of actual liberalization experiences within the region and around the world. It is not only that the transition toward market economies in the Eastern European countries appears to have led to rapidly widening income inequality but that such outcomes have been frequent elsewhere also, including both industrialized countries and a number of developing ones, most prominently several from Latin America (Berry and Stewart, 1997). Dramatic increases in inequality occurred in Chile and Argentina and perhaps also in Uruguay, the Dominican Republic, and Mexico concurrent with market-oriented policy packages that included trade liberalization as a central feature. Though there is a good possibility that Costa Rica has somehow avoided paying the price of increased inequality, the regional record as it now stands suggests that the "normal" outcome is a sharp deterioration in income distribution, with no clear evidence that this shift is temporary in character.

This book does not focus on the implications of the end of the debt crisis and the previously mentioned policy shift for economic growth. Whether aggregate growth will or will not be rapid (say 5% per year for the region) is tremendously important, of course, since even a fairly severe worsening of income distribution over the medium term might not be too difficult to weather if average incomes were rising fast enough to spread some of the fruits of growth to those at and near the bottom of the income pyramid. At this time, however, it is not at all clear that growth will be rapid enough to push distributional concerns into the background. The new model is still relatively untried; most of the impressive growth performances in the LDCs—in particular those in East Asia—have taken place in less market-friendly contexts, with Hong Kong and post-1985 Chile perhaps the only very notable exceptions. The obvious problems that a number of LAC countries have been suffering in the management of their exchange rates, the continuing proclivity toward overvaluation, and the resulting sluggish growth are all causes for concern (Helleiner, 1994). Finally, in spite of the newfound access to foreign capital, gross domestic investment has not yet approached its precrisis level of about 25%. The prudent response, therefore, is to be worried about the possible implications of any sharp deterioration in distribution along with the other unwelcome evidence—that temporary jobs, part-time jobs, and more generally job insecurity are a growing feature of labor markets in the region.

The first chapters of this book provide two perspectives on the region's recent experience in terms of inequality and poverty and their relation to the economic cycle and to economic policy. Next, the contributors review the experiences of six Latin American countries—Argentina, Chile, Mexico, Colombia, Ecuador, and Brazil. The foci of these six chapters vary both because the relevant country experiences differ in timing and content and because available information varies a good deal; but all attempt to address the impact of recession, recovery, and policy reform on key labor market variables. The final chapter presents overall conclusions.

Five of the countries studied underwent a sharp deterioration in their income distribution around the time of the introduction of market reforms. (Brazil's experience is too recent to provide evidence on this point.) The chapters by Altimir and Berry express serious concern on this count. A main element of optimism—emphasized in the work of S. A. Morley (1995)—is that economic recovery does tend to reduce poverty. Further analysis will, we trust, clarify many of the causal mechanisms at work; this will be a high priority since it is clear that distribution has already worsened markedly in most of the countries of the region and that, as a result, most remain in a danger zone from a social and political point of view.

Note

1. This is an apparent implication of recent analyses (e.g., Morley, 1995) that conclude that inequality tends to rise with recession and fall with prosperity.

Part 1

Comparative Analyses of Poverty and Income Distribution in Latin America

1

Confronting the Income Distribution Threat in Latin America

Albert Berry

Latin America has long been noted for the extreme inequality of incomes and opportunities characteristic of nearly all countries in the region. In this chapter, I focus on how labor-market outcomes and especially the distribution of income have been related to economic events and to policy changes, with a view to predicting the distribution of benefits from expected future growth. The chapter's immediate raison d'être is the accumulating evidence that the market-friendly policy shift since the 1980s has been systematically associated with an abrupt and important deterioration in income distribution.

Before turning to a look at the empirical evidence on recent income-distribution trends in Latin American and Caribbean (LAC) countries in which the focus is on the timing of changes in distribution and the hypotheses suggested by that timing, I review some of the interpretations put forward to explain the generally negative trends in distribution and/or other worrisome aspects of labor-market outcomes.

Possible Explanations for Negative Distributional Trends

There is little by way of verified theory to explain levels and trends in inequality in Latin America or in developing countries generally; deficient databases and limited quantitative analysis have conspired against a better understanding. Kuznets's (1955) hypothesis that income distribution typically worsens, then improves over the course of development has received a great deal of discussion but remains controversial. Limited discussion has also revolved around the distributional implications of Lewis's labor surplus model (1954) and the proposition that as a country's labor market begins to tighten up the distribution of income may be expected to improve (Berry, 1983). Among structural features, the distribution of agricultural

9

land as well as of other productive assets (Loehr and Powelson, 1981), the distribution of education (Ram, 1989), the size structure of firms, and the degree of openness to international markets have all received some attention either in a static sense and/or as features whose change may be predicted to contribute to distributional trends over time (Bourguinon and Morrisson, 1989; Fields, 1984). It is well recognized that the speed and pattern of technological change could have a significant effect on distribution. There has been less analysis than in developed countries of the impact of the economic or business cycle, partly because the sort of cycle so prevalent in the industrialized countries has not been generally present in a similar form in the less-developed countries (LDCs), but Morley's recent work (1995) advances this line of research for LAC.

My central concern here is with the impact of the market-friendly policies adopted in varying degrees by most LAC countries over the last decade or so, including trade and foreign investment liberalization, privatization and general downsizing of the public sector, labor-market reforms, and so on. It is useful to review some of the major ideas put forward in the literature.

1. There are competing ideas as to why liberalization, or openness to the international economy, matters, and which aspects of it matter but not much disagreement that it does matter. The Heckscher-Ohlin theory emphasizes differences in factor proportions between exportables and importables. Other theories relate the rate of technology adoption and the type of technology adopted to the degree of openness (Pack, 1992). Less often mooted is the "economies of scale in trade" hypothesis whereby, regardless of what happens at the production level, there are important economies of scale in the commercial and financial aspects of international trade. This helps to explain why large firms dominate trade in many sectors and smaller firms are less involved. To the extent that factor proportions are closely related to firm size (there is much empirical evidence for this relationship), one would expect globalization to favor the larger firms and hence to raise the total returns on capital and lower those on labor. Unlike the Heckscher-Ohlin hypothesis, which implies that trade would affect income distribution differently according to countries' relative factor endowments (e.g., by raising the labor share in labor-abundant countries and lowering it in capital-abundant countries), this theory suggests one negative effect of trade on distribution in all countries, an effect that would accentuate the negative static Heckscher-Ohlin effect in capital-abundant countries and partially or wholly offset the positive Heckscher-Ohlin effect in labor-abundant countries.

A debated aspect of the open or free trade policy question is the appropriate way to think of economies in Heckscher-Ohlin terms, in particular the number of factors of production that must be distinguished. Results can be reversed according to whether a model with a single labor factor is closer to reality than one with two or more categories of labor that bear different relationships of substitution or complementarity with other factors. Simple two- or three-factor models tend to view agriculture as the sector most penalized by protection, whereas the evidence from several LAC countries has suggested that some agricultural activities are among the most protected.

2. Symmetrical with the traditional two-factor trade theory is the proposition that foreign investment should improve the functional distribution of income in the host country by raising the ratio of capital to labor and hence the ratio of wages to returns on capital. Hanson and Feenstra (1994), who link foreign investment to widening wage dispersion between higher-skilled and lower-skilled workers in Mexico, suggest a different mechanism, one in which activities that are shifted from the source country to the host country are less capital- and skill-intensive than average in the former and more capital- and skill-intensive than average in the latter, with the result that their departure from the former lowers the unskilled wage/skilled wage ratio in the source country and their arrival in the latter lowers the ratio in the host country.

3. There is a considerable literature in developed countries that reports that unions, minimum wages, and other types of labor-market legislation usually have the effect of narrowing earnings differentials, either because they prevent the exploitation of relatively undefended workers or because they prevent differences in ability from being fully reflected in earnings levels. In developing countries, though this view has also been prominent, there is a competing view that the protection of the labor elite increases the inequality of labor income. The effect on overall distribution is theoretically unclear, since it depends in part on how much of the rents taken by protected labor are at the expense of capital (and which among the groups of capital owners pay them) and how much are at the expense of the rest of labor (if indeed they are). This issue has been very little addressed from an empirical point of view in LAC countries or other LDCs, but the evidence reviewed in the later chapters from Chile, Argentina, and other countries makes it clear that it merits serious attention. Also relevant to this hypothesis (and to some of the others) is the frequent recent finding that the earnings differentials not explained by such standard analytical variables as level of education, experience, and sector have risen substantially in recent years. Perhaps previously unimportant differences among people in training, education, and skills become important as a result of changes in technology; differences in capacity to adjust to new technology could show up in short-run differences in productivity that were not previously present. To the extent also that labor institutions tend to dampen

the variance of income within categories defined by variables like these, the waning influence of those institutions could let differences appear that were previously latent but repressed.

The often-assumed link between a widening of observed wage dispersion and a worsening of income distribution appears less than certain in many LDCs. Often the wage series available do not represent the labor force in general; for example, formal sector manufacturing wages may not move too closely with average wages in the formal and informal sectors taken together. If large informal sectors and a high level of self-employment exist, wage series alone are not reliable guides even to the distribution of earner income, let alone those of family income or consumption. Also, with the sectoral and occupational composition of the labor force sometimes changing fairly quickly (a tendency accentuated by the rapidly rising female participation rates in some countries), average wages of all employed workers may move rather differently from those of specific categories. Analysis of wage structure is as important in LDCs as in developed countries, but the subsequent mappings from those trends onto income distribution constitute an important challenge.

4. Public sector activities create incomes (or "rents," depending sometimes on how one views them) for the worker and sometimes for those who are well connected. Most observers feel these are generally middle-class and middle-income people and that the shrinking of the public sector will accordingly be felt mainly by the middle deciles of the distribution. But much may also depend on the indirect effects of the downsizing. If former public sector employees proceed to "bump down" some in lower income categories, the ultimate (general equilibrium) effect might be more complicated.

5. To the extent that the prevalence of small (and medium-sized) enterprise has a lot to do with the demand for labor, especially relatively less-skilled labor, the size and growth rate of this sector may determine future income inequality. One hypothesis to explain Taiwan's relative income equality is the dominance of small farms and small firms over the formative part of its development process. Brazil is at or close to the other end of this spectrum and so is its level of inequality. South Korea's industrial structure was more like Brazil's during the early part of its growth boom, but over the last couple of decades small and medium-sized enterprises have greatly increased their share of employment and output (Cho, 1995); simultaneously the level of inequality has fallen (Nugent, 1989).

6. Much income inequality is directly related to an unequal distribution of human capital, which in turn reflects the functioning of the education and training process. Educational access is related to income distribution, especially in countries with important private educational sectors. Both the predictions based on the character of the ongoing technological

revolution and some evidence from industrial and developing countries that wage dispersion by education and skill levels has recently been rising imply that this is a major issue.

Although all of these factors no doubt play a role in the evolution of income distribution, not all are likely to be behind the sharp recent changes witnessed in many LAC countries. This probably includes both educational and small enterprise policy and performance. However, trade policy, labor policy, size of public sector, technology change, and business cycle factors are all obvious possible candidates for explaining the trends of income inequality.

The Distribution Record of Latin America and the Caribbean

Growth and Trickle-Down Prior to the 1980s

As the Latin American countries progressed through the 1960s and 1970s, it appeared that severe poverty might be more or less eradicated by another decade or so of "growth without redistribution," that is, growth within the context of an essentially unchanged and very high level of income inequality. This outcome was a possibility because Latin America's average income was higher than that in most of the Third World.

Over the period 1950–1980 the region's per capita income rose by about 3% per year. With the poverty line that Altimir (1982) applied across countries for 1970, poverty incidence was about 38% of households. The growth record over 1950–1970 would suggest that poverty incidence in 1950 (using the same poverty line) had been around 65%; over 1970–1980 it probably fell further to somewhere around 25%. Had per capita income growth continued over the last two decades of the century at the 3% per year observed over 1950–1980, poverty incidence would probably have fallen to about 10–15%;[1] with reasonably effective poverty redressal policies (targeted employment schemes, food schemes, etc.) of the sort that can more easily reach a large share of the poor when the incidence of poverty gets down to this relatively low level, it would have been realistic to think that no more than a few percent would have been critically poor or indigent.

Although most countries of the region did not witness major shifts in income distribution during the 1970s, some patterns hinted at possible improvements in the not-too-distant future. Thus, the sharp increase in real wages of lower-skilled workers in Brazil during the "economic miracle" of the late 1960s and early 1970s and the less dramatic increase in real wages in agriculture and some other sectors of the Colombian economy suggested that these two economies might be on the verge of a tighter labor market and continuing wage increases, especially among those lower-skilled workers (Pfefferman and Webb, 1983; Berry, 1990). In the case of Colombia, urban income distribution did, in fact, improve over at least the latter part of the 1970s.

The Crash, Halting Recovery, and Policy Response

A happy outcome was of course not forthcoming, due to the economic downturns and the difficult recoveries that followed. The timing of the economic crises varied somewhat, with the Southern Cone countries already in difficulty by the mid-1970s, whereas for most of the others the onset was signaled by the international debt crisis of the early 1980s. Particularly severe short period (2–4 years) declines in per capita income were suffered by Costa Rica, Chile, Peru, and Venezuela, and gross domestic product (GDP) per capita fell by over 20% during the 1980s in Argentina, Venezuela, Peru, Bolivia, and Nicaragua (though the first two regained some of that ground in 1991–1992). For the region as a whole, per capita national income fell by about 13% from 1980 to 1985 and has fluctuated a little with no significant movement either way since then. A brief spurt of modest growth from 1985 to 1987 petered out by the late 1980s, the last three years of which all produced average growth of less than 1%; the period 1990–1994 saw modest growth of 6% in per capita GDP, though only 4% in per capita national income because of further negative shifts in the region's terms of trade (ECLAC, 1994: 37, 47). With this sort of macroeconomic performance, there had to be many "losers" during this period. The only countries that did not suffer a net decline in gross national income per capita between 1980 and 1992 were Colombia, Uruguay, and Chile, but in the latter two cases this was mainly because the recession hit earlier.

The debt crisis provided the push to induce or oblige the region to jettison its trademark import-substituting industrialization (ISI) strategy based on protectionism for a more liberalized trading system, as well as to move toward adoption of the other elements of what is now a standard package of reforms of labor markets, financial markets, and the public sector. Some countries had already taken significant steps away from the traditional combination of protectionism and overvalued exchange rates and the resulting bias against exports. Both Colombia and Brazil had moved to encourage exports in the late 1960s; Colombia's adoption of a crawling peg exchange rate put an end to the systematic overvaluation of earlier years. These approaches were qualitatively similar to the East Asian practice of encouraging exports while continuing to protect against imports. Chile went much further as the Pinochet regime introduced the most liberal free-trade free-market system in the region, including a real import liberalization bringing tariff rates down to 10% by 1980. Though they were raised somewhat in the mid-1980s, the average was back down to 15% as the decade came to a close (UNCTAD, 1992: 44). Argentina had an important liberalization episode between 1976 and 1982 in which the average effective rate of protection fell from 158% to 54% (Gelbard, 1990: 46). In the second half of the 1980s, most of the countries of the region initiated significant reforms, varying in detail and in timing and having few if any close precedents in the developing (or the developed) world.

Distribution and Poverty Effects of the Policy Reforms: Evidence from Country Experience

Although considerable uncertainty still surrounds the precise evolution of income distribution during the crisis and adjustment periods in most of the countries of Latin America, and it is difficult to sort out the effects of policy changes from those of the crisis itself and of longer-run structural trends dating back to the precrisis years, analysis of the record is nevertheless quite rewarding. There was a clear preponderance of negative shifts in distribution around the time of the introduction of policy reforms, an impact not readily explicable by other obvious candidates like stage of the cycle, rate of inflation, and so on.

The evidence that, taken together, points strongly at the policy package as a possible source of increasing inequality, comes from Chile, Argentina, Uruguay, Mexico, the Dominican Republic, Colombia, and Ecuador. In no case with data of satisfactory quality do we have clear evidence of the opposite pattern. Costa Rica is a special and important case since it appears to be an exception, with distribution probably remaining roughly constant. Preliminary analysis for Jamaica indicates that expenditure distribution improved over 1991–1993 as a phase of trade liberalization was being initiated, so it may enter the category of "exceptions" as well. Several other countries did not undertake the reform package far enough back in time for useful data to have yet been generated, and for others the data are of questionable quality. The discussion that follows is organized around groups of countries whose experiences appear to share a number of relevant characteristics.

Chile, Argentina, and Uruguay

The three Southern Cone countries differ from the rest of the LAC nations in that all introduced significant liberalizing economic reforms in the early or mid-1970s, before similar efforts were undertaken elsewhere in LAC.[2]

These cases thus offer a longer period during which possible impacts of the reforms might have been felt. Argentina and Chile suffered unusual worsening of their income distributions, with high unemployment an aspect of the period in question in Chile and falling labor incomes for the lower deciles the dominant feature in Argentina. Uruguayan data are somewhat suspect in terms of quality and comparability over time, but they too suggest a major deterioration of distribution.

Chile's experience is the most important from our perspective, since the policy experiments date well back in time and, despite some vacillation, their basic direction has been maintained subsequently. There have been two severe recessions since 1970, the first associated with Salvador Allende's overthrow, when GDP fell by 23% over the period 1972–1975, and the second with a set of internal and external factors including the international debt crisis that led to a sharp decline in GDP between 1981 and 1982. After each collapse, growth resumed quickly and was strong, but the recessions' impact was still to hold average annual growth over 1970–1992 to only 3.2%, in spite of an impressive 6% annual growth rate since 1984. Since 1973 the economy has undergone the most radical policy "reforms" of any nation in the region.

As of the late 1960s, inequality was a little less severe than in most other LAC countries.[3] The data for greater Santiago indicate a sharp improvement during the Allende administration, followed by a sharp reversal after the military coup, such that by 1976 household income inequality was markedly worse than in the pre-Allende period and no longer superior to the levels observed in most other LAC countries (Berry, 1995: Table 2).[4] Less frequent but possibly more comparable data on the distribution of consumption among greater Santiago households show one of the largest deteriorations ever recorded statistically in a developing country, occurring primarily between 1969 and 1978 but also over the decade that followed (see Table 1.1).

Since it is reasonable to assume that distribution at the end of the Allende years was better than that of 1969 (to which the data refer), it would

Table 1.1   The Quintile Distribution of Consumption Among Households in Greater Santiago, 1969, 1978, and 1988 (percent of total consumption)

Quintile	1969	1978	1988
1	7.6	5.2	4.4
2	11.8	9.3	8.2
3	15.6	13.6	12.6
4	20.6	21.0	20.0
5	44.5	51.0	54.9
Total	100.0	100.0	100.0

Source: Ffrench-Davis, 1992: 16.

appear that the worsening was dramatic over the first five post-Allende years, consistent with the evidence on the household distribution of income. If the national trend in consumption distribution was like that of Santiago, the consumption decline in the bottom quintile of households over the years 1969–1978 would have been on the order of 40%.[5] Meller reports an increase in poverty incidence from 17% in 1970 to 45% in 1985, with the 1985 poverty line not more than 6% above that of 1970 in real terms (Meller, 1992a: 23). Even if these figures may somewhat exaggerate the trend, there is no doubt that poverty increased sharply.[6] A special and interesting feature of the Chilean experience was the combination of government-sponsored make-work policies for low-income groups and targeted poverty redressal, which seem to have limited the most serious poverty impacts of the negative income trends just discussed.

A number of the policy steps taken by the Pinochet regime would have been expected to foster inequality. The extensive privatization of state enterprises, mainly carried out during the severe recession of 1972–1974, led to an acute concentration of ownership and the formation of large conglomerates (Meller, 1992a: 27). Curtailment of agricultural credit to small farmers led to land concentration as well. Preferential financing to small entrepreneurs was cut back. Perhaps most important was the reform of labor legislation, which relaxed worker dismissal regulations, suspended unions (to 1979, when they were again authorized to operate, but with many restrictions), and greatly reduced the social security tax paid by the employers and other nonwage costs as well. After the second crisis (1981–1983), wage indexation to inflation was abolished and replaced by a real wage "floor," specified to be the real wage prevailing in 1979. Wealth and capital gains taxes were eliminated, profit tax rates were substantially reduced, and public employment was greatly cut back. Unemployment rates (for greater Santiago) rose to unprecedented levels in the neighborhood of 20–25% (depending on the definition used). Only in 1989 did this rate fall below 10%, but since then the fall has been continuous, to just 5% in 1992 (ECLAC, 1992: 42). The coverage of the minimum wage was restricted considerably, and its level fell in the 1980s. Fringe benefits had been greatly reduced from their 1970 level, and public expenditure per capita in health care, education, and housing had also decreased. According to R. Ffrench-Davis (1992: 15) average wages in 1989 were still 8% lower than in 1970; as of 1992 they were probably marginally above the 1970 level,[7] a very slow recovery indeed.

One feature of the post-1975 period that probably contributed to increasing income inequality is an increase in the relative income of persons with university education vis-à-vis those with less education. D. J. Robbins's (1994) analysis indicates that the increase was not primarily the result of shifts in the composition of employment among industries but rather a phenomenon within sectors. It may reflect a greater relative pay-off to higher education under a more open economy or the dismantling of union power and changes in labor legislation in Chile.

Until the early 1980s, Argentina had a long period of very slow growth—only a total of 4% between 1974 and 1988 with a dramatic fall of 13% at the heart of the crisis (1980–1982). Accompanying this macroeconomic failure was an unusually sudden and large increase in inequality; the Gini coefficient among income earners in greater Buenos Aires rose from about 0.36 over the period 1974–1976 to 0.44 in 1978 (see Table 3.7).[8] Since then the level of concentration has fluctuated without a clear trend; after falling in the early 1980s, inequality reached a temporary peak in 1989 (under intense inflation) and fell back to the previous level, from which it has varied little, although the share of the bottom 30% has continued to fall somewhat. From an average of 11.6% over 1974–1976, it fell to the 10.5% range in the early 1980s and was down to 8.5% by 1994.[9]

One apparent determinant of short-run movements in the level of earner inequality is the real exchange rate; its role is suggested by the short-run inverse relationship, from 1970 to 1987 at least, between the real exchange rate (Argentine currency per dollar) and both the real wage and the ratio of the real wage to per capita income (Berry, 1990: 31). It is plausible, given the prominence of wage goods among Argentina's exports, that an increase in the real exchange rate (through devaluation, for example) would, by raising the relative price of wage goods, lead to a decrease in the real wage rate and a worsening of the distribution of income. But it is clear that the longer-run worsening of the income distribution cannot be fully explained by this link with the real exchange rate since net worsening in distribution occurred over periods when there was no net increase in the real exchange rate. Other factors must therefore have been at work. Possibly structural changes wrought by the change in trade policy worsened inequality; the liberalization episode of 1976–1982 referred to earlier led not only to a fall of 11% in manufacturing output between 1976 and 1982 but to an reduction in employment of 37%, as output per worker rose by a striking 41% (Gelbard, 1990: 54). Many small and medium-sized firms went out of business, and many large firms reduced employment, increased capital stock, and improved technology. It is also possible that the very large capital flight from the country played a role by reducing the capital available to complement the labor force. Changes in labor policy almost certainly played a significant role; the bulk of the increase in inequality since the mid-1970s occurred between 1976 and 1978 as the new military government fixed wages, repressed trade unions, eliminated collective bargaining and the right to strike, and reformed the labor code to the detriment of workers (Cortés and Marshall, 1993). Unlike Chile, however, Argentina's experience at this time was not characterized by high levels of unemployment.

The tearing down of labor-market institutions would not obviously worsen income distribution in countries with small "protected" segments of the labor force and large unprotected ones, since the beneficiaries of such protection are both few and relatively high in the income hierarchy. In relatively advanced and highly urbanized countries like Chile and Argentina, a negative effect on distribution is quite plausible since the protected group is large and encompasses more of the poorer members of society. Such an effect might be especially strong in an economy where large rents come from high-productivity mining (Chile) or agriculture (Argentina) and where the public sector and other service activities have been living off those rents. When the public sector shrinks and wages are more closely linked to the marginal product of labor in the private sector, one might expect wages to fall more than in many other types of economies.

Uruguay's story has fascinating similarities to and differences with each of the other two countries. Protectionism and monetary mismanagement have prevailed over most of the postwar period, and average growth has been very slow. For such a small economy, Uruguay has been relatively closed, with the ratio of exports to GDP sometimes as low as the 10–14% range. Economic stagnation and high inflation gradually engendered social and political instability in the 1960s, leading eventually to a military coup in 1973. The new economic team installed in 1974 introduced a program of price stability, relaxed some of the existing controls on foreign trade and capital movements, and liberalized labor markets (Allen and Labadie, 1994: 10). The military's distaste for strikes showed in reaction to a general strike called by the National Confederation of Workers (CNT); the strike was quickly disbanded, employers were given the right to fire anyone who did not return to work, and 12,000 public and 4,000 private sector workers were fired (Allen and Labadie, 1994: 12). Neither the union movement nor collective bargaining played any visible role for ten years. Meanwhile, import licensing and quotas were abolished between 1974 and 1977, the level and dispersion of tariffs was reduced, and export taxes on agricultural goods were cut. Average growth from 1974 to 1978 of about 4% per year was led by export-oriented industrial activities—production of clothing, leather goods, shoes, and fishing equipment (Favaro and Bensión, 1993: 195); the investment rate rose from 10% to 19%. The fiscal deficit remained high, however, because of increased spending on the military and on public investment projects, which offset spending decreases on wages and transfers. Attempts to restrict monetary growth were offset by inflows of cash, especially from Argentina. The initial trade reforms of 1974 were followed by a trade liberalization program that attempted to simplify the tariff structure and to reduce the level of protection gradually to the target of 35%; but the plan to shift resources toward tradables was not fulfilled because the impact of the trade liberalization was more than offset by exchange rate overvaluation, which was part of the stabilization effort.

The defeat by a significant margin of a 1980 referendum called by the military on constitutional change marked the first step toward the reopening of the political system (Allen and Labadie, 1994: 14). Unions started to reappear as it became clear that the military wanted to hand the reins over to the civil society, and the new movement proved at least as militant as the old. Wage councils were reinstituted in 1985, along with the return to democracy (Allen and Labadie, 1994: 15). A couple of years of fast recovery were once again followed by stagflation.

It seems clear that inequality increased after the early 1960s, but the timing, degree, and characteristics of the worsening are not well understood. The data for the Montevideo household distribution suggest a very large increase between the early 1960s (Gini coefficient around 0.37) and the early 1980s, but the pattern is not continuous (Berry, 1995: Table 5; Indart, 1996), and some of the early 1980s observations might be outliers. A conservative guess, based on a comparison of the average of the three figures for the period from 1961–1962 to 1967 (0.385) to that of the three over 1980–1984 (0.441) would be an increase of 5 or 6 points. The reported inequality of earned income among Montevideo households rose very fast over the 1970s but then dropped a little in the first half of the 1980s (Melgar, 1981, 1988). No clear significant trend is in evidence from then until 1992, but tentative data for 1993 suggest a drop in that year (Melgar, 1995, as reported in Indart, 1996). This may signal a new, more egalitarian pattern in Uruguay, or it may simply be a statistical bleep.

The 1970s are of particular relevance because of the important policy changes introduced at that time. Most of the evidence points to a substantial increase in inequality, including the sharp fall in wages and the apparently sharp widening in the earnings differentials across educational levels. E. Favaro and A. Bensión (1993: 276) suggest that the opening of the economy, the reduction in the relative size of the government, and the prohibition of labor union activity all contributed to increasing inequality. They believe that the behavior of the labor market during previous decades was greatly influenced both by the unions and by the state's participation in the wage boards, determination of wage levels, and employment of a significant share of the labor force. These factors, they feel, weighed in favor of a more uniform wage structure than would have resulted from market forces and created disincentives for more skilled workers.[10] This view, expressed with different details, is also held by S. G. Allen and G. J. Labadie (1994). The Uruguayan experience is widely interpreted as one in which, whatever their impact on distribution, labor-market rigidities and imperfections have been an important drag on economic growth.

Mexico and the Dominican Republic

Mexico and the Dominican Republic did not undertake major policy reforms until the 1980s. In each country economic crisis hit in the early

1980s. The Mexican experience is of special importance and interest because of the country's recent entry into North American Free Trade Agreement (NAFTA) as the first developing country to enter a free trade area with large developed countries.

Mexico grew rapidly during the 1970s (second only to Brazil among major LAC countries) but then ran afoul of its debt buildup and achieved an average growth of only about 2% since 1980, with the 1990s performance still in that range in spite of the major policy reforms of the late 1980s. In contrast to oil-importing Brazil, whose balance of payments was negatively affected by the oil price hikes of the 1970s, Mexico eventually benefited from the high price of its oil exports, but by the late 1970s it was attempting to maintain a level of expenditures inconsistent with its tax effort, and it turned to heavy foreign borrowing to make up the difference. The debt crisis brought an output decline of about 8%, a serious bout of inflation, and a sharp decline in real wages of about 30% from 1982 to 1986. The slow growth and instability of the early 1990s have been associated with a large capital inflow and resulting overvaluation of the exchange rate.

Mexico's industrial development was nurtured under a rather typical import-substitution policy regime that provided moderate levels of effective protection to manufacturing and included a number of sector-specific infant industry programs that gave increasing emphasis over time to export targets and to price competitiveness (Ros, 1994: 208). Policies were overhauled in the 1980s in response to the debt crisis; liberalization began in the late 1980s. Current trade patterns and industrial structure are a continuation of past trends, with this "smooth" transition attributed by some (e.g. Ros, 1994: 209) to a combination of successful import substitution in the past and the fact that the debt crisis and declining terms of trade forced macroeconomic policy to provide unprecedented levels of exchange rate protection, which facilitated the adjustment of industrial firms to a more open economy.

Over Mexico's long period of rapid growth up to the debt crisis in the early 1980s, it appears that most wages rose substantially (Gregory, 1986) and that inequality either fell (as argued by Hernandez-Laos and Cordoba, 1982) or stayed almost constant. Alarcón and McKinley (1994c) report, however, that the Gini coefficient of total household income (grouped data) rose from 0.43 in 1984 to 0.475 in 1992, most of the increase having occurred by 1989 (see Table 1.2).[11] The main winners were the top decile, whose share in total household distribution rose from 32.8% in 1984 to 37.9% in 1989 (Alarcón, 1994: 87).

The increased inequality among households resembles that observed in other countries of the region. What is unusual about the Mexican case is the dramatically increased concentration among wage and salary earners; the Gini coefficient rose moderately from 0.419 in 1984 to 0.443 in 1989,

Table 1.2   Selected Data on Distribution in Mexico, 1984, 1989, and 1992

	1984		1989		1992	
	Share of Total Income	Gini & Pseudo-Gini	Share of Total Income	Gini & Pseudo-Gini	Share of Total Income	Gini & Pseudo-Gini
Households ranked by household income (grouped data)						
Total	100.0	0.429	100.0	0.469	100.0	0.475
Wages	46.9	0.444	46.4	0.430	45.5	0.466
Profits	7.1	0.468	10.2	0.634	8.4	0.613
Services	4.7	0.427	6.5	0.623	7.3	0.635
Agriculture/livestock	10.4	0.395	4.9	0.257	4.5	0.328
Nonmonetary	21.2	0.390	22.6	0.455	26.1	0.429
Urban[a]	—	0.407	—	0.453	—	—
Rural[a]	—	0.403	—	0.410	—	—
Households ranked by per capita household income (individual data)[b]						
Total	—	0.488	—	0.519	—	—
Urban	—	—	—	0.499	—	—
Rural	—	—	—	0.442	—	—

Source: Alarcón and McKinley, 1994: Table 2, except as noted.
Notes: Calculations are based on grouped data. Households are ranked by total household income.
a. From Alarcón, 1994: 112.
b. Ibid., p. 87, 121.

then leaped to 0.519 in 1992 (Alarcón and McKinley, 1994c: Table 4), probably one of the highest Gini coefficients among wage-income earners observed anywhere. The variance within virtually all groups exploded over the period 1989–1992 but most especially at higher levels of education, in the border states, in urban areas, in export manufacturing industries and, surprisingly, among union workers. Although there was no increase in income variance among "poor" workers (including domestic servants, helpers and unskilled laborers in industry, street vendors, and urban agricultural workers; see Alarcón and McKinley, 1994c: 18), for the "elite" occupations (professionals, managers, supervisors, etc.) at the other extreme the Theil L indexes more than doubled. The group most clearly achieving a relative gain over the two periods were those with higher education (Alarcón and McKinley, 1994c: Table 7). An independent source of evidence (data from the annual industrial surveys) indicates that the earnings gap between nonproduction and production workers in manufacturing has been widening since 1985, after a previous downward trend. In that earlier phase, the ratio of nonproduction workers' wages to those of production workers' fell from nearly 3.0 in 1965 to its low of about 1.85 in 1985; it then moved back up to about 2.2 by 1988 (Hanson and Feenstra, 1994: Figure 3).

The Mexican story involves a number of as-yet-unresolved puzzles. Though the stresses of the crisis beginning in 1982 were severe and though certain income gaps (e.g., between poor and nonpoor states) did widen, the overall measured increase in inequality was modest according to the household distribution data. But the sharp widening of wage dispersion in the 1989–1992 period and the evidence of widening gaps between more and less skilled workers are cause for concern. Has increased openness,[12] the declining importance of traditional labor market institutions, or technological change played a role?

R. C. Feenstra and G. Hanson attribute the widening wage gap by skill level to the inflow of foreign capital; Mexico's foreign direct investment (FDI) boom of the late 1980s was large in relation to the existing capital stock. The key idea in their interpretation is that a movement of capital from an industrial to a developing country (in this case the United States and Mexico, respectively) lowers the relative wages of unskilled workers in both countries because the activities transferred to Mexico when capital moves in that direction will be more skill-intensive than the previous Mexican average but less skill-intensive than the previous U.S. average. As predicted by the theory, the relative wage movement in Mexico parallels that observed of the United States. In Mexico the increase in the ratio of skilled to unskilled wages was greatest in the border region (50% for both hourly and annual wages; see Hanson and Feenstra, 1994: 33).

The Dominican Republic's economy grew rapidly until 1977. The external crisis hit in the early 1980s and led to an adjustment program composed of fiscal, monetary, and exchange rate elements that continued until 1986, by which time the adjustment had taken place and growth had returned. The new 1986 government stimulated the economy through an ambitious program of public investment, in pursuit of which it shrunk real current expenditures, which contributed to a fall in the real wages of government workers (Sanatan and Rather, 1993: 54). Inflation broke loose in this period, after relative stability up until 1984. Just prior to the major devaluations beginning in 1984, a combination of overvaluation and declining terms of trade had pushed the ratios of current price exports to GDP and imports to GDP to quite low levels (under 15% and under 20%, respectively) for the Dominican Republic; they then rose sharply to around or over 30%. The constant price series have been less volatile.

I. Sanatan and M. Rather (1993: 55) report that after a small decline in inequality between 1976 and 1984—with the Gini coefficient apparently falling from 0.45 to 0.43—there was a sharp jump to 0.51 in 1989. The authors blame inflation, among other things, for the deterioration. Its timing means that the growing trade ratios may also have played a role.

Colombia and Ecuador

Colombia and Ecuador are among the relative latecomers to the market-friendly policy package, both pushing it vigorously only in the early 1990s. Colombia has the distinction of being perhaps the only country to adopt the package when not under severe pressure to do so. Though the postimplementation period is too short to provide definitive answers with respect to the labor-market effects of the *apertura* (opening) and other recent reforms, there appears to have been a sharp reversal of a previous (and perhaps unique) equalizing trend in the urban distribution of income.[13] Urban unemployment, however, has remained low by Colombian standards, though some industries have clearly been hurt by import liberalization.

Since the late 1960s, Colombia's macroeconomic performance has also been among the best in the region. Aggregate GDP growth averaged 4.4% over 1970–1993, second only to Brazil's 5.1%, and the economy was least affected by the debt crisis and accompanying recession. In the early 1990s (through 1994), growth has been a little above average for the region, at about 3.5% per year. This creditable performance, which dates from the late 1960s, has been based on generally good exchange rate management since the switch to a flexible rate in 1967; a trade regime offering incentives both for import substitutes and for exports; and a relatively prudent fiscal and monetary policy, under which fiscal deficits never reached the unsustainable levels of a number of other LAC countries and monetary growth was accordingly more modest. Growth did slow in the early 1980s as a result of the Dutch disease effects of coffee and foreign indebtedness booms between 1975 and 1982, reflected in the real appreciation of the peso and a mini-episode of import liberalization around 1980. Export promotion was downgraded, not as a result of an explicit decision but as a result of short-term macroeconomic considerations. The deteriorating balance-of-payments situation, affected by the onset of the Latin American debt crisis, led to a rapid reversal of more than a decade of import liberalization; the economy became more closed with the constant (1975) price import/GDP ratio falling from 22% in 1982 to 14.4% in 1984 and then fluctuating in the 16–18% range through 1991 (see Table 6.1). Industrial growth had returned by the mid-1980s, but the presumably falling returns from the ISI elements of the model and the acute change in the external conditions facing the country led to a radical turnabout in policy in 1990–1991, and the adoption of a more explicitly outward-oriented strategy (Ocampo, 1994: 145). Cesar Gaviria's administration (1990–1994) came to power committed to continuing and accelerating an already initiated process of liberalization, which was accompanied by a partial freeing of exchange controls, more open access to foreign investment, and a liberalization of the labor market. The apertura was carried out quickly, though its effects on imports were delayed. Growth, which had recovered and averaged 4.5% over the period 1985–1990, fell to a low of under 2.5% in 1991, from which it gradually accelerated to somewhere in the range of 4–5% in 1993–1994.

The abrupt *apertura* of the early 1990s had been preceded by a brief episode of liberalization (early 1980s), then a sharp reduction in openness, and finally a gradual reopening through the rest of the 1980s. Labor-market reforms occurred mainly around 1990, though union power was clearly weakened by the recession of the early 1980s. Estimates of income distribution reported by Albert Berry and Jaime Tenjo (see Table 6.3) reveal a significant decline in urban inequality between 1976 and 1990, mainly focused in the period up to the early 1980s; the decline was more striking among wage and salary earners (whose Gini coefficient fell from 0.50 to 0.41 for the three cities studied by Berry and Tenjo) than among persons ranked by per capita family income (where the decline was from 0.52 to 0.46—see Table 6.4).[14] An important part of the story is the unusually marked decline in earnings differentials across educational levels and between genders, declines especially concentrated in the late 1970s while the economy was still growing rapidly and in the early 1980s when it was not (Tenjo, 1993). Rural earnings were also showing considerable improvement at this time (Ministerio de Agricultura, 1990: 228).

Inequality probably bottomed out in the late 1980s, after which it increased sharply, especially among wage and salary earners (for whom the Gini coefficient rose from 0.41 in 1990 to 0.47 in 1993), but significantly also among persons generally (for whom it rose from 0.47 to 0.51). The 1990–1993 period saw significant declines in the income share of the first six deciles of earners (30.8% to 26.6%), whereas the only major gainer was the top decile (36.2% to 40.4%, see Table 6.3). In percentage terms the biggest losers were the lowest deciles; the first decile saw its share fall by 23% from 1.93% to 1.48%, about the level of the late 1970s. Trends in level of concentration of each of the major components of personal income parallel those of total income (see Table 6.4). The very similar time patterns of the distributions of labor and of business incomes suggest close links between the markets in which the two types of income are determined. The reversal of the former positive trend in the level of inequality mainly reflects the increasing concentration of business income.

The dearth of data on rural incomes makes it impossible to know for sure whether the time trends observed in urban areas hold for the nation as a whole. A best guess is that there was not much change between 1988 and 1992, the years for which surveys are available. A significant widening of the average urban-rural income gap does appear to have occurred between 1990 and 1993 (Lora and Herrera, 1994), which, together with a constant level of inequality in rural areas (at least over 1988–1992), could imply a larger increase in inequality at the national level than for the urban areas alone. Given the uncertainty and incompleteness of the rural data, it must be conceded that the national trends could be better than the urban ones, as argued by J. L. Londoño (1996: 15).[15] This matter will be settled only by more in-depth analysis on the rural side.

Ecuador experienced rapid economic growth during the 1970s, when the country became an oil exporter. The domestic reinvestment of export earnings led to an intense process of ISI and agricultural modernization. During the late 1970s, as oil exports stagnated, growth was achieved at the cost of foreign borrowing. As the external situation deteriorated, this strategy became unsustainable. Two natural disasters added to the woes of the 1980s—coastal floods in 1983 and a major earthquake in 1987. The initial downturn in 1981–1983 was less severe than in many other countries—GDP dropped about 3% and national income per capita by about 10%—but the recovery has been weak and halting, in spite of a moderate advance in the early 1990s. Only in 1992 did per capita income reattain its precrisis level.

Ecuador implemented structural adjustment policies from 1981 onward. Generally the process can be characterized as gradual, slow, selective, highly conflictive, and still incomplete. A stable political consensus on economic policies was never reached. Although trade barriers were reduced from 1984 on, the most important step was adopted in 1990, when import tariffs were reduced to somewhere within the range of 5% to 80% (with most products—except vehicles—between 5% and 30%) and most import restrictions were lifted. The result was a dramatic expansion of consumer goods imports by a factor of nearly five between 1990 and 1994. Labor deregulation was pursued continuously during the period; real minimum wages declined and labor legislation was reformed to "increase flexibility and eliminate rigidities unattractive to foreign investors" (de Janvry et al., 1993: 79). The reduction of the state apparatus was also pursued throughout the 1980s (except for a right-wing "populist experience" between 1986 and 1988) and speeded up in the early 1990s. Between 1982 and 1990, public sector employment fell from 13.5% to 11.4% of total employment. Public expenditure, meanwhile, plunged dramatically from 21.6% of GDP (current prices) in 1981 to 11% in 1992 (see Table 7.3). Public consumption and social services (education and health) have been particularly hard hit.

The evolution of the functional income distribution points strongly toward increases in inequality in 1980–1984 and 1987–1991 (see Table 7.5). Urban household survey data available since 1987 corroborate that evidence, pointing to a sharp increase in income concentration around 1990 (see Table 7.6). The Gini coefficient among wage and salary earners (based on unadjusted income data) jumped from an average of 0.431 in 1988–1990 to an average of 0.483 in 1992–1993. Household income distribution followed a similar, albeit smoother, ascending path. The evolution of real income by income stratum discloses a severe deterioration for the poorest half of the population, exceeding 25% for the bottom quintile, an unstable or slightly declining situation for the next 45%, and a sharp improvement (of 25%) for the richest 5% (see Table 7.6); income of the top decile relative to the bottom decile rose from twenty-four-fold to thirty-fold (based on unadjusted data). Carlos Larrea (see Table 7.8) estimates urban poverty incidence to have risen from 66.3% in 1988 to a peak of 75.3% in 1990, after which a decline occurred in 1993.

The timing of this recent accentuation of inequality suggests that trade liberalization and the reduction of public employment could have played a role. Concentration as measured by the Gini coefficient increased between 1988–1990 and 1992–1993 for both wage and nonwage income—3.3% and 7.3%, respectively—and for both formal and nonformal activities—9% and 4.6%, respectively. This pattern is consistent with rapidly rising incomes for a subset of business people leading to the increased variance both within the nonwage category and within the formal sector; a negative impact of trade liberalization on small-scale enterprises could have contributed to this as well. Though the increase was less marked, wages became more concentrated as well. There was a strong decline in real minimum wages after 1980 that, together with some labor-market deregulation, could have played a role in the declining labor share.

Costa Rica: Reform Without Widening Gaps?

On the evidence available to date, Costa Rica appears to be the only LAC country to undertake significant market-friendly reforms without suffering a large widening of income differentials—an increase in the Gini coefficient of, say, 5 percentage points or more.[16] Costa Rica brought a tradition of social and political stability to the trials of the 1980s and came off a strong postwar economic performance in which average GDP growth exceeded 6% over the period 1950–1980. A good social service system gave it the highest life expectancy in Latin America, with the exception of Cuba, and the absence of an army allowed it to allocate more resources to civilian uses. Growth in the 1970s was fragile, however, based on an expansionary monetary and fiscal policy; a fortuitous increase in coffee prices in 1976–1977, and an investment boom, much of which was financed by foreign savings. The second oil price hike in 1979, rising interest rates, and the world recession brought a sharp 14% decline in GDP over 1980–1982, a 23% fall in income per capita, and a 25% cut in real wages. At the depths of the trough, a new president with ties to labor and (through his party) to previous social legislation took office, buoyed by a high level of public support and confidence. Over the next few years an adjustment program was put in place, including tax increases; weakening of the power of unions (union strength had lain mainly in the public sector);

privatization; and new incentives for exports, especially nontraditional ones.

The program has been relatively successful in reestablishing a decent growth performance of over 4% per year (through 1994) after returning to its precrisis GDP level in 1985. Policy changes were less extreme, more gradual, and less erratic than in Chile. Real wages did not long remain low because the indexing mechanism that linked nominal wage increases to past inflation was left in place with only mild modification, so that when tightened monetary and fiscal policy brought inflation quickly to heel, real wages moved back to or near their previous peak in only three or four years. The national unemployment rate also returned quickly to its normal range, around 5%.

Costa Rica's income distribution, while unequal, has been less so than in such extreme cases as Brazil. J. D. Trejos and P. Sauma (1994) report that measured inequality among households fell during the crisis and again during the adjustment period (which they date as 1982–1986), then rose sharply from 1985 to 1987 and tended to fall after that (Berry, 1995: Table 8). The increase between 1985 and 1987 could reflect the first effects of the liberalization, but it could also be due to a change in survey methodology at that time.[17] Qualifications related to the uncertain quality of the Costa Rican data notwithstanding, the best guess at this time is that there was no significant, lasting negative impact of the post-1986 reforms on the level of inequality in Costa Rica. Trejos and Sauma (1994) report Gini coefficients of essentially the same magnitude in 1993 as in 1980. The nearly 3 percentage point decline between 1980 and 1985 is balanced by the 4% increase over 1985–1987. Since there is some likelihood that the latter increase is illusory, there is a corresponding possibility that the level of inequality (i.e., the Gini reflecting these families and the types of income included) actually fell between 1980 and 1993 and that it was about constant between 1985 and 1993. In that case, Costa Rica stands as an exception to the general tendency for such reforms to be associated with sharply increased inequality.

One broad interpretation of the Costa Rican experience is that it shares many elements with other LAC countries but includes differences in degree, timing, and abruptness. For example, although the earnings differentials by skills do stop falling, they do not increase sharply at the time of economic liberalization. And though the variance of salary incomes rose for a couple of years after liberalization began, it then continued its downward movement. It is possible that when changes are made more gradually as in Costa Rica, they do not produce as great a negative impact on distribution as when the same degree of policy change takes place more quickly.

Paraguay: The Export-Oriented Agriculture Growth Model

Although Paraguay has not undertaken the sort of policy reforms that are the main topic of discussion here, its experience is worth mentioning because it is unique among Latin American countries in having pursued an outward-oriented growth strategy based on the rural economy, more or less systematically since the 1950s (Weisskoff, 1992a: 1531). It is the most agricultural of the countries reviewed and, in some general sense, at an earlier stage of development than most of the others. W. Baer and L. Breuer (1986: 125) note that the massive Itaipu hydroelectric project, begun in the early 1970s, sidetracked the country's export-oriented growth strategy during that decade, bringing in massive capital, creating inflation, and leading to an appreciation of the currency that restrained export growth. Even then, however, agriculture grew fast, though more on the basis of internal demand. Completion of the Itaipu project in the early 1980s led to a crisis, but after two years of negative growth recovery began and then accelerated, led once again by export agriculture. Through 1980, although exports were growing fast along with the economy, the ratio of exports to GDP eased down a bit to just 14%, after which it shot up to 34% in 1989.

R. Weisskoff (1992a: 1531) describes the agricultural growth strategy as "based on increasing inputs of land, labor and machinery in a mix of old and new technologies" and as resulting in "the successful expansion of a wide range of crop and livestock activities." Some exports (e.g., cotton) were produced by small peasant farmers using oxen but also hybrid seed and chemical fertilizers; soybeans and wheat are grown on medium-sized farms with machinery and international technology (Weisskoff, 1992a: 1538). Cattle are the domain of the *latifundia* (large farms). Although all groups have participated, Weisskoff concludes that export-led growth has gone hand-in-hand with the growth of structural inequities and repression of peasant organizations. Since the political opening of 1989, land invasions and occupations have increased, as has expulsion by armed groups.

Weisskoff (1992b: 173) reports sharp increases in inequality across the three census years (1972, 1982, and 1988) for which he constructs national distributions; the Gini coefficient (calculated from his quintile shares) rises from 0.531 in 1972 to 0.564 in 1982 to 0.596 in 1988. During the 1972–1982 period, during which per capita GDP rose from $1,230 1980 purchasing power parity dollars[18] to $2,016, the average of the bottom quintile edged up a bit from $221 to $231; in the next six years, which saw no net change in the national average family income, the figure for this group collapsed to $131. Simultaneous with this apparently continuous widening of income differentials at the economywide level, the urban distribution was in fact improving; the locus of the increase in inequality was agriculture, where the share of the top decile rose dramatically from 50.4% in 1972 to 75.7% in 1988.[19] This may seem surprising given that the *minifundia* (small farms) sector did participate in the export growth process; probably the repressive political regime tilted the distributional outcomes in the negative direction. In any case, this experience does not provide positive evidence on the distributional merits of agriculture-based export strategy. It is consistent with the less quantified record from countries like Mexico and Ecuador, which indicates that the main benefits are likely to go to high-income families.

Is Paraguay's experience indicative of what might be expected in other countries that pursue an export-oriented strategy built on agriculture? Does this experience belie the hope, in countries where agriculture is important though less dominant than in Paraguay, that freer trade will raise the incomes of the rural poor? The answers to these questions are of obvious importance because the hope has been that liberalization of trade and investment would raise rural incomes. It is also of importance since acceptable quality data on rural income trends are lacking in a number of the countries analyzed (including Chile, Argentina, Uruguay, Ecuador, and Colombia), leaving open the possibility that events in agriculture may have offset the general worsening observed in the urban economy.

The evidence from other countries, while not quantitatively linked to overall income distribution as in Weisskoff's work, suggests that Paraguay's experience with export-oriented agricultural growth is probably among the most negative in terms of its distributional consequences. At the same time, it provides few grounds for strong optimism that the rural-agricultural side of the outward-orientation picture will be positive enough to greatly alter the conclusions reached on the basis of urban data.[20] In their impressively detailed review of three cases (Paraguay, Chile, and Guatemala), M. R. Carter, B. L. Barham, and D. Mesbah (1996) emphasize the range of possible results. They note that in all three cases the amount of labor absorbed in the boom crop decreases as the size of the farm operation grows, so it is important that small farms be participants in the production of export items.

> The social welfare impact of the export booms thus depend in the short run on which classes adopt the crops: in the longer run, these impacts depend on the patterns of structural change that shift land between classes (and secondarily, alter levels of employment). If adoption of export crops favors smallholders, as it has in the Guatemalan highlands, then the positive impacts on the rural poor will tend to be magnified, and more and more so over time if the boom renders smallholders more competitive in the land market.
>
> In the frontier region of Paraguay, the boom in wheat has given rise to precisely the opposite interaction. The boom, which directly favors

large-scale farmers who absorb relatively little labor per hectare, has occasioned a pattern of structural change over time in which the shift of land to large farms has accentuated the negative impacts of the boom on the rural poor, creating a highly exclusionary growth trajectory that leaves peasants out as both producers and workers.

The Chilean experience falls somewhere in between these two cases. The fruit export boom has bypassed the traditional minifundia sector and the small-scale farm sector created from the remnants of the agrarian reform. Over time, land has shifted from smallholders to larger holdings. At the same time, export crops on large farms seems to absorb more labor than the traditional crops (and farms) that they displace. The effects on social welfare of this partly exclusionary process have probably been aggravated by the restructuring of the workforce toward more seasonal labor. (Carter, Barham, and Marsbah, 1996: 57–58)

The best type of export crop for the rural poor would be one that they could adopt on most of their land and grow competitively with larger farmers. The Guatemalan experience with vegetable exports from the highlands is clearly the most positive in this sense and hence the most promising from a distributional point of view. The contract-farming regime appeared to be the competitively dominant way of organizing production, but its dominance is proving to be short-lived. Exporters have begun to shift from contract farming because of increasing costs associated with quality measurement, in particular problems with pesticide residues, which have been threatening entry into the U.S. market. Intense supervision of smallholders' pesticide use appears infeasible because of the costs of monitoring (Carter, Barham, and Marsbah, 1996, 43). This experience thus falls short of the ideal both in that small farmers are not able to devote as much of their resources to these export items as would have been desirable to raise their incomes and in that its sustainability is now in question.

On the whole, Carter, Barham, and Mesbah (1996: 58–59) conclude that "more competitive biases seem to be working against small-scale producers than working for them" and hence that "informed pessimism is in order." Larger farms are often favored by the human capital intensity of many export crops, by product perishability and the resulting need for vertical integration, and by the absence of insurance markets. Cooperative institutions, which can raise small-farm competitiveness, have been declining in recent years in much of rural Latin America due to reduced foreign assistance, macroeconomic crises, austerity programs, and rapid changes in agrarian structure.

Puerto Rico: Outward Orientation with Improving Distribution?

Another case whose special features may provide interesting lessons is Puerto Rico. It is outward-oriented, has registered one of the developing world's fastest rates of growth of per capita income since 1950, and has been blessed by a falling level of income inequality. From 1950 to 1990 per capita GDP rose at an annual rate of 3.95%. W. J. Baumol and E. N. Wolff (1996: 883) judge that this growth performance should serve to dispel the idea that Latin Americans are at the opposite end of the spectrum from the East Asians in terms of "drive, entrepreneurship and ability to produce a vibrant and expanding economy." Its experience may also be construed as a test of the effects of a strongly outward-oriented strategy. Exports have regularly surpassed 50% of output, there are few restrictions on capital flows or on labor, and the manufacturing sector is composed almost entirely of outside capital.

In terms of the possibly transferable lessons to be learned on the growth front, one must consider the roles of outside funds contributing to the high investment rate; of unimpeded access to U.S. mainland markets; and of ease of emigration—43% of the total Puerto Rican population lives on the U.S. mainland (Sotomayor, 1996: 50), which has lowered population growth to an average of just 1.25% from 1950–1990. Our main interest here, however, is the distribution implications of such a growth process.

Drawing on U.S Bureau of the Census data for 1969, 1979, and 1989, O. J. Sotomayor (1996) reports that both poverty and inequality declined unambiguously in the 1970s and 1980s. The source of this improvement, however, was not the growth and distribution of earned income but rather that of unearned income, and in particular transfers from the U.S. federal government. The Gini coefficient of the distribution of total household cash income among households (ranked by that income, I presume) fell from 0.565 in 1969 to 0.522 in 1979 and to 0.505 in 1989, with the headcount and other indices of poverty also moving down (Sotomayor, 1996: 52). The share of the top quintile fell sharply in the 1970s but rose a bit in the 1980s, when the share gains registered by the lowest income groups were at the expense of the third and fourth quintiles.[21] While this overall decrease in household income concentration was taking place, the already high Gini coefficient for wage income rose further (0.63 in 1969 to 0.67 in the other two years), as did that for all earned income (wages and income from self-employment). But this effect was more than offset by the big increase in transfer income, mainly in the form of federal aid (i.e., aid from the United States) to local governments and income in the form of food stamps, social security, and public assistance. Such transfers rose dramatically (167% in the 1970s and 10% in the 1980s; see Sotomayor, 1996: 51) to push their share of total household cash income up from 14.9% in 1969 to 29.6% in 1979, tapering off to 27.4% in 1989.

The slower rise of wage/salary compensation than of output over the two decades (29% per capita versus 86% per capita) reflects rising profits, a large share of which presumably returned to the U.S. mainland.[22] Median wage rates rose slowly for low-skilled workers (those with less than high-school degree) in the first decade (14.2%) and not at all in the second, but for high-skilled workers there was virtual constancy in both decades.

Sotomayor judges that without the transfers the level of income concentration would have increased, as suggested by the fact that the concentration of earned income did increase, and that poverty would have stayed constant or risen (depending on the measure), whereas in fact it fell significantly. This belief is based on the presumption that the transfers had no more than small (negative) effects on earned incomes, that is, that they did not greatly diminish income-generating employment.[23] In any case, it is safe to judge that in the absence of the large flow of transfers, the very high level of inequality characterizing Puerto Rico would not have fallen. No example of an outward-oriented Latin American country achieving an improvement in distribution through the combination of market outcomes and its own redistributive efforts has yet been identified.

Conclusion

The LAC countries are launched on a different, more outward-oriented and less interventionist economic strategy than the ISI approach they followed during most of the postwar period. The new model shows clear signs of working well in some countries but has been slower than might have been hoped in allowing the region to recover its former growth. Unless growth accelerates quickly in the next few years, and in some countries even if it does, it will once again be overoptimistic to assume that growth will prove an adequate antidote to poverty. The reasons are summarized in what follows.

1. Distribution has worsened significantly, if not dramatically, in most countries undertaking market-friendly economic reforms.

Slower than expected growth is one source of dampened hopes. But the main one is the accumulated evidence, reviewed previously, that the economic reforms have been systematically associated with severe accentuation of (primary) income inequality. Among LAC counties for which the statistical evidence is adequate to reach any conclusions on this issue, the only probable exception to this generalization is Costa Rica; Jamaica and Peru may turn out to be as well, but this remains to be seen. In general, insufficient data are available to judge whether the distribution of secondary income (after allowing for taxes, transfers, and public provision of goods) has moved differently from the primary distribution. Effective targeting of the poor has made a positive impact on inequality in some cases, but the reduction of government activity, as well as the changes in tax systems toward the greater use of indirect taxes, may have had a regressive effect.

The country experiences reviewed above suggest that the "normal" observed increase in inequality accompanying reforms is 5–10 points as measured by the Gini coefficient of primary income (see Table 1.3). It seems likely that this increase is typically the result of a jump in the share of the top decile, most of this accruing to the top 5% or perhaps to the top 1% (as in the cases of Colombian and Ecuadorean households), whereas most of the bottom deciles lose. In the three Colombian cities analyzed in Chapter 6, the income of the top 5% of households rose from thirteen to twenty times the income of the bottom decile. The share of the bottom decile (the biggest loser in percentage terms) fell from 1.75% to 1.45% of total recorded income. At a moderate GDP per capita growth rate of 2% per year, it will require nearly ten years of distribution-neutral growth to recover the "lost ground" implicit in this income share decline. If per capita income growth could be accelerated to, say, 5%, the recovery period would be only four years. In Ecuador, where the percentage decline for the bottom decile was sharper (from 2.2% to 1.5%), nearly twenty years of distribution-neutral growth at 2% per year per capita would be needed (about eight years at 5%).

2. *The close association between adoption of market-friendly
   economic reforms and accentuation of inequality is evident
   and a cause for serious concern.*

No definitive conclusions as to what underlies the observed increases in inequality can be derived from the comparison of country experiences alone. Drawing on both those experiences and the limited microeconomic evidence on the various elements of the reform package and on other hypothesized causes, I tentatively suggest that ongoing technological change, more open trade regimes, the dismantling of labor institutions, and the "socialization" of debts (whereby the state makes itself responsible for certain private external debts that might otherwise threaten macroeconomic or financial stability) have all had negative impacts on distribution. The effect of the scaling down of the public sector (directly and via the privatization of public enterprise) seems more open to question. Increasing foreign investment has also been proposed as a source of increasing inequality (in Mexico, for example), but judgment should probably be reserved on this point also. Many questions remain with respect to how these various factors interact among themselves or complement each other, both in terms of their growth effects and their implications for income distribution.

Trade and labor-market reforms have been consistent elements of the reform packages instituted in the LAC countries where distribution has worsened significantly. In each case it is easy to see mechanisms whose

Table 1.3 Summary of Relationships Between Economic Reforms and Distribution (countries for which data are available)

Country	Main Period of Worsening	Main Period, Degree of Worsening	To Present, Degree of Worsening	Main Period of Worsening, Characteristics
Argentina (greater Buenos Aires)	1976–1978	8 points, followed by some easing	8 points	Liberalization, labor repression, no net growth
Chile (greater Santiago)	1974–1976	7–9 points	7–9 points	Liberalization, labor repression, sharp recession
Uruguay (Montevideo)	1976–1979 or 1982–1984	9 points or 7 points	Not available	Liberalization, labor repression, growth *or* recession, increased exports, transition toward democracy
Mexico	late 1980s	3–5 points	3–5 points	Liberalization, some labor reform, slow growth
Dominican Republic	1984–1989	8 points	Not available	May have coincided with adjustment
Colombia (three major cities)	1990–1992	4–7 points	4–7 points	Liberalization, labor-market reforms, moderate growth
Ecuador (urban)	1989–1991	5 points	5 points	Liberalization, labor reforms, slow growth
Costa Rica	1985–1987 (?)	0–4 points (?)	–1 to +3 points	Liberalization, mild labor reforms, moderate growth

Sources: For Argentina, Table 3.7, this volume; for Chile, Berry 1995: Table 2; for Uruguay, Berry 1995: Table 5 and Indart 1996; for Mexico, Table 1.2, this volume; for the Dominican Republic, Sanatan and Rather 1993: 55; for Colombia, Table 6.3, this volume; for Ecuador, Table 7.6, this volume; for Costa Rica, Trejos and Sauma 1994 and Berry 1995: Table 8.

Notes: Distribution worsening measured in percentage point increases of the Gini coefficient. Depending on data availability, the Gini coefficient may refer to income earners, households ranked by household income, households ranked by per capita income, or other distributions available. Completeness of income coverage varies with the case, as is discussed in the text. The (?) attached to the Costa Rican case reflects the special data uncertainty, which implies that no worsening may have occurred in this instance.

effects on distribution *might* be negative, and in each case there is at least some empirical evidence suggesting that those mechanisms are at work. In the case of trade, for example, it appears likely that the comparative advantage of the region does not lie in unskilled labor-intensive products. Import liberalization appears to shift the price vector in favor of better-off families. Although optimists have argued that the opening up of trade should be expected to raise the relative incomes of agricultural workers, recent evidence on this point is not encouraging. A significant feature of the 1984–1989 period in Mexico was the contribution of a widening gap between urban and rural incomes to the overall increase in inequality and of the sharp decline in income from agriculture and livestock as a share of rural income (Alarcón, 1993: 139, 148). In Colombia, an unprecedented increase in the gap between urban and rural incomes has appeared within the last two years, coincident with the process of liberalization. It is increasingly clear that in such countries a major part of the agricultural sector cannot compete easily with an onslaught of imports, and its labor resources are unlikely to move quickly to other sectors.[24] In Paraguay, export-based agricultural growth seems to have contributed to a big increase in inequality. Meanwhile, labor-market reforms appear to open the way for wider wage and salary differentials among individuals. A tentative guess would be that these two elements of reform packages may underlie most of the negative trends in distribution.[25]

The "socialization" of international and other debts in order to save teetering financial and other enterprises has doubtless had a significantly negative impact on distribution, as shown in the case of Chile by P. Meller (1992a). This was, however, a crisis-response policy, less germane to our present concerns than the now ongoing financial liberalizations (assuming that such liberalizations do not henceforth lead to financial crises, as they sometimes did during the 1970s and 1980s; see Diaz-Alejandro, 1985). Solid evidence has yet to come in as to their distribution impacts, but there are plenty of reasons to suspect that these could be negative and that the optimists will here, as in the area of trade policy, prove to have been excessively optimistic.

The impact of foreign investment is another area in which the conventional wisdom, based on a two-factor model in which an increase in the capital stock would raise the relative returns to labor, may be off target for the LAC region. But further analysis will be necessary before much can be said with confidence in this area. The same goes for the impact of the downsizing of the public sector.

3. *Neither theory nor the record has provided much evidence on*
   how lasting the negative distributional effects will turn out to be.

Since many of the economic reform episodes reviewed above are recent, it might be hoped that many of the accompanying negative effects are temporary, associated with the transition to a new model, and likely to peter out with time and the adjustment of economic actors to the new reality. It is now two decades since inequality began to rise in Chile; and although no further increase seems to have occurred since the late 1980s, neither has a decline begun. More generally, it does not appear likely that simple recovery from the recessions that have racked the LAC countries will reverse the increases in inequality. S. A. Morley's conclusion that the best policy to reduce poverty in economies mired in stagnation and underutilization of capacity is to get the economy moving is certainly valid. It may be true, as he argues, that economic downturns were the main factor underlying the increases in inequality observed in some LAC countries during the 1980s, but the evidence presented above suggests that most of the observed worsening has other origins.

4. It is urgent to achieve better combinations of growth and distribution than those of the last two decades.

All country experiences no doubt have valuable lessons built into them, but those of Chile, Colombia, and Costa Rica are perhaps the most interesting from the perspective of learning how to guide policy more effectively in future. Costa Rica is the one country that may have come through a reform process without a major deterioration of distribution. Colombia appears to have achieved the most significant prereform improvement in distribution, at least in the urban areas. And Chile undertook the reforms earliest, suffered high social costs thereafter, but has also pioneered a number of impressive policy experiments of relevance to other countries.

Some priority policy areas seem clear: education and training systems, clearly important in light of the danger that low-skilled persons are being left behind; small and medium-sized enterprise policy, important because of the major role this sector plays in the creation of productive employment; poverty redressal, whether through better targeting or otherwise, in light of evidence that considerable social spending has not been very efficiently carried out in the past and that under conditions of rapid economic change such systems must be unusually adept in order to do their job well. Although there is much agreement on these broad directions, the precise policy formula most likely to bear fruit in each of these areas is much less clear. Designing it has high priority. Better information and more analysis of the determinants of income distribution will be needed for policy to become more professional in this area.

On the rural-agricultural front, the patterns of change are less clear. The optimism of those who felt that simply loosing the chains on agricultural exports would quickly reduce rural poverty has been premature and naive, if the unfolding events in Paraguay and several other countries are any guide. Although probably due more to the preceding economic crisis than to the reforms that have followed it, the social strains evident in rural Mexico, Central America, and other areas highlight the need for an effective policy response. As Carter, Barham, and Marsbaugh (1996: 60) put it:

> The political, social and economic consequences of exclusionary growth can be devastating and are therefore worth trying to prevent. . . . The extreme social conflicts erupting in Central America and the extent of Brazilian rural poverty and its spillover into issues ranging from street children, urban squalor, and crime to environmental degradation should serve as motivating examples.

On the positive side, the more inclusive rural policies developed in East Asian countries may have played an important role in the subsequent development successes of those countries (Wade, 1990). Whether meaningfully inclusionary policies are possible without major structural reform (e.g., significant land redistribution) remains a big unknown in this part of the developing world. Although some pessimism on this front is no doubt warranted, policymakers must clearly confront the challenges in the hope that some useful policy adjustments are possible.

Notes

Albert Berry is a professor of economics at the University of Toronto. He thanks Albert Fishlow, Gustavo Indart, Adriana Marshall, and Samuel Morley for comments on an earlier version of this chapter.

1. If this extra period of growth brought with it a significant tightening of the labor market, it might have been realistic to expect the income share of the bottom few deciles to rise (though perhaps not the very bottom decile).

2. As noted above, Brazil and Colombia had already taken serious steps to encourage exports by the late 1960s but had not (at that time) undertaken an important liberalization of imports nor imposed changes on the institutions governing their labor markets.

3. Comparable 1967–1968 data from the Estudios Conjuntos Sobre Integración Económica Latinoamericana (ECIEL) study revealed a Gini coefficient for the distribution of income among households of 0.451 in Santiago, 0.487 in Lima, an average of 0.473 in four Colombian cities, and an average of about 0.43 in two Venezuelan cities (Musgrove, 1978, 36).

4. Most of the published distribution data refer only to greater Santiago, but it is probably fairly representative of the country, as suggested by the similarity of measured inequality for the few years for which both city and national data are available.

5. Over that period average private consumption per person fell by about 13 percent and the share of the bottom quintile by 32 percent. The short-run movements of the various available distributions coincide rather closely. The main question is how large a total shift occurred between the pre-Allende period and the late 1980s, when inequality began to level off. The figures on consumption distribution, important both because of their presumed greater accuracy than income data and

because they should be a good measure of welfare, show an incredible 12 point jump in the Gini coefficient (from 0.31 to 0.42). The household income distribution series suggests an increase of about 5 points in the Gini coefficient between 1970 (which seems representative of the late 1960s, judging by the series for income recipients) and 1987–1989; the Gini coefficient of the household per capita distribution rose by about 6.5 points. The probable increase in the Gini of the most interesting distributions was thus somewhere between important (6 points) and dramatic (12 points).

6. The high incidence of television sets (over 70%), refrigerators (49%), radios (83%), and bathrooms (74%) even in the lowest quintile throws some question on the 45% poverty figure. Some of these items probably became much more prevalent due to the low prices that came with the import liberalization around 1980. Possibly some of the poor went into debt at this time to acquire them.

7. If the series cited by Ffrench-Davis (1992) (the source of the wage data is Instituto Nacional de Estadistica) is consistent with that reported by Economic Commission for Latin America and the Caribbean (ECLAC) (1992: 44), which shows an increase of 11.7% over 1989–1992, then the 1992 figure is 3% above that of 1970.

8. Data on the distribution among households in the greater Buenos Aires region and among income earners in the country as a whole seem to move parallel to those just cited for those time periods when they are available, which does not in either case include much beyond 1980. As a result, it has been necessary to use the Buenos Aires earner data, but with considerable confidence that they do not misrepresent the trends that actually occurred among households in the nation as a whole (Berry, 1990).

9. Fiszbein's figures on the distribution of income among households, cited in Morley (1994: 8), show a sharp increase in the Gini coefficient from 0.40 in 1985 to 0.45 in 1988, and Psacharopoulos et al. (1993) show a big increase between 1981 (0.41) and 1989 (0.48). These are not greatly different from the earner distribution trends presented by Adriana Marshall (see Chapter 3).

10. Favaro and Bension (1993: 276) claim that these disincentives contributed to considerable emigration by this group. But this appears inconsistent with the fact that if the emergence of a more uniform wage structure took place prior to 1968, then it did not quickly lead to emigration, which was in fact most significant between 1973 and 1975, when there were no unions in Uruguay (communication from Gustavo Indart).

11. Evidence that the number of super-rich has increased rapidly in Mexico (two Mexicans were included in *Forbes* magazine's 1991 list of billionaires; the 1994 list included twenty-four) may mean that these data understate the increase in inequality, since household surveys essentially never include evidence from that very small group of very rich families. Only after more detailed analysis, involving a wider range of methodologies, will the Mexican story become clearer.

12. At least two econometric studies have addressed the relationship between trade liberalization and employment and/or wages in the manufacturing sector. Feliciano (1993) finds no impact of liberalization on industry-level employment. Revenga (1994), using panel data over 1984–1990 for medium-to-large plants, does obtain a negative and significant coefficient for the impact of the tariff (or tariff equivalent) reduction on employment. Although such studies are valuable in assessing the impact of liberalization on manufacturing, they do not provide a guide to its economywide impacts.

13. The statistical evidence is matched by a growing concern in Colombia that the new "model" is having an adverse effect on income distribution (Sarmiento, 1993).

14. These figures are consistent with the fairly generally accepted view that income inequality decreased in Colombia between the early 1970s and the 1980s, both in urban areas and for the nation as a whole and both for earners and for households (Londoño, 1989, 1995). There is some disagreement as to the timing of the decline and when it came to an end (see Chapter 6).

15. Londoño (1993) accepts that the distribution of labor income became more concentrated between 1988 and 1993 but estimates that a correspondingly marked decrease in that of nonlabor income for the economy as a whole offset the former effect, such that the Gini coefficient of income among households (the ranking criterion is not noted) was essentially unchanged between 1988 and 1993.

16. Other possible candidates, both of which have liberalized too recently for the evidence to be clear at this time, are Peru and Jamaica. The latter case is discussed by Handa (1995).

17. Communication from T. Gindling. Problems of comparability might be somewhat less severe in estimates of the distribution of income among earners, but our estimates of distribution among (paid or unpaid) workers reveal the same sort of abrupt worsening in 1987 as characterizes the household estimates.

18. One purchasing power parity dollar of 1980 refers to an amount of currency that will buy the same amount of an average international bundle of goods as would a 1980 dollar.

19. Weisskoff's analysis relies on Asunción data for the three census years (1972, 1982, and 1988) and constructs agricultural distributions for the same years on the basis of landholding and farm income surveys. The estimates are based on allocation of total national accounts of sectoral income across component population cells. As a result, they incorporate an upward bias relative to estimates from unadjusted household survey data that miss much of the capital income and hence understate the degree of inequality.

20. As Carter, Barham, and Marsbah (1996: 33) note, the proponents of policies to encourage agricultural exports focus on the macroeconomic benefits and on potential improvements in productivity and employment. Opponents generally expect that such exports will have negative impacts on the rural poor and on the environment because of lessening access to land, insufficient and uncertain labor opportunities, and rising food prices.

21. Unfortunately, the figures are somewhat suspect (although the author claims they are fully comparable over the three years) since the lowest decile had in 1969 only 0.01% of total income, and an implausibly low share in 1979 as well. In other words, there were many zero-income households, suggesting either a too-short income reporting period or serious reporting errors. The reported income shares of the bottom four deciles rose over the twenty years, especially those of the lowest deciles.

22. The household figures reported here do not include much capital income, and the national accounts estimates for that income source are not conceptually comparable, so no attempt was made to estimate degree of reporting of such incomes (Sotomayor, 1996: 54).

23. Sotomayor cites Santiago's (1992) study of the aggregate data, which finds a significant but small negative impact of the level of transfers on participation. He does not take into account the possibility that hours worked could be negatively affected even if the participation rate was not. He observes correctly that

since these transfers are net income gains to the region, they may have positive macro effects and thus contribute to income generation and poverty rates in that way.

24. Even more striking is the experience of Paraguay, unique among Latin American countries in having pursued an outward-oriented growth strategy based on the rural economy, more or less systematically since the 1950s (Weisskoff, 1992a: 1531). Some of the exports (e.g., cotton) were produced by small peasant farmers, using hybrid seed, chemical fertilizers, and other modern inputs. Yet Weisskoff's (1992b: 173) estimates indicate the inequality increased sharply between 1972 and 1988, the Gini coefficient (calculated from his quintile shares) rising from 0.531 in 1972 to 0.564 in 1982 to 0.596 in 1988.

25. It is important to distinguish the increases in inequality that coincided, in a number of countries, with the recessions suffered by those countries and are analyzed in detail by Morley (1995), from the increases which persisted after the subsequent recoveries. The downturns were often associated with high levels of inflation and with sharply falling real minimum wages. It is likely that the falling minimum wage played a significant role in the increases in inequality in several of those countries. But our main concern is with the increase in inequality that remains after countries have emerged from the crises in question. Here too it is likely that the lowered real wages have been important, but perhaps somewhat less so than during the crises themselves.

2

Income Distribution and Poverty Through Crisis and Adjustment

Oscar Altimir

Most Latin American countries are painfully recovering from the protracted crisis they suffered during the 1980s and from the traumatic adjustments they had to undergo in order to lay the bases for a new phase of sustained growth. The net transfer of resources to the region, which before the crisis represented more than 2% of regional gross domestic product (GDP), suddenly became negative. Between 1982 and 1989, the Latin American countries' net export of capital was equivalent to almost 4% of their aggregate GDP. The turnaround in the net transfer of resources was thus tantamount to a loss of 6% on domestic resources during this period.

After the external adjustment and recession that reduced regional per capita GDP by 10% between 1980 and 1983, most Latin American economies wavered between recession and inflation, muddling through the external debt tangle and its domestic sequels for most of the decade. At its close, per capita product was still at the 1983 level, and real national per capita income was 15% lower than in 1980. From 1991 to 1993, however, growth has been steadier, there have been signs of a reactivation of private investment along with the return of significant capital flows, the trend toward price stabilization has become generalized, and most of the huge fiscal adjustments of the previous years have held fast.

Although in some countries the stabilization processes remain fragile, most Latin American economies are now working on new foundations. These are characterized by a firmer orientation toward exports (whose volume has, in many cases, at least doubled during the past decade), trade

This slightly modified version appeared first in Oscar Altimir, "Income Distribution and Poverty Through Crisis Adjustment," *CEPAL Review,* No. 52 (LC/G. 1824-P), Santiago, Chile, Economic Commission for Latin America and the Caribbean (ECLAC), April 1994.

liberalization, fiscal austerity, more prudent management of monetary policy, and greater reluctance to resort to state regulation of economic activity.

For the poor and lower to middle-income groups, however, the severe economic crisis of the 1980s involved damaging declines both in real income and in access to and quality of social services. Almost all countries experienced acute redistributions of income among households during this crisis decade, in most cases with regressive net outcomes at the end of the decade. At the same time, regressive changes in relative incomes and the fall of real per capita income during the first half of the decade, when most economies suffered recessionary adjustments or had only just begun to recover, led to significant increases in absolute poverty, which in only a few cases have been partially reversed with the stabilization and growth processes of more recent years.

Economic recovery and the abatement of inflation are bringing relief on the poverty front, but there are increasing grounds for suspecting that the new modality under which the economies are functioning and the new rules of public policy involve greater income inequalities and more precarious employment situations than in the past, in a certainly tighter fiscal environment.

The Approach Adopted

The Database on Income Distribution and Poverty

Income distribution statistics in Latin America are of varied reliability and are not directly comparable with each other.[1] Among the many factors distorting their comparability, underestimation of income affects both income levels and their concentration. In order to somehow sidestep this obstacle, the analysis of changes in the distribution of income is based on pairs of available estimates for a given country (see Table 2.1) that are selected for being similar and therefore are apparently comparable with regard to the concept of income, the technique for measuring income, and the geographical coverage of the surveys used to collect the data as well as the units and criteria used by the respective authors in processing or adjusting the survey data.[2] However, in many cases proven or likely differences in any of these aspects invalidate the possibility of going beyond these pair-wise comparisons and simply pooling estimates—across countries, for example.

The poverty estimates for the 1980s (see Table 2.2, p. 49) are those provided by the Economic Commission for Latin America and the Caribbean (ECLAC, 1991c and 1992a). They are the result of applying, to the distributions of households by per capita income (previously adjusted

Table 2.1 Changes in Income Distribution During Selected Periods: Ten Latin American Countries

Country	Period	Source	Coverage[a]	Income Concept[b]	Changes in Concentration (%)		Changes in Shares of Income Groups (% of total income)		
					Gini Coefficient	Ratio of Top 10% to Lowest 40%	Lowest 40%	Middle 50%	Top 10%
Argentina	1970–1974	Altimir (1986)	MA	HI	4	9	-0.7	-0.7	1.4
	1974–1980	Altimir (1986)	MA	HPCI	10	28	-2.1	-1.2	3.3
	1980–1986	ECLAC (1991b)	MA	HPCI	11	27	-1.5	-3.2	4.7
	1980–1989	Psacharopoulos et al. (1992)	MA	HPCI	17	47	-2.9	-3.0	5.9
	1985–1990	Beccaria (1991)	MA	HPCI	—	-33[c]	-1.4[d]	-3.4[e]	4.8
	1979–1987	ECLAC (1991b)	RU	HPCI	4	32	-2.3	-1.3	3.6
Brazil	1979–1989	Psacharopoulos et al. (1992)	N	HPCI	7	9	2.7	-5.5	2.8
	1987–1989	Hoffman (1992)	U	IR	7	28	-1.3	-2.4	3.7
	1987–1990	Hoffman (1992)	U	IR	8	31[f]	-2.1[g]	-2.8[h]	4.9
	1987–1990	ECLAC (1991b; 1993a)	MA	HPCI	2	9	-1.0	—	1.0
			RU	HPCI	-6	-18	0.4	6.3	-6.7
Chile	1968–1974	Heskia (1980)	MA	HI	1	53	-5.1	5.2	-0.1
	1974–1980	Heskia (1980),	MA	HI	-10	-23	-2.0	1.8	-3.8
	1981–1983	Riveros (1985)	MA	HI	21	60	-2.8	-6.2[h]	9.0[i]
	1968–1983	Riveros (1985)	MA	HI	2	14	-1.1	-0.5[h]	1.6[i]
	1969–1978	ECLAC (1979), Rodriguez (1985)	N	HI	23	38	-1.6	-6.2	7.8
	1978–1988	Ffrench-Davis, Raczynski (1987)	MA	HE	—	54[j]	-4.9	-1.6[h]	6.5[i]
		Ffrench-Davis, Raczynski (1987)	MA	HE	—	23[j]	-1.9	-1.7[h]	3.6[i]
	1987–1990	ECLAC (1991b; 1991d)	U	HPCI	-2	-3	0.4	-0.4	—

(continues)

Table 2.1 continued

Country	Period	Source	Coverage[a]	Income Concept[b]	Changes in Concentration (%)		Changes in Shares of Income Groups (% of total income)		
					Gini Coefficient	Ratio of Top 10% to Lowest 40%	Lowest 40%	Middle 50%	Top 10%
Colombia	1978–1988	Londoño (1990)	N	IR	-1	-3	-0.2	0.3	-0.5
	1980–1986	ECLAC (1990)	MA	HPCI	-3	-12	0.2	0.8	-1.0
			RU	HPCI	-5	—	0.4	3.0	-3.4
	1980–1989	Psacharopoulos et al. (1992)	U	HPCI	-9	-27	1.9	3.2	-5.1
	1986–1990	ECLAC (1991b; 1993a)	MA	HPCI	-2	-1	-0.4	2.7	-2.3
			RU	HPCI	-9	-2	1.9	1.4	-3.3
Costa Rica	1981–1988	ECLAC (1991b)	MA	HPCI	7	22	-1.5	-1.6	3.1
			RU	HPCI	14	3	-1.9	-3.2	5.1
	1981–1989	Psacharopoulos et al. (1992)	N	HPCI	-3	-10	1.4	-1.9	0.5
	1988–1990	ECLAC (1991b; 1993a)	MA	HPCI	-6	-13	1.1	1.1	-2.2
			RU	HPCI	-6	-15	0.4	3.0	-3.4
Mexico	1977–1984	ECLAC (1988), Lustig (1992)	N	HI	-9	-41	2.8	0.7	-3.5
	1984–1989	Lustig (1992)	N	HI	—	28	-1.4	-3.7	5.1
Panama	1979–1989	Psacharopoulos et al. (1992)	N	HPCI	16	66	-3.5	-2.8	6.3
Peru	1985/1986–1990	Psacharopoulos et al. (1992)	MA	HPCI	2	5	-0.7	0.5	0.2
Uruguay	1973–1979	Melgar (1981)	MA	PHI	32	100	-4.7	-8.3	13.0
	1979–1981	Melgar (1981), Melgar, Villalobos (1987)	MA	PHI	-2	-4	-1.2	6.3	-5.1
	1981–1986	ECLAC (1991b; 1991c)	MA	HPCI	7	20	-1.2	-2.4	3.6
	1986–1989	ECLAC (1991b; 1991c)	MA	HPCI	-9	-19	1.4	3.1	-4.5
			RU	HPCI	-7	-12	1.5	0.1	-1.6
	1981–1989	Psacharopoulos et al. (1992)	U	HPCI	-3	-7	0.8	-0.2	-0.6

(continues)

Table 2.1 continued

Country	Period	Source	Coverage[a]	Income Concept[b]	Changes in Concentration (%)		Changes in Shares of Income Groups (% of total income)		
					Gini Coefficient	Ratio of Top 10% to Lowest 40%	Lowest 40%	Middle 50%	Top 10%
Venezuela	1981–1986	ECLAC (1991b)	MA	HPCI	8	19	-2.5	-1.7	4.2
	1981–1989	Psacharopoulos et al. (1992)	RU	HPCI	18	46	-2.6	-3.1	5.7
	1986–1990	ECLAC (1991b;1993a)	N	HPCI	3	8	-0.4	-1.3	1.7
			MA	HPCI	-4	-7	0.8	-0.4	-0.4
			RU	HPCI	—	3	—	-0.6	0.6
	1987–1989	Marquez, Mukherjee (1991)	N	HPCI	6	11	-0.2	-3.5	3.7
	1989–1990	Marquez, Mukherjee (1991)	N	HPCI	-4	-14	0.9	1.8	2.7

Notes: a. MA: metropolitan area; RU: remaining urban areas; U: urban areas; N: nationwide.
b. HI: household income; PHI: primary household income; HPCI: household per capita income; HE: household expenditure; IR: income of recipient.
c. Ratio of top 10% to lowest 30%.
d. Corresponds to lowest 30%.
e. Corresponds to middle 60%.
f. Ratio of top 10% to lowest 50%.
g. Corresponds to lowest 50%.
h. Corresponds to middle 40%.
i. Corresponds to top 20%.
j. Ratio of top 20% to lowest 40%.

for income underestimation),[3] country-specific poverty lines representing minimum normative budgets of private consumption based on minimum food budgets that adequately cover nutritional requirements.[4] The poverty lines used for different years of the 1980s were held constant in real terms, an approach that is acceptable for a period of recession and recovery.[5]

In this chapter, I use only headcount ratios as the poverty measure, which are available for several years of the past decade, for each country considered.[6] These are given in Table 2.3, which also includes the incidence of extreme poverty or destitution, defined as the proportion of households with a per capita income less than the value of the minimum food budget.

National measures of poverty are derived from urban and rural estimates. However, it should be borne in mind that headcount estimates for rural areas are of considerably shakier quality than those for urban areas. On the one hand, the norms used to draw rural poverty lines have an unavoidable urban bias in spite of taking into account urban-rural differences in prices and consumption. On the other hand, available measurements of rural incomes and of their distribution are usually even less accurate than those of urban incomes from the same survey. Finally, some of the rural estimates are no more than educated guesses based on relevant but indirect data (Altimir, 1991).

The set of countries considered in this chapter includes the major Latin American nations as well as some others for which comparable inequality and poverty measurements were also available, both at the beginning of the decade and at some later point in time. It excludes predominantly rural countries, such as Guatemala and Honduras, even though poverty estimates have been produced by ECLAC, because the method of analysis used here and the variables on which it rests capture mainly urban phenomena. Poverty measurement and analysis in such cases should be based on surveys, poverty yardsticks, and explanatory variables more closely applicable to rural conditions.

In this database, income generally measures household disposable cash income,[7] including both primary income (wages and salaries and entrepreneurial income) and other monetary income (pensions, transfers, rentals, interest, etc.) after direct tax payments. It therefore excludes imputed income from public goods and services provided free of charge or heavily subsidized and hence fails to reflect the redistributive effects of such public expenditure. These income measurements do not capture the incidence of indirect taxes on real income, either.

The Method of Analysis

Although my ultimate concern is with changes in social stratification and with disentangling those changes that are permanently reshaping Latin

Table 2.2 Estimates of Poverty and Indigence: Nineteen Latin American Countries, 1980, 1986, and 1990[a]

| | Poverty[b] | | | | | | Indigence[c] | | | | | |
| | 1980 | | 1986 | | 1990 | | 1980 | | 1986 | | 1990 | |
Area	Millions	%	Millions	%	Millions	%	Millions	%	Millions	%	Millions	%
Households												
Nationwide	24.2	35	32.1	37	37.0	39	10.4	15	14.6	17	16.9	18
Urban	11.8	25	18.7	30	22.7	34	4.1	9	7.0	11	8.7	13
Rural	12.4	54	13.4	53	14.3	53	6.3	28	7.6	30	8.2	30
Persons												
Nationwide	135.9	41	170.2	43	195.9	46	62.4	19	81.4	21	93.5	22
Urban	62.9	30	94.4	36	115.5	39	22.5	11	35.8	14	44.9	15
Rural	73.0	60	75.8	60	80.4	61	39.9	33	45.6	36	48.6	37

Sources: 1980 and 1986: ECLAC, 1991c; 1990: ECLAC, 1992a.

Notes: a. Based on data for Argentina, Brazil, Colombia, Costa Rica, Guatemala, Mexico, Panama, Peru, Uruguay, and Venezuela, for 1980 and 1986; and also for Chile, Honduras, and Paraguay for 1990. Poverty and indigence ratios calculated for these thirteen countries have been applied to the population of nineteen to arrive at the absolute numbers presented.

b. Corresponds to household per capita income below poverty lines equivalent to twice the country-specific minimum food budgets, which range from $22 to $34 (1988 dollars) per person per month, for urban areas.

c. Corresponds to household per capita income below the value of the country-specific minimum food budgets used to draw the poverty lines.

Table 2. 3 Incidence of Poverty and Indigence: Ten Latin American Countries, 1980s (percentage of households)

	Poverty			Indigence		
	Urban Areas	Rural Areas	National Level	Urban Areas	Rural Areas	National Level
Argentina						
1980	7	16[a]	9	2	4[a]	2
1986	12	17[a]	13	3	6[a]	4
1990	19[b]	—	—	—	—	—
1991	15[b]	—	—	—	—	—
Brazil						
1979	30	62	39	10	35	17
1987	34	60	40	13	34	18
1990	39	56	43	17	31	20
Chile						
1980	32[c]	41[c]	33[c]	13	—	14
1987	37	45	38	11	16	12
1990	34	36	35	—	15	—
Colombia						
1980	36	45[a]	39	13	22[a]	16
1986	36	42	38	15	22	17
1990	35	—	—	12	—	—
Costa Rica						
1981	16	28	22	5	8	6
1988	21	28	25	6	10	10
1990	22	25	24	7	12	10
Mexico						
1977	—	—	32	—	—	10
1984	23	43	30	6	19	10
Panama						
1979	31	45	36	14	27	19
1986	30	43	34	13	22	16
1989	34	48	38	15	25	18
Peru						
1979	35	65[a]	46	10	38[a]	21
1985/86	45	64	42	16	39	25
Uruguay						
1981	9	21[a]	11	2	7[a]	3
1986	14	23[a]	15	3	8[a]	3
1989	10	23[a]	15	2	8[a]	3
Venezuela						
1981	18	35	22	5	15	7
1986	25	34	27	8	14	9
1990	33	38	34	11	17	12

Sources: ECLAC (1991b; 1991c; 1992a).
Notes: a. These estimates should be considered "educated guesses" based on relevant but indirect information.
  b. Author's estimates based on Beccaria and Minujin (1991).
  c. Author's estimates based on Pollack and Uthoff (1987). Also see Altimir (1991).

American societies from those related to peoples' transitory accommodation to hard times, I am able here to focus only on aggregate changes in the relative distribution of welfare and the incidence of poverty, leaving out changes in the composition of households and in their economic strategies, including their ways of participating in the labor market. Moreover, the analysis is limited to changes in the distribution of private income.

With these limitations, I have tried to assess the distributive costs of the crisis and adjustments. These go beyond the "social costs," sometimes measured as losses in aggregate welfare, but they are far less than the total social costs, if we recognize that the social structure is more than just the distribution of welfare and that living conditions are not determined only by income.

Evaluating the specific nature of the costs is another matter. The distributive changes recorded by available income distribution measurements incorporate the effects of adjustment, institutional changes involving policy reform, and underlying restructuring processes as well as those of failed adjustment and the acceleration of inflation. However, since the crisis of the 1980s is the reflection of an epoch-making transformation of Latin American development, the measured distributive losses are attributed to the changes—including the periods of instability and inflation, failed policies, or policies involving overadjustment—that have marked such processes in some countries.

The focus is not on the interaction of macroeconomic variables (which has been analyzed elsewhere),[8] but on the relationships between changes in income distribution and poverty and the processes of adjustment, policy reform, and structural mutation underlying the changes in those macroeconomic variables.

Understanding the links between distributive changes and policy reforms poses methodological and time-related problems. Economic policy reforms generally oriented toward facilitating or promoting sustainable growth on the basis of freer trade and private investment may have short-term effects on income distribution as a result of the package of stabilization and adjustment policies. In the longer term, reforms may have negative distributive effects if a trade-off between growth and more equitable income distribution is observed or is to be expected on the basis of the pattern of growth promoted by the particular reforms undertaken. Whether economic restructuring promoted by policy reforms and by the new structural circumstances involves more unequal distribution of income is a matter whose empirical verification can only occur in the long term. For the moment, we can only consider what appear to be the "normal" or more or less "stable" distributive structures once each economy regains a sustained growth path.

Even though the distributive costs of external adjustment, stabilization, fiscal adjustment, and economic restructuring are intertwined, the characteristics and sequencing of policy packages certainly make a difference in terms of the magnitude and duration of distributive losses (see, for example, Garcia, 1991). However, the income distribution and poverty estimates in our database are too scanty to give more than very broad hints in this regard.

Moreover, in many instances the periods of analysis imposed by the availability of data include adjustment or stabilization policies, followed by a period in which the policies fail, followed by the acceleration of inflation; thus the data cover the distributive costs of both kinds of processes.

The basic assessment criteria I have used in this study are, on the one hand, to compare distributive changes and changes in macroeconomic and labor market variables during similar macroeconomic phases in the course of the adjustment process in different countries and, on the other hand, to compare the distributive situations before and after adjustment in each country.

Consequently, the analysis is carried out for different phases of the macroeconomic evolution of each economy during the 1980s, the underlying hypothesis being that different relationships between distributive changes and macroeconomic changes may prevail during instability, recession, recovery, and growth close to the production frontier. The scarcity of distribution measures for each country and their failure to match the same macroeconomic phases in the various countries inhibits my attempting a formal econometric exercise.

In the selection of macroeconomic variables, both their availability and their analytical relevance were taken into account. The implicit conceptual model links changes in inequality with variations in real national per capita income;[9] the real exchange rate as a proxy for relative prices; public consumption expenditure at constant prices[10] as a proxy for government employment; and real wages, inflation, real urban wages, and urban labor underutilization (i.e., urban unemployment and informal employment). Changes in urban poverty are, in turn, related to variations in real per capita income, inequality, and the real minimum wage. Changes in rural poverty, however, are linked to changes in real per capita income, agricultural output, and the real exchange rate.

There are a number of measurement limitations that hinder a rigorous association between observed changes in income distribution and poverty and observed changes in macroeconomic variables. Foremost among them is the fact that observed income distributions from household surveys of the type generally used for these estimates (i.e., those including questions on labor) measure incomes in a specific month of the year, whereas measures for most of the relevant macroeconomic variables are made available on a yearly basis, with quarterly data being much more difficult to obtain. Moreover, the years for which income distribution or poverty measurements are readily available do not always correspond to relevant phases of the conjunctural movements of the economy (which in many cases have been numerous and often of different direction) or to periods when a specific policy package was in force.

The analysis of associations between distributive changes and macro variables focuses on the distribution of income and poverty in urban areas, with only a summary analysis of changes in rural poverty. There are various reasons for disaggregating the analysis. First, as noted previously, income distribution and poverty measurements at the national level incorporate or mix urban and rural measurements of very different degrees of reliability or accuracy, making the common assumption of "constant bias over time" (the idea that any bias due to incomplete reporting, for example, will tend to be similar across the various readings of inequality level in a country) less tenable. Also, most of the available macro variables have a different relationship with either urban or rural incomes (e.g., the exchange rate), or a tenuous or remote relationship with rural incomes (e.g., unemployment or informal employment), or almost no bearing at all on them in the short run (e.g., urban wages); hence, analysis based on aggregate income distribution or poverty at the national level blurs their differential explanatory value.

Furthermore, for some countries or periods, only measurements for urban areas are available. To be sure, this is a hindrance for distributional analysis. However, it is a less serious problem than in other developing regions, since in most of the Latin American countries considered more than 60% of the population is urban (more than 80% in the Southern Cone countries and Venezuela) and less than half the poor are rural (20% or less in the Southern Cone and Venezuela).

Finally, the distributive changes of the 1980s are also assessed in the context of the previous trends of the 1970s (i.e., before the crisis), when different growth processes were in place and—in some countries—before policy reforms were undertaken.

The Record of the 1970s

Inequality

Analysis of changes in income distribution and growth in the main countries of the region during the 1970s prior to the crisis years of the 1980s (Altimir, 1992) suggests, as summarized in Table 2.4, the following:

1. Countries that experienced disrupted growth, such as Argentina, Chile, and Peru, suffered significant increases in inequality, with this effect not obviously related to the quite different degrees of income concentration that characterized them at the beginning of the decade.

2. In countries (such as Costa Rica or Uruguay) that had moderate average per capita growth rates (between 2% and 3%) over the decade and in which income concentration, at its beginning, was at an intermediate level, there was a deterioration in the distribution situation.

3. Three countries (Colombia, Mexico, and Venezuela) that had solid average sustained per capita growth rates (over 3% per year) significantly reduced their previously high (Gini coefficients over 0.5) income concentration.

4. In contrast, the high and sustained per capita growth rate (close to 6% per year) of Brazil during the 1970s was not accompanied by a reduction in the very high income concentration (Gini coefficient of around 0.6) established during the previous decade.

Poverty

Changes in the incidence of absolute poverty depend on growth of average real income, changes in the distribution of income, and (where relevant) the shifting of poverty lines over time.[11] Using comparable estimates of the incidence of poverty for 1970 and around 1980, O. Altimir (1992) highlights the following results for ten countries (see Table 2.4).

1. Argentina, Chile, and Peru, a group of countries with increasing inequality and low and unstable growth during the decade, as a consequence of economic shocks and institutional disruptions, registered either discouraging or downright dismal results on the poverty front. In Argentina the incidence of poverty at the national level may have increased only slightly and in Peru it may even have decreased, if the respective "educated guesses" about the decrease in rural poverty are accepted, but in both countries urban poverty tended to increase. In Chile, there was a virtual explosion of poverty in both urban and rural areas.

2. In the two countries that experienced moderate growth and increasing inequality (Costa Rica and Uruguay), urban poverty either remained unchanged or increased, with rural poverty decreasing or remaining about constant, respectively.

3. Those countries that attained high rates of per capita growth and decreasing inequality (Colombia, Mexico, and Venezuela) showed significant reductions of absolute poverty, both in urban and rural areas.[12]

4. Brazil's rapid economic growth resulted in the reduction of poverty, even in spite of the lack of improvement of the relative income distribution;

Table 2.4 Growth Rates and Changes in Income Distribution and Incidence of Poverty: Ten Latin American Countries, 1970s

Growth	Changes in Income Concentration	Changes in Incidence of Poverty		
		Nationwide	Urban	Rural
Slow growth (<1%)				
Argentina	I	M	I	D
Chile	I	I	I	I
Peru	I	D	I	D
Moderate growth (2–3%)				
Costa Rica	I	D	M	D
Panama	—	M	I	D
Uruguay	I	—	I	M
Rapid growth (>3%)				
Brazil	M	D	M	D
Colombia	D	D	D	D
Mexico	D	D	D	D
Venezuela	D	D	D	D

Source: Altimir (1992).
Note: I: Increased; M: maintained similar level; D: decreased.

however, if some shifting of the poverty line is accepted to allow for the possible effects of such a growth process on the prevailing style of living, the incidence of poverty in urban areas would have remained more or less constant.

5. The incidence of poverty in rural areas showed a downward trend during the 1970s in almost all of the countries considered, irrespective of the rate or stability of their growth, with the marked exception of Chile.

6. Rural-urban migrations, which were particularly intense in the 1970s, may have been more important than the improvement of economic conditions in rural areas in explaining the absolute reduction in the number of rural poor in Argentina, Brazil, and Venezuela. In contrast, improved rural economic conditions have been more important than migrations in reducing absolute rural poverty in Colombia, Mexico, and Panama and in bringing down the incidence of rural poverty in Costa Rica and Peru. In Chile, rural-urban migrations merely cushioned the general rise in the incidence of poverty.

The 1980s: A Review of Ten Countries

Income concentration and poverty increased in the urban areas of almost all Latin American countries during the crisis of the 1980s, as is evident from Tables 2.1 and 2.3. Colombia is the only clear exception, while Mexico and Costa Rica appear to have softened to some extent the distributive deterioration caused by the adjustments of the decade, and Panama only suffered when it was affected by political and international conflicts. Brazil, which already had a high degree of inequality, also suffered relatively in the additional deterioration. Chile, Argentina, and Uruguay experienced severe distributive losses during different phases of their reform and adjustment processes of the last two decades, and their record of the 1980s has to be considered in this context. Peru and Venezuela also suffered heavy distributive losses from different combinations of shocks and policy failures. The changes in income concentration[13] and urban poverty in each country and period are compared with the changes in relevant macroeconomic and labor-market variables summarized in Table 2.5.

The exceptional case is Colombia, where all available data show an improvement of income distribution during the decade: between 1978 and 1988 there was a relatively slight reduction of income concentration among wage earners (Londoño, 1990), while between 1980 and 1986 there was a significant decrease in the share received by the upper decile of households, mainly in favor of the middle strata; moreover, up to 1990 that improvement deepened, favoring also the lower four deciles of households. However, the incidence of urban poverty in 1990 was roughly similar (around 35%) to the 1980 and 1986 levels.

These results are roughly consistent with the initial conditions before the crisis, the macroeconomic trends of the period, and the traditionally prudent style of Colombian economic policy. When the financial crisis of the 1980s broke, Colombia was not heavily indebted; adjustment did not take place until 1984–1985, and even then the policy followed was a gradual one, deliberately aimed at minimizing wage and employment losses. In fact, during the rest of the decade economic policy included job creation and the sustaining of wage levels among its objectives (Garcia, 1991).

In 1986, when Colombia's comparatively mild external adjustment had just been completed, real per capita income was already 5% higher than in 1980, and real wages were 12% higher. However, urban unemployment was 4% (i.e., almost half again) higher than in 1980, and 2% more of the urban labor force (i.e., 27%) was employed in informal activities. The 1986–1990 period was one of growth with stability, of sorts, for the Colombian economy. Real per capita income expanded more than 4% over the period, with exports, public consumption expenditure and private consumption leading the expansion. Unemployment correspondingly decreased (by more than 3%) as did the importance of informal employment, while real wages increased slightly up to 1989 and decreased significantly only in 1990, by which time the macroeconomic situation had deteriorated somewhat.

In Mexico, available measurements show a significant decrease in inequality accompanied by a reduction of poverty at the national level

Table 2.5   Changes in Macroeconomic and Labor Variables and in Income Distribution in Different Phases of the 1980s:
Ten Latin American Countries

Countries	Periods	Macroeconomic Variables[a]			Labor Market[b]						Changes in Income Distribution[c]	
		RNIpc	REER	INF[d]	RW	RMW	NALU	NALI	UU	RGCpc	Concentration (Gini coefficient)	Urban Poverty
Periods of recessionary adjustment to external shocks												
Argentina	1980–1993	-23	77	I	-1	37	10	1	81	-19	I?	I+?
Brazil	1979–1983	-13	26	I	-18	-5	20	24	8	-7	M	I
Chile	1981–1983	-22	34	I	-11	-19	32	5	111	-8	I	I
Colombia	1980–1993	-5	-12	D	8	7	12	9	21	7	D	M?
Costa Rica	1980–1983	-26	40	I/D	-18	-1	12	12	42	-30	I?	I+
Mexico	1981–1984[e]	-12	40	I	-30	-32	12	7	36	-14	I?	I?
Peru	1982–1984	-12	14	I	-25	-20	32	31	35	-22	—	I+
Uruguay	1981–1986	-19	55	I	-13	-14	—	—	60	-14	I	I+
Venezuela	1981–1986	-30	51	—	-19	6	24	6	78	-21	I	I+
Periods of recovery after external adjustment												
Argentina	1983–1986	—	—	D	8	7	10	8	19	24	I	I?
Brazil	1983–1987	19	13	D/I	37	-23	-11	-1	-45	42	I	D
Chile	1983–1987	12	72	—	-3	-27	-25	-16	-37	-23	I	—
Colombia	1983–1986	10	67	I	4	6	4	-2	18	-3	D	M
Costa Rica	1983–1988	8	15	I	8	16	-4	8	-25	11	I?	D?
Panama	1982–1986	10	—	—	16	13	—	—	26	-3	—	M?
Peru	1984–1987	16	—	D/I	40	-3	-15	-7	-46	28	—	D?
Uruguay	1986–1989	13	12	M/I	6	-12	—	—	-20	-20	D	D
Venezuela	1986–1989	-6	52	I	-38	-15	-5	4	-20	-20	I	I
Periods of recession due to domestic imbalances												
Argentina	1986–1989	-13	34	I/H	-19	-62	14	8	36	—	I	I+
Brazil	1987–1989	-1	-31	I	-11	-1	-6	-6	-11	17	I	I
Mexico	1984–1987	-8	44	I	-16	-17	21	36	-32	-20	I?	—

(continues)

Table 2.5 continued

Countries	Periods	Macroeconomic Variables[a]			Labor Market[b]						Changes in Income Distribution[c]	
		RNIpc	REER	INF[d]	RW	RMW	NALU	NALI	UU	RGCpc	Concentration (Gini coefficient)	Urban Poverty
Panama	1986–1989	-22	—	—	-1	-1	—	—	61	-22	I?	I
Peru	1987–1990	-30	-49	I/H	-69	-64	—	—	73	-58	I?	I
Periods of disinflation and recovery												
Argentina	1990–1991	5	-24	D	-7	39	—	14	-13	—	—	D
Mexico	1987–1989	2	-11	D	-2	-16	9	—	-7	-10	I?	—
Periods of growth after recovery												
Chile	1987–1990	18	5	I	11	27	-15	1	-45	-3	D	D
Colombia	1986–1990	4	31	I	-5	-5	-13	-7	-25	20	D	D
Costa Rica	1988–1990	—	-4	D/I	2	5	-4	1	-14	20	D	I
Venezuela	1989–1990	10	4	D	1	-5	2	—	8	-9	D	—

Sources: Changes in macroeconomic and labor variables: ECLAC and PREALC unpublished information. Distributive changes: ECLAC (1991b; 1991c; 1992a) and sources from Table 2.1, p. 45, this volume.

Notes: a. RNIpc: real national per capita income; REER: real effective exchange rate; INF: inflation.

b. RW: real urban or industrial wages; RMW: real minimum wage; NALU: nonagricultural labor force underutilization (per active person), equal to NALI+UU; NALI: nonagricultural labor force in informal activities (PREALC definition); UU: urban unemployment rate; RGCpc: per capita real government consumption expenditure.

c. I: increased; I+: greatly increased; D: decreased; M: maintained; "?" indicates most likely presumption for the phase (see text) in the context of the changes observed in Tables 2.1 and 2.3 (this volume) for a longer period.

d. I: increased; D: decreased; M: inflation rate was maintained; H: entered into hyperinflation.

e. This period includes a transient recovery.

between 1977 and 1984 and a subsequent deterioration between 1984 and 1989, a period during which the government's policy stance radically changed (Lustig, 1992). The 1984 observation falls in the midst of the first adjustment and stabilization program, at a time when a moderate economic recovery from recessionary adjustment was taking place (Lustig, 1992). However, real wages had dropped almost 30% in two years, and per capita public consumption expenditure had decreased 14%. It is likely that the improvement in concentration with respect to 1977 (quite apart from the ever-present possibility that the two measurements are not comparable) conceals a deterioration from a substantially better distributive situation reached during the period of vigorous growth (6% a year) prior to the crisis, particularly in urban areas.

Be that as it may, there is evidence of an increase in inequality between 1984 and 1989, when the Mexican economy had a moderate rate of growth and inflation was under control, after absorbing an oil shock (real per capita national income was still 7% lower than in 1984), and in a period when fiscal discipline and policy reforms were progressively gaining ground. Over this time span, per capita public consumption expenditure was reduced more than 30% in real terms, and urban real wages declined a further 26%. At the same time, unemployment dropped to levels below those registered during the oil boom and informal employment increased 10 percentage points, to more than 30% of the nonagricultural labor force. Both developments, consistent with the remarkable flexibility of real wages, must have cushioned the negative impact on the incomes of poor and lower- to middle-income households (Lustig, 1992).

Costa Rica has been traditionally characterized by political and economic stability, and the adjustment of its economy during the 1980s was significantly aided by official transfers from the United States. Nevertheless, the distribution of urban incomes worsened between the beginning and the end of the decade, although the improvement of rural incomes may have helped to maintain the previous concentration of income at the national level.[14] The deterioration that took place between 1981 and 1988 was only partially reversed during the subsequent two years, and this reversal favored the middle strata more than the poor. Consequently, urban poverty increased significantly between 1981 and 1988 and also advanced a little more up to 1990.

There is evidence that impoverishment was acute during the recessionary external adjustment of 1981–1982, while later stabilization and recovery in 1983–1986 brought absolute poverty down to levels close to those registered prior to the crisis (Trejos, 1991). At least, this is what appears to have happened at the national level; real devaluation may have increased the incomes of the rural poor, as argued by S. A. Morley and C. Alvarez (1992), while the real rise of wages in formal activities after the adjustment may have improved the situation of the lower-middle strata. However, the deterioration of real incomes in informal activities, which had expanded, may have increased the number of the urban poor.[15]

In the subsequent period marked by policy reform (especially trade liberalization) and unstable expansion, the available evidence indicates a relative stabilization of the incidence of poverty at the national level (Trejos, 1991; ECLAC, 1992a) but also, as already indicated, a tendency for urban poverty to increase, in the context of a reduction of real wages, a gradual decline in real per capita income, and relative stability of the real exchange rate. However, the expansion of public consumption expenditure in real terms (20% per capita) must have helped the observed improvement of the relative position of middle-income groups.

The external shocks that set off the crisis in other Latin American countries had a delayed and milder impact on the economy of Panama, which only suffered a brief stagnation of economic activity in 1983–1984. In spite of a 23% rise in real per capita income and a 14% increase in real wages between 1979 and 1986, urban poverty fell only slightly, to less than 30% of households. The political crisis cum international conflict that pushed the Panamanian economy into recession in 1988–1989, however, brought real per capita income to 5% below the 1979 level—although this was not so with real wages—reduced per capita public consumption expenditures more than 20%, and forced up open unemployment of the urban labor force by 10 percentage points. As a result, the concentration of income significantly increased, as did poverty, which spread to 34% of urban households.

The already highly unequal income distribution of Brazil, which had not improved even during the previous decade of high growth, worsened further during the 1980s. The inequality of the distribution of household income remained relatively stable during the 1981–1983 recession and later recovery and improved slightly and briefly in 1986, in the climate of growth and temporary stability created by the Cruzado Plan. Between 1986 and 1989, however, with the acceleration of inflation and the beginning of the present recession, income concentration increased, though there is evidence (Hoffmann, 1992) that in 1990 inequality of household income improved somewhat. Consequently, the distribution of income in 1989 was more concentrated than in 1979, and poverty affected 5% more of urban households, while real national per capita income and industrial wages remained at about the same level as at the end of the previous decade. Unemployment had risen by more than 3 percentage points, as had informal employment. However, expansion of public consumption expenditure (55% growth in per capita terms between 1979 and 1989) must have helped to cushion the relative deterioration of the middle-income groups. The fall of economic activity and incomes in 1990, which was accompanied by a 20% real reduction of industrial wages, increased urban poverty by 4 additional percentage points to almost 39% of households.

External shocks and policy reforms under the authoritarian rule of the Pinochet regime, along with the ensuing instability and low average economic growth, caused major changes in income distribution and poverty in Chile during both the 1970s and the 1980s. Income distribution suffered significant deterioration: not only was the short-lived redistribution that lasted up to 1974 reversed, but the distributive pattern of Chilean society underwent a complete change.

By 1980, after the recovery from a deep recession (per capita GDP was only 6% higher than in 1970), implementation of a radical trade liberalization program, reversal of agrarian reform, and institutional reforms that allowed for greater labor-market flexibility but also for labor repression (Ffrench-Davis and Raczynski, 1987), the upper decile of households was receiving at least 5% more of total income than in 1968, to the detriment of the shares—and real incomes—of both the middle and lower strata. Real wages were still more than 10% lower than in 1970, 17% of the labor force was unemployed, and 28% was in informal activities. Absolute poverty virtually exploded, both in urban areas—from 12% in 1970 to around 28% in 1980—and in rural areas, bringing the incidence of poverty at the national level to about 30% of all the households (Altimir, 1991).

During the 1982–1983 crisis, the existing inequality was further aggravated, although perhaps only marginally, compared with the worsening of the previous period, and urban poverty increased still further.[16] The deterioration may have continued until 1987, when real per capita income and real wages were, respectively, still 12% and 5% lower than in 1980; per capita public consumption expenditure had shrunk more than 30%; and unemployment still affected 17% of the labor force, although the share of informal activities had been reduced. Under those circumstances, urban poverty had risen by about 4 percentage points and the distribution of income had further concentrated in favor of the upper quintile, whose share of expenditure increased by almost 4% of the total with respect to 1978, to the detriment of the middle and lower strata, the latter of which suffered a relatively greater loss.

Only between 1987 and 1990, with the Chilean economy reaching full utilization of its capacity and with progressive reforms of the labor laws, did the distributive picture improve somewhat. Real per capita income increased 18% and real wages 11%, and unemployment was reduced by almost 6 percentage points, to about 7% of the labor force. At the same time, urban income concentration decreased slightly in favor of the lower income groups, and urban poverty was reduced by 2 percentage points, while rural poverty decreased more significantly, bringing the incidence of poverty at the national level to less than 35% of households.

Major distributive changes have also taken place in Argentina since the 1970s, under successive spells of economic instability and political disruption. After a military regime came to power in 1976, policy reforms were introduced to liberalize prices, trade, and the financial market but not employment and wages (which were repressed for most of the period). Economic activity followed a stop-go pattern in the context of a situation of high inflation, in spite of the explicit anti-inflationary policy stance that permeated three successive stabilization programs (Canitrot, 1981).

Between 1970 and 1980, income concentration significantly increased: the upper decile of households enlarged its share of total income by almost 5 percentage points, while the lower strata lost almost 3 percentage points. Urban poverty increased by 2 percentage points, to 7%. Most of this deterioration, however, took place after 1974.[17] In 1980, real per capita income was roughly similar to the 1974 level, though real wages in manufacturing were still 14% lower, and unemployment was very low.

The sizable fluctuations in economic activity, magnitude of the external shocks and ensuing adjustments, and swings in relative prices associated with high and accelerating inflation during the 1980s were accompanied by movements of the relative distribution of income, although these were perhaps not as intense as the macroeconomic ebb and flow (Beccaria, 1991). By 1986, income concentration had further increased with respect to 1980, involving a dramatic change from the beginning of the 1970s: the share of the upper decile had grown about as much as it had in the previous decade, but this time at the expense mainly of the middle-level strata. Urban poverty had increased 6 percentage points (i.e., almost doubled), to more than 12% of households. Although the economy was recovering under a successful stabilization program, real per capita income was 22% below the 1980 level, unemployment was 3 percentage points higher, and informal employment 2 percentage points higher; however, real wages were 6% higher than at the beginning of the decade.

After 1986, the acceleration of inflation and the fall in real wages were accompanied by a further deterioration of relative income distribution, which reached its high point in 1989; with the burst of hyperinflation and recession reaching its trough, income concentration stood at its peak. In 1990, income concentration among individual recipients receded to the still high level reached in 1988 (Beccaria, 1991). Between 1986 and 1990, poverty may have spread to an additional 6% of urban households, and the situation improved only in 1991, when prices stabilized and economic recovery began.

Uruguay is the other Southern Cone country in which policy reforms had been already undertaken in the 1970s, under authoritarian rule, with significant distributive consequences. Starting in 1974, financial markets were liberalized and price controls were gradually eliminated, while wages continued to be administered and, from 1979, a trade liberalization program was put into effect. The 1973–1981 period was one of relatively high growth (3.4% per capita a year); nevertheless, the distribution of income deteriorated sharply between 1973 and 1979 at the expense of both the middle and lower strata, improving somewhat later, but only to the benefit of the middle-income strata. This evolution closely followed that of the relationship between real national per capita income and real wages: the former increased 12% between 1973 and 1979, while the latter dropped 32%; and between 1979 and 1981 real income expanded 4% but real wages rose about 17%. However, urban poverty increased by 4 percentage points between 1970 and 1981.

External shocks and ensuing adjustments slashed real per capita income by 19% between 1981 and 1986; real wages fell 8%, and unemployment increased 4 percentage points, while per capita public consumption expenditure was reduced more than 30%. Income concentration increased yet again, and urban poverty expanded by 5 additional percentage points to 14% of households. As a net result of economic recovery and later stagflation, real per capita income in 1989 was 13% higher than in 1986 and real wages were 6% higher, while unemployment had decreased 2 percentage points. Consequently, the distribution of urban incomes improved, and urban poverty decreased by 4 percentage points. Thus, at the end of the decade, the relative distribution of income and the incidence of absolute poverty were roughly similar to those at its outset, while real wages were substantially lower and unemployment somewhat higher than in 1981.

Continuing deterioration of real national income in Venezuela between 1980 and 1986 caused by the fall in oil revenues and the ensuing reduction (around 20%) of real wages and per capita public consumption expenditure were accompanied by a significant worsening of the distributive situation. Between 1981 and 1986 urban poverty increased 7 percentage points, while the relative distribution of income also became more unequal.

Economic policy failed to adjust to the fall in oil prices in 1986; external and fiscal imbalances widened, and the rate of inflation trebled. The orthodox stabilization program implemented at the beginning of 1989, along with the first trade and price liberalization measures, brought a recession and sharp falls in public consumption expenditure and real wages. Previous gains in employment were reversed, and informal activities expanded. Consequently, poverty increased,[18] and income distribution apparently "equalized downwards." The rise in oil earnings caused by the Persian Gulf conflict in 1990 and ensuing public expenditure in 1991 fueled an extraordinary—and unsustainable—expansion of economic activity. This, however, was mainly to the advantage of the upper- to middle-income strata; urban poverty in 1990 was still 9 percentage points higher than in 1986 and 16 percentage points higher than in 1981 (i.e., almost double). However, there is evidence indicating that by 1991, at least at the national level, poverty may have receded somewhat.[19]

The worsening income distribution in the urban areas of Peru in the 1970s was further aggravated during the 1982–1985 crisis and external adjustment in a climate of increasing violence. By the end of 1985 and the beginning of 1986, when the economy was recovering under the drive of an unsustainable heterodox stabilization program implemented by the newly elected Garcia government, real national per capita income and real wages in the private sector were still 9% and 5% lower than in 1979, while an additional 10% of the nonagricultural labor force was employed in informal activities, pushing the total above 40%. At that time, urban poverty still affected 45% of urban households, 10 percentage points more than in 1979.

Although there are no comparable observations for later years, there is some evidence that by 1990, in the midst of hyperinflation and economic collapse, poverty may have expanded by more than half with respect to 1985–1986, and it worsened still further in 1991, when the Fujimori government put into effect the present stabilization program.[20]

Rural Poverty

For most of the countries in my sample there is evidence of a decrease— however slight in some cases—of the incidence of rural poverty in the course of the 1980s, thus continuing the trend toward abatement that was manifest in the previous decade. The only clear exceptions are Panama and Venezuela, where that trend appears to have reversed by the end of the 1980s, and possibly Argentina, for which a slight increase of rural poverty has been estimated. Chile is a special case, since the rural impoverishment of the 1970s continued well into the following decade, to be reversed only in the latter part of the decade (see Table 2.3).

Those exceptional cases of increasing poverty are associated with falls in real per capita income, but the reverse does not hold true: of nine recorded spells of rural poverty reduction, this coincided with an increase in real national per capita income in only four cases;[21] in the remaining five, rural poverty decreased along with declines in real national income. In contrast, there is a close association of rural poverty reduction with expanding agricultural output, which holds good in eight of the nine cases, suggesting that peasants somehow share in general rural prosperity. In contradiction to conventional wisdom, however,[22] the association is weaker with real devaluation of the exchange rate, since it is observed in only four of the cases (see Table 2.6).

All this suggests that, in the absence of major institutional reform,[23] slow-moving structural changes in the rural milieu affect the process of

Table 2.6   **Changes in Rural Poverty and in Relevant Macroeconomic Variables:
Eight Latin American Countries, 1980s (percentage change over
each period)**

Country	Period	Changes in Rural Poverty[a] (%)	Changes in Macroeconomic Variables (%)		
			Per Capita Real National Income	Agriculture GDP	Real Exchange Rate
Argentina	1980–1986	4	–23	12	75
Brazil	1979–1987	–3	4	41	43
	1987–1990	–6	–7	–	–38
Chile	1980–1987	11	–13	33	89
	1987–1990	–19	18	14	5
Colombia	1980–1986	–7	5	11	47
Costa Rica	1981–1988	–3	–5	18	–6
	1988–1990	–10	–	10	–4
Panama	1979–1986	–4	23	11	—
	1986–1989	11	–22	7	—
Peru	1979–1985/1986	–2	–9	12	–9
Venezuela	1981–1986	–3	–30	23	51
	1986–1990	12	3[b]	1	59

Source: Unpublished ECLAC information.
Notes: a. Taken from estimates in Table 2.3, this volume.
  b. 1986–1989: –6%.

reduction of rural poverty more than short- or even medium-term changes in macroeconomic variables, although these may be able to slow down or even temporarily reverse such a process.

These slow-moving changes are in part reflected in the continuous transfer of rural poverty to the urban areas through migrations. In the 1980s, these have been less intense than in the previous decade, but they were nevertheless substantial. In most of the countries, rural-urban migrations were the main force sustaining the trend toward the reduction of poverty in rural areas, although they may not have been sufficient—as they had been in the 1970s—to prevent an absolute increase in the rural poor.

Transient and Permanent Changes in Income Distribution

In order to shed some light on whether and to what extent changes in inequality during the decade of crisis and adjustments may be permanent, it is crucial to consider the different macroeconomic phases through which the Latin American countries have passed and the structural circumstances in which each of them is situated at present, as well as the nature and depth of policy reforms undertaken. Changes in macroeconomic and labor variables and distributive changes in selected periods corresponding to different macroeconomic phases of the 1980s are summarized in Table 2.5.[24]

Income Distribution and Poverty in Different Phases of Adjustment Processes

Recessive adjustment to external shocks at the beginning of 1980 had adverse effects on inequality and devastating effects on urban poverty all over Latin America. Income concentration certainly increased in Argentina, Chile, Uruguay and Venezuela and perhaps also in Costa Rica and Mexico, while in Brazil inequality apparently remained unchanged through the rapid adjustment of 1981–1984 (Hoffmann, 1992). In all these cases, urban poverty increased during the period of adjustment, along with underutilization of the urban labor force[25] (which rose by between 10% and 20%, depending on the country), and there were sizable falls in real per capita income, real average wages,[26] and real per capita public consumption expenditure.

Colombia stands out as an exception, partly because of its lower initial debt burden. The economy went through a smooth external adjustment—even with real currency appreciation—with a reduction of inflation, which allowed for real rises in minimum and average wages and even for the real expansion of per capita consumption expenditure. Such was the background for the probable improvement of income distribution and the lack of aggravation of absolute poverty. Although Panama also underwent a mild adjustment in 1982–1984, with rising real wages but an increase in unemployment, in this case there is no indication of the distributive changes over that period.

The recovery following external adjustment brought relief on the poverty front only in certain countries. In Brazil, the recovery may be associated with the cumulative rise in real per capita income (close to 20%) and real wages (37%) and with decreasing labor underutilization, in spite of a probable increase in inequality.[27] If Peru also experienced a slackening of urban poverty during this phase—which is not known for certain, but is likely—this may have been due to a similar configuration of changes in the level of activity and the labor market. The decrease of poverty in Uruguay—along with inequality—and perhaps in Costa Rica and Panama and the possible maintenance of its lower incidence in Colombia are also associated with changes in income and the labor variables in the same direction, but to a less spectacular extent.[28]

In contrast, recovery in Argentina, Chile, and Venezuela was accompanied by further increases in urban poverty, although for different reasons. In Argentina, the unsteady and only partial recovery and the increase in unemployment and informal labor apparently outweighed the modest rise in real wages and the temporary abatement of inflation. In Venezuela too, until 1989, the recovery had been partial and subject to adverse external shocks, with accelerating inflation, while shrinking (–38%) real wages and per capita consumption expenditure (–20% in real terms) outweighed the very modest decrease in labor underutilization, providing the background for increases in inequality and urban poverty. In the case of Chile, greater labor-market flexibility led to a deterioration in equity in the medium run; the 1983–1987 recovery was vigorous, and underutilization of the labor force decreased significantly (although it still remained at more than a third of the urban labor force). Real wages and per capita public consumption expenditure barely held steady, in a context of moderate and roughly constant inflation, while both inequality and absolute poverty increased.

Those countries that again plunged into recession, after recovering from external adjustment, due to pervasive internal imbalances, additional external shocks, and accelerating inflation combined with stabilization efforts, experienced further increases in inequality and absolute poverty.

In Argentina and Peru, such imbalances resulted in hyperinflation and brought Brazil to the brink of it; real incomes and wages plunged and labor underutilization increased, as did absolute poverty and income inequality. Argentina's emergence from hyperinflation in 1990 stopped the fall and even brought some marginal improvement in inequality, although it did not prevent a further increase in poverty. The acceleration of inflation in Brazil took place along with some economic expansion and further increases in per capita public consumption expenditure, albeit with stagnating real per capita income and falling real wages; however, the 1990 stabilization package brought about disinflation with recession, which apparently increased poverty still further.

External shocks in 1985–1986 and stabilization efforts in Mexico also led to a new recessionary spell; the increase in informal activities and the drop in real wages suggest that there may have been a further increase in urban poverty and that—jointly with the fall in per capita public consumption expenditure—part of the observed increase in inequality up to 1989 may have taken place during this period. Panama's deep recession of 1988–1989, triggered by political and international conflicts, increased urban poverty and possibly also inequality.

The two cases of stabilization and recovery from high inflation and recession in the late 1980s (Argentina in 1990–1991 and Mexico in 1987–1989) included moderate increases in real income and in the utilization of the urban labor force and also moderate reductions in real wages. In the case of Argentina, urban poverty decreased from the high level of incidence attained during the previous spells. In the case of Mexico, however, there is no evidence of a similar abatement of poverty or of a decrease in inequality.

In almost all of the few observable instances of sustained or even unsustainable growth after recovery, such circumstances brought about an improvement of the relative income distribution and some decrease in urban poverty. Only in Costa Rica in 1990 was there a rise in urban poverty, with the acceleration of inflation and particularly as a consequence of the elimination of subsidies and the increase in public service rates. In both Colombia and Chile inequality and poverty decreased; in the latter case, the rise in real incomes and wages was more substantial, but in Colombia there was an expansion in real per capita public consumption expenditure. In Venezuela, there are indications of a reduction of income concentration in 1989–1990, in spite of falling real wages and increasing unemployment.

Permanent Changes in Income Concentration

Let us consider first the countries that have already attained a stage of full-capacity growth. Colombia is the only one in which income concentration at that stage is actually lower than before the crisis, but in Costa Rica in 1990 urban inequality was only slightly higher than in 1981. In both countries, real wages and per capita public consumption expenditure were higher than at the beginning of the decade (see Table 2.7).

In Chile, in contrast, after regaining a medium-term growth path, the income structure is significantly more concentrated than before the crisis and certainly much more than the relative income distribution prevalent at the end of the 1960s, before the socialist-populist experiment and the authoritarian structural reforms of the 1970s (see Table 2.1). This, in spite of an almost recovered real wage. In Venezuela, income concentration is higher than before the crisis, after recovery evolved into rapid, albeit unsustainable, growth; in this case, both real wages and per capita public consumption are substantially lower than before the crisis.

Although they were not yet on a full-capacity growth path in 1989, Mexico and Uruguay were approaching the culmination of their respective recoveries; at that stage, income inequality had nearly returned in both cases to prerecession levels.[29] In Mexico, this occurred in spite of drastic reductions in real wages and public consumption expenditure, whereas in Uruguay both variables were more moderately eroded.

The countries that were still laboring under recession and instability at the end of the 1980s (Argentina, Brazil, Panama, and Peru) showed degrees of inequality substantially higher than those prevailing before the crisis. Stabilization and recovery in Argentina brought only some improvement of income inequality, but this nevertheless remained high

Table 2.7 Inequality, Urban Poverty, and Macroeconomic Variables at the End of the 1980s, Relative to Precrisis Levels: Ten Latin American Countries (indices)

Country	Year	Base Year	Macro Phase[a]	Application of Significant Policy Reforms	Inequality (Gini coefficient)	Urban Poverty (incidence)	GDP	RNIpc[b]	RGCpc[c]	NALF[d]	RW[e]	RMW[f]	REER[g]
Argentina	1990	(1980=100)	D&R	Recent	113	205	93	69	—	88	77	40	185
Brazil	1990	(1979=100)	RDDI	Partial	108	130	127	97	158	98	85	55	89
Chile	1990	(1981=100)	SGAR	Yes	113	107	126	104	69	108	96	76	240
Colombia	1990	(1980=100)	SGAR	Partial	91	96	135	110	125	99	106	108	192
Costa Rica	1990	(1981=100)	SGAR	Yes	103	138	128	95	115	103	102	134	90
Mexico	1989	(1977=100)	D&R	Yes	100?	>95	147	106	76	89	54	41	111
Panama	1989	(1979=100)	RDDI	No	116	111	116	95	99	—	108	93	—
Peru	1990	(1979=100)	RDDI	Recent	—	190	94	72	62	—	36	24	40
Uruguay	1989	(1981=100)	RAEA	Yes	98	109	100	92	86	—	93	76	173
Venezuela	1990	(1981=100)	UG	Recent	110	188	105	72	68	93	48	63	240

Source: ECLAC data bank.

Notes: a. D&R: disinflation and recovery; RDDI: recession due to domestic imbalances; SGAR: sustained growth after recovery; RAEA: recovery after external adjustment; UG: unstable growth.

b. RNIpc: per capita real national income.

c. RGCpc: per capita real government consumption expenditure.

d. NALF: index of the proportion of nonagricultural labor force employed in formal activities (opposite of NALU—underutilization of nonagricultural labor force per active person).

e. RW: rural urban or industrial wages.

f. RMW: real minimum wage.

g. REER: real effective exchange rate.

compared with the precrisis level, which was substantially higher than that prevailing before the disruptions of the 1970s. However, in the spells of recovery after external adjustment, income distribution improvements—where they exist—only took place along with real wage increases, as outlined previously; these wage increases are less likely during the stabilization processes still faced by Brazil and Peru and have not occurred during the current Panamanian recovery. Consequently, one should not expect significant equity improvements in these countries as a consequence of stabilization and recovery. Indeed, full deployment of policy reforms and associated adjustment measures—particularly on the fiscal front—may still bring a medium-term increase in income inequality. Furthermore, if the experiences of Colombia and Chile are taken as examples, all these countries can expect only a modest reduction of income inequalities later, when they attain a sustained growth path.

In sum, "normal" distributive patterns in the coming phase of sustained growth, when this materializes in most Latin American countries, once they have recovered from the crisis and its sequels, completed structural adjustments, and deployed policy reforms, tend to be more unequal—at least in the urban areas—than those prevailing in the last stages of the previous growth phase, during the 1970s.

Only Colombia, Costa Rica, and Uruguay—and, just possibly, Mexico—have managed to restore their previous lower degrees of inequality (see Table 2.7). It is no accident that this should have happened in countries in which social justice values have traditionally imbued institutions, objectives of equity have been quite consistently incorporated in policy design throughout the adjustment phase, and both adjustment and policy reforms have been approached gradually and pragmatically.[30] This suggests that the tendencies that increase inequality of primary earnings (before the eventual connections involved in public social spending) can be partially corrected by economic policy design and implementation.

Prospects for Poverty Alleviation

Even without any significant changes in the relative distribution of income,[31] absolute poverty will be reduced by economic growth, and this will take place more quickly—at least in economists' estimates—if constant poverty lines are used, or more sluggishly if shifting poverty yardsticks are deemed normatively more appropriate.

The recovery of the 1970s, outlined earlier, shows urban poverty decreasing only in rapidly growing economies that either maintained or reduced their concentration of household income. In Colombia, Mexico, and Venezuela, where equity improved, the reduction of urban poverty showed elasticities of −0.4 to −1 with respect to the increase in real per capita income and of −0.4 to −2 with respect to real wages. In Brazil, where there was no significant improvement in income concentration, such elasticities were lower (see Table 2.8).

Recession and recovery in the 1980s left most Latin American countries with a sometimes markedly higher incidence of poverty in urban areas than before the crisis. Only Colombia and possibly Mexico were able to end their respective recovery phases with less urban poverty than before the recession, in both cases because of a decrease in inequality (see Table 2.7).

Available poverty estimates seldom paint a sharp differentiation between periods of recession and those of recovery. When they do, the beneficial effects of recovery on poverty appear weaker than the negative effects of the previous recession. In Uruguay, the elasticity of poverty with respect to real income in the 1986–1989 recovery was −2.1, while during the recession it had been −3. In Argentina, disinflation plus recovery abated poverty as elastically (−4) as recession had increased it, but the recovery itself was then very incipient. In Venezuela, however, the completion of recovery did not prevent poverty from widening still further. In other instances (Brazil, 1979–1987; Costa Rica, 1981–1988; Chile, 1980–1987; and Peru, 1979–1986) the culmination of the recovery phase left the economy with a greater degree of inequality and a higher incidence of urban poverty. In Costa Rica, not even sustained growth after 1988 was able to prevent the increase in urban poverty as a consequence of price deregulation.

In most cases, real wages at the end of the recovery process were lower than before the crisis, which helps to explain the weaker effect of recovery on poverty. Although in Argentina and Brazil at the culmination of the respective heterodox stabilization programs and in Costa Rica real wages were higher, that fact appears to have been offset by other factors that increased inequality and, particularly in the first case, by the fall of real per capita income. In Colombia and Panama, in contrast, higher real wages have reinforced the effect of the recovery of real income in preventing an increase in urban poverty. This was not so, however, in Mexico, where real wages in 1984 were substantially lower than before the crisis (see Table 2.8).

However, the few observable growth spells at the end of the 1980s (Colombia, 1986–1990; Chile, 1987–1990) show elasticities with respect to real per capita income (−0.7 and −0.4, respectively) similar to those recorded in the 1970s in rapidly growing economies where income inequality was decreasing. Only in Chile, however, has poverty reduction been more elastic with respect to real wages than to real incomes, as had happened in all cases in the 1970s (see Table 2.8).

Table 2.8 Changes in Urban Poverty and Their Relation to Changes in Income Concentration and Real Income in Different Periods: Latin America

Country	Period	Changes in Income Concentration[a]	% Variation				Elasticity of Urban Poverty in Relation to:		
			Urban Population	RNIpc[b]	RW[c]	RMW[d]	RNI[e]	RW	RMW
Growth periods in the 1970s									
Brazil	1970–1979	M	-14	67	48	-1	-0.2	-0.3	14
Colombia	1970–1980	D	-21	44	17	27	-0.5	-1.2	-0.8
Mexico	1970–1984	D	-30	31	15	-20	-1.0	-2.0	1.15
Venezuela	1970–1981	D	-30	71	—	-3	-0.4	-0.4	10
Periods of recession and recovery in the 1980s									
Argentina	1980–1986	I	71	-23	7	47	-3.1	10	1.5
	1986–1990	I	52	-15	-22	-64	-4.0	-2.4	-0.8
	1990–1991	—	-22	5	-7	39	-4.4	3.1	-0.6
Brazil	1979–1987	I	13	3	19	-27	4.2	0.7	-0.5
	1987–1990	I	15	-6	-29	-26	-2.5	-0.5	-0.6
Chile	1980–1987	I	14	-13	-5	-31	-1.1	-2.8	-0.5
Colombia	1980–1986	D	—	5	12	13	—	-0.1	—
Costa Rica	1981–1988	I	31	-5	16	27	-6.5	1.9	1.1
Mexico	1977–1984	D	-6	14	-34	-40	-0.4	-0.2	0.2
Panama	1979–1986	I	-3	23	14	-6	-0.1	-0.2	0.5
	1986–1989	—	13	-22	-1	-1	-0.6	-13	-13
Peru	1979–1986	—	29	-7	-5	-39	-4.1	-5.8	-0.7
Uruguay	1981–1986	I	56	-19	-13	-14	-3.0	-4.3	-4.0
	1986–1989	D	-29	13	6	-12	-2.1	-4.8	2.4

(continues)

Table 2.8 continued

Country	Period	Changes in Income Concentration[a]	% Variation Urban Population	% Variation RNIpc[b]	% Variation RW[c]	% Variation RMW[d]	Elasticity of Urban Poverty in Relation to: RNI[e]	Elasticity of Urban Poverty in Relation to: RW	Elasticity of Urban Poverty in Relation to: RMW
Venezuela	1981–1986	I	39	–31	–19	6	–1.3	–2.1	6.5
	1986–1990	D	32	3	–41	–19	9.4	–0.8	–1.7
Growth periods in the late 1980s									
Chile	1987–1990	D	–8	18	11	27	–0.4	–0.7	–0.3
Colombia	1986–1990	D	–3	4	–5	–5	–0.7	0.6	0.6
Costa Rica	1988–1990	D	5	–2	2	5	–2.8	2.5	1.0

Sources: See Tables 2.1 and 2.3, this volume, for data in changes in income concentration. Other data based on author's calculations from unpublished ECLAC and PREALC information.

Notes: a. M: maintained similar level; D: decreased; I: Increased.
b. RNIpc: per capita real national income.
c. RW: real urban or industrial wages.
d. RMW: real minimum wage.
e. RNI: real national income.

Rural-urban migrations will continue to exert pressure on the ability of the economies to alleviate urban poverty. If the experience of the last two decades (Altimir, 1991) is any indication of what might happen, in the relatively less urbanized countries with a high incidence of poverty in the rural areas, the migrating rural poor may swell the ranks of the urban poor at a rate equivalent to an absolute increase of 1.3–2.0% a year.

To sum up all this evidence, it is likely, on the one hand, that countries accomplishing their recovery into full-capacity growth will undergo a change in their ability to reduce urban poverty in the short run, requiring relatively more expansion of economic activity than in the recovery phase for each percentage point of poverty reduction. On the other hand, medium-term growth with no improvement of income inequality would permit only a slow process of poverty abatement: slower than in the cases of high growth and equity improvement of the 1970s and slower than during recent growth spells in Colombia and Chile, when income distribution also improved.

Conclusions

After overcoming the difficult period of the 1980s, Latin American countries are entering into a new era of potential growth under a different pattern of development and a new style of state intervention. The adjustments to absorb both exogenous changes, those required in order to adapt to resource availability and utilization, and the structural changes still under way have caused most Latin American societies to suffer more unequal distribution of income and a higher incidence of poverty among their people. The few exceptions are the result of deliberate and persistent concern for equity in economic policy design and implementation. Moreover, the prospects for poverty alleviation through growth alone, without improvement of the relative distribution of incomes and vigorous social policies, appear so limited as to be disheartening and seem likely to be counterproductive for social integration and, ultimately, for sustained growth (ECLAC, 1990).

Given the unlikely prospect that primary earnings will become less unequal even if there is deliberate concern for this in economic policy, the improvement of equity and particularly the abatement of absolute poverty will have to lean much more on social policy and its effectiveness. With fiscal resources reduced or still constrained by the debt burden, however, the scope for welfare transfers will be restricted to no more than the provision of a basic social safety net, with preference being given to social expenditures that can be considered as investment in human resources.

Eventual gains in equity of income distribution will depend on the spread of productivity improvements and their actual appropriation by households. The structural transformations under way tend to increase the productivity of capital and total factor productivity, thus enhancing labor productivity in the economy at large. However, for income distribution to improve on the basis of differential productivity gains, three developments are required. First, employment in formal or modern activities must be extended, along with productivity increases, to a larger proportion of the labor force, thus absorbing underemployment. Second, those productivity increases must be effectively translated into proportional wage rises. Third, the capital per worker in the labor force remaining in the informal, small business, and traditional sectors of the economy must increase dramatically.[32]

In order to attain these objectives it is necessary, in addition to raising the productivity of capital in general, to increase the skills of the different segments of the labor force while restructuring the availability of skills so as to enhance the technological capabilities of the productive system at large. For this purpose, and in order to ensure long-term progress, heavy investment in human resources (education, training and retraining, nutrition, and health) must supplement investment in fixed capital (ECLAC, 1992b). Indeed, there are some grounds for substituting investment in human capital for investment in physical capital, insofar as a greater contribution to total factor productivity can be expected from the former, in a long enough term.

Fulfilling these requirements involves substantial amounts of investment resources, partly originated and handled in the marketplace but also partly raised and allocated by the state. At the same time, in order for higher skills to be reflected in workers' income, pay structures must meet the double challenge of being both institutionalized and flexible.

The efficient absorption of capital by the underemployed, effective widespread access to the acquisition of skills and their efficient application to production, and correspondence between contributions to productivity and earnings all call for substantial organizational improvements at the company level and profound institutional reforms in public policy.

Abating structural poverty follows the same lines as general improvements in income distribution but poses different obstacles that must be overcome if policies are to be effective. On the one hand, the physical capital required may be lower than in modern activities, but the skills gap is greater. On the other hand, effective public policies are more demanding in terms of organizational requirements and institutional creativity. Finally, the remedies must address the whole vicious circle of circumstances that reproduce poverty from one generation to another.

Strategies for equity improvement must take these differences into account. The usual way in which social policy is designed—which actually restricts access mainly to the strata above the poverty line, for which such policies may be more easily implemented, and thus leaves the poor to fend for themselves—may lead to further progress for a segment that is already integrated into society and actually endorse the disintegration of the poor strata into a segregated underclass. At the other extreme, a unilateral strategy focusing only on the poor may further weaken the low and middle strata of the population, where a rich reservoir of skills, social cohesion, and political dynamism is located. What is required is a two-tier strategy that recognizes the differences between the poor and the nonpoor working population, in terms of potential, response, and deterioration of lifestyles, and aims at integrating both universes into a single dynamic society.

Notes

Oscar Altimir is the deputy executive secretary of ECLAC.

1. See Altimir (1987) for a review and discussion of the reliability of income measurements from different types of surveys in Latin America and their comparability problems.

2. For a detailed compilation of the income distribution statistics available for each country and the selection of comparable pairs, see Altimir (1992). In particular, the manner of selection based on the similarity of data and their treatment makes it possible to compare Gini coefficients—and calculate their variations, as is done in Table 2.1—which have been computed on the basis of similarly grouped data.

3. For the method of adjustment applied, see Altimir (1987), and for the details of the adjustments, see ECLAC (1991c).

4. See ECLAC (1991c) for details on these country-specific minimum food budgets and how they were set. Minimum food baskets were drawn on the basis of the composition of food consumption of those strata of households that in each country attained with some latitude the minimum nutritional requirements, although such reference baskets were adjusted to these minima as well as to mean national availability of each foodstuff and were freed of high-price-per-calorie or nutritionally superfluous items. Therefore, the criterion to establish the minimum food baskets was one based on habits, taking into account availability and cost, rather than one of minimum cost, taking into account availability and habits, as used in Altimir (1979) in order to obtain estimates for the 1970s.

5. For a discussion of the case for shifting poverty lines during periods of economic growth, see Altimir (1991).

6. ECLAC (1991c) also includes estimates of poverty gaps, but only for 1986.

7. Income in kind and imputed income, such as receipts from family subsistence activities or rent of owner-occupied dwellings, is either explicitly excluded or so poorly measured as to be considered excluded in most of the surveys in the database, which are labor or income surveys. Only a minority of them are income and expenditure surveys, which are more successful in measuring such items (see Altimir, 1987).

8. See, for example, Bianchi, Devlin, and Ramos (1985; 1987) and ECLAC (1986).

9. That is to say, the per capita product after net factor payments and the effect of terms of trade variations; therefore, this variable incorporates the direct (i.e., accounting) effect of external shocks represented by changes in the terms of trade and in accrued interest on the foreign debt.

10. That is to say, public consumption expenditure at current prices deflated by the GDP deflator. This is different from public consumption expenditure in real terms as estimated in the national accounts, which in Latin American practice reflects, at best, government employment.

11. Contrary to the widespread fashion of using poverty lines constant over time in real terms, there is a strong argument for shifting even *absolute* poverty lines over time, in a context of growth and societal progress (see Altimir, 1991).

12. Even if the poverty lines were shifted upward because of high growth, poverty would still have gone down, although to a lesser degree.

13. Even reliable income distribution measurements are not able to capture income received by the country's residents from assets held abroad. Capital flight during the initial years of the crisis was substantial, particularly in Argentina, Mexico, and Venezuela (see Cumby and Levich, 1987). With the yields current at the time, property income on assets accumulated abroad by the private sector of those countries may have represented around 3% of household disposable income in Argentina and Mexico and as much as 5% in Venezuela. These proportions have most likely increased the share of the upper decile or quintile in total household income, adding to the changes recorded in Table 2.1 for the first half of the decade. Similarly, the later fall in international interest rates and related yields should have been reflected in an inverse change (of about half the size of the previous one) in the "total" (i.e., from domestic and foreign sources) share of the upper-income groups.

14. Morley and Alvarez (1992: Tables 7b and 7c) argue that the real devaluation that was required for external adjustment presumably increased agricultural wages after 1981, although the bulk of the devaluation occurred in that year. They also note that between 1981 and 1989 rural nominal incomes in the lower deciles of the national distribution increased more than those of urban households in the same deciles.

15. Morley and Alvarez (1992: Table 7h) note that among urban households between 1981 and 1986 there was a sharp deterioration of nominal wages in non-basic services compared with industry.

16. Pollack and Uthoff (1987) estimate that absolute poverty increased by 8% (from 40% to 48%) in Greater Santiago.

17. See Altimir (1986) for the evolution of income distribution and Beccaria and Minujin (1991) for the evolution of absolute poverty during the period.

18. Marquez (1992) estimates that, at the national level, poverty affected 28% of households in 1985, 32% in 1987, and 41% in 1989.

19. Marquez (1992) puts the incidence of poverty at the national level in 1991 at 35% of households, compared with 41% in 1989.

20. See Figueroa (1992: Table 2) and Abugattas and Lee (1991: Table 4). However, comparison of the distribution of Lima households by size of per capita consumption expenditure using the observations from the 1985–1986 and 1990 surveys of the standard of living (Psacharopoulos et al., 1992) shows little increase in inequality; this may reflect another case of "downward equalization" by recession, with the real consumption of the poor falling by almost 7% a year and the real consumption of the richest decile by almost 6% a year.

21. Brazil (1979–1987), Colombia (1980–1986), Chile (1987–1990), and Panama (1979–1986).

22. At least this is true if no allowance is made for time lags between real devaluation, reallocation of resources to tradables, ensuing expansion of agricultural output, and eventual participation of peasants and laborers in such expansion.

23. Such as agrarian reform, as in Peru, or its reversal, as in Chile, both in the 1970s.

24. The intervals between measurements of poverty (Table 2.3) or income distribution (Table 2.1) usually cover more than one phase of economic evolution; in these cases, the changes in distribution shown in the table are also based on the evidence referred to in the text.

25. The indicator of underutilization of the urban labor force used here is the sum of the rate of open (urban) unemployment and the proportion of the nonagricultural labor force engaged in informal activities, estimated by PREALC.

26. In Argentina, however, real wages recovered and the minimum wage increased sharply in 1983 at the end of the military regime, even with accelerating inflation. In Chile, real average wages (in formal activities) rose up to 1982, in a context of moderate inflation, high labor underutilization (almost half of the nonagricultural labor force), and a new labor regime that gave the labor market total flexibility (Garcia, 1991).

27. However, the conspicuous increase in real per capita public consumption expenditure (42%) must have improved the relative position of some middle-income strata.

28. Mexico's brief and mild recovery in 1984 did not significantly alter the results of the previous recessive phase, although "the very circumstances that triggered it contributed in part to its demise" along with worsening terms of trade in 1985 (Lustig, 1992: 34–36).

29. However, if prerecession (i.e., around 1981) inequality in Mexico was even lower than the level observed in 1977, as suggested earlier, postrecovery inequality would have been somewhat higher than that previous mark.

30. The gradual approach was abandoned in Mexico in the last phase of the reform process, but it must be borne in mind that this phase coincided with the preparations for the incorporation of the country into the North American Free Trade Agreement (NAFTA).

31. Including, to be sure, the absence of changes in either the composition of households or their work and resource utilization strategies, which is a highly artificial assumption.

32. The capital for those remaining in such activities should perhaps be doubled, but even so this would demand much less capital than the amount required for each job created in the more modern or larger-scale activities.

Part 2

The Experience of Individual Latin American Countries

3

State Intervention, the Labor Market, and Inequality in Argentina

Adriana Marshall

From 1976 on, the inward-oriented growth strategy that had prevailed in Argentina since the 1940s definitively ceased to underlie economic policymaking. Alternative routes to economic growth were pursued, but in fact this policy transition, which came after ten years of uninterrupted growth (1964–1974), ushered in a long period of decline, and stagnation was accompanied by pervasive inflation. In 1990, aggregate gross national product (GNP) was below the 1975 level; GNP per capita declined at an average annual rate of –1.4% between 1976 and 1989; and the gross domestic product (GDP) and employment shares of manufacturing fell. In spite of an increase in the profit share after 1976, a combination of widespread financial speculation, conspicuous consumption, interest payments on the external debt, and massive capital flight conspired to depress the rate of investment in productive equipment, which plummeted in 1981–1983 (–18.2% per year) and continued to fall between 1983 and 1989 at an average annual rate of –5.1%.

These severe problems were addressed by a series of stabilization plans, some of which achieved momentary success, as was the case with the "heterodox" Austral Plan of 1985. In 1991–1994 yet another economic program, agreed upon with the International Monetary Fund (IMF), was implemented. It was based on deregulation, a tight fiscal policy and large-scale privatization, a fixed exchange rate, and the opening up of the economy to imported manufactures. One important aim, attained in 1992, was Argentina's incorporation in the Brady Plan for the renegotiation of the foreign debt. The economic program was applied thoroughly and had a deep impact, both positive and negative, in a relatively short period. Stabilization was achieved and maintained. High interest rates ensured a continuous inflow of foreign exchange, essential to maintaining the exchange rate fixed in 1991. Cuts in government expenditure, increased tax revenues, and, particularly, privatization eased the fiscal deficit. Economic activity, including manufacturing, recovered. Aggregate GNP boomed during two consecutive years at rates near 9%; in 1991 it reached and in 1992 finally surpassed the 1980 level.[1] In contrast to these positive effects, the explosion of imports due to trade liberalization measures resulted in a growing trade deficit, even though exports, including nontraditional manufacturing goods, were showing an upward trend initiated in 1988. In 1995, the economic program was still under way and inflation was under control. Growth remained high in 1993 and 1994 (an average of 6.7%) but became negative in 1995, and unemployment jumped to unprecedented levels. Currently the economic debate centers on whether it will be possible to go beyond mere recovery to resume sustained growth.

The 1976–1994 period witnessed significant changes on the supply side of the labor market, such as the decrease in internal migration to industrial centers, the growth of female labor-force participation rates, and an overall improvement in education. The structure of labor demand also experienced substantial modification: a relative fall of employment in manufacturing and construction and an expansion of employment in small firms; changes in skills demanded; an increase in the presence of women in the employed labor force due not only to their own increased willingness to participate but also to changes in the structure of demand; an expansion of precarious forms of employment, as more extensive use was made of temporary labor and, due to widespread evasion of payroll taxes, fewer and fewer workers were covered by the social security institutions. In addition, unemployment increased and real wages deteriorated. The mechanisms of wage determination also changed, as is discussed later. Mirroring these processes, income distribution became more uneven, with the first and sharpest increase in inequality occurring between 1976 and 1978. The climax was reached in 1989, when inequality, unemployment, and poverty were intensified by hyperinflation in the midst of political turmoil.

Many of these labor-market and distributional changes may be traced back to the state's active intervention through its social and economic policy instruments. In the context of their envisaged economic growth strategies as well as their shorter-term stabilization goals, the successive governments, inter alia, manipulated wages and dealt with trade unions and collective bargaining, devised stimuli for manufacturing exports, reformed the tax system, and decided on the level and composition of public expenditure. Though not all of the measures taken brought the desired results, they had direct and indirect effects on labor demand and supply, the distribution of income, and living standards. In particular, I will argue that governments' views on the economic role of wages and the subsequent policy choices—pre- and postdebt crisis and "adjustment"—were one major factor behind both the initial increase in inequality in the late 1970s and the long-term permanence of the more uneven income distribution pattern. To this determinant were added the effects of persistent economic stagnation and its sequels—unemployment growth and weakened trade unions—and of accelerating inflation. At least since the 1930s, the state had intervened in the process of wage determination in different forms, and wages had been repeatedly controlled by the state (Cortés and Marshall, 1993), but from 1976 to 1988 they were administered systematically and without the interruption of periods of free wage bargaining.

In this chapter, I highlight the major labor-market and distributional effects of policies implemented from the mid-1970s on, paying special attention to the economic program applied in 1991–1994. Four years is perhaps too short a period to permit an accurate assessment of the impacts of the latter program, but one can note certain patterns that appear to be superimposed on the longer-term structural tendencies. In any case, only the resumption of stable economic growth will permit a disentangling of the ephemeral changes from those that are more permanent.

In what follows, the central policy measures applied in each period as well as the economic strategies behind them are briefly reviewed; a more detailed account is provided for the 1991–1994 program. Next, labor-market trends are examined, and an attempt is made to identify policy impacts on the volume and structure of labor supply and on labor requirements. Wages and income distribution are then analyzed, and finally, the distributional effects of changes in taxation and social expenditure are discussed.

Economic and Social Programs, 1976–1994

The military government's (1976–1983) neoliberal economic program was an attempt to overcome the constraints faced by inward-oriented industrialization (market size, external restrictions, high levels of protection) in the context of the new international order (Cortés and Marshall, 1993). Wage cuts, trade liberalization, and financial reform were intended to foster growth, modernize the economy, and bring inflation under control. The reduction of labor costs was considered to be indispensable for restoring growth. However, a short-lived investment boom (1977–1980) was soon followed by falling investment levels. Trade liberalization (1979–1981), which had been expected to encourage the modernization of Argentinean manufacturing and to increase its external competitiveness, led instead, together with the overvaluation of the Argentine currency and high interest rates, to the dismantling of local manufacturing industries (Kosacoff, 1993). Easy international credit contributed to an unprecedented growth of external indebtedness that, to make matters worse, was matched by capital flight rather than by increased domestic investment. The GNP share of the public sector did not decline despite the rhetoric on the "state's subsidiarity" and the need to curtail state expenditure. In brief, the economic program was not successful, and this period ended with the stagnation of manufacturing and a large fiscal deficit due to the government's decision to accept responsibility for the overwhelming privately incurred external debt.

On the labor-market side, the military government fixed wages, repressed trade unions and eliminated collective bargaining as well as the right to strike, and reformed the labor code to the detriment of workers (Cortés and Marshall, 1993).[2] In 1976, money wages, thought to be at an "artificially" high level due to trade union intervention, were frozen while prices were liberalized. Wage policy aimed also at increasing wage dispersion, which was considered to have been excessively narrowed by trade union interference; wage disparities were now expected to stimulate labor mobility, reflect productivity differentials across firms, and, by further segmenting the labor force, undermine the basis of centralized collective negotiation and union strength (Marshall, 1988a). Measures to widen wage differentials were also applied within the public sector.

Tax reforms of this period included an increase in personal contributions to social security; the elimination of employer payroll taxes for the state pension scheme and for the public housing fund, revenues that were replaced by the generalization of the value-added tax; tax exemptions to personal income out of distributed profits; and a shift to taxes that can be more easily passed on to the consumer. With taxation on income and profits representing only 10% of taxation revenues, Argentina's tax structure already was, by international standards, extremely regressive, and this characteristic was exacerbated by the reforms.[3] The pressure of direct and indirect taxation on labor income increased (Marshall, 1988a).

The Radical Party government elected by the end of 1983 under President Raúl Alfonsín had initially planned to base economic growth on the increase in manufacturing exports, but inflation and trade balance difficulties soon led it to give priority to stabilizing prices and obtaining foreign exchange for servicing the external debt inherited from the previous government. It did so by reducing consumption so as to cut imports and expand exports. Its programs centered on stabilization plans against inflation and balance-of-payments disequilibria (Cortés and Marshall, 1993), while efforts were being made to renegotiate debt repayment conditions. The so-called heterodox Austral stabilization plan that in principle implied wage and price control was launched in 1985; because its success in curbing inflation lasted only two years, it was followed by new stabilization packages that also proved unable to check the acceleration of the rate of price increases. Meanwhile, government incentives failed to stimulate firms to invest as expected. Schemes to promote investment and growth of manufacturing exports in the form of tax exemptions were often utilized in a fraudulent way. Investment continued to fall, and domestic capital held abroad did not return. The government term concluded with the deepening of the crisis and hyperinflation.[4]

The labor policy of the Radical government centered on wage control. Reinstatement of collective bargaining still did not permit wage negotiation until 1988. Wages were administered up to 1988 on the assumption that wage increases would bring about balance-of-payments difficulties by reducing the export surplus and expanding imports and would accelerate inflation due to the "premature overheating" of the economy (Marshall, 1989: 50).

Among the main taxation reforms were the elimination of the earlier extension of the value-added tax to wage goods; the reinstatement of employer payroll taxes for the state pension scheme, though at less than their historical level; measures to improve the control of tax evasion; specific taxes on sales of fuels, gas and telephone services to provide funds for social security; and the creation of the "forced savings" scheme, a temporary tax on personal incomes above a stipulated threshold. These measures were not sufficient to alter the overall regressiveness of the taxation system (Marshall, 1993). Taxes on personal income increased, but only from 5.5% of total taxes collected in 1983 to 6.2% in 1988 and from 1.0% of GNP to 1.2%.[5]

The *Justicialismo* (Justice Party) won the next elections (mid-1989), and this new government under President Carlos Menem adopted neoliberal views once again, as had the earlier military government of 1976–1983. After several failed attempts at reducing inflation, a new economic program was applied beginning in 1991. It implied a radical transformation of the traditional "rules of the game" in Argentina's economy. Having some points in common with policies put in practice by Economy Minister José Alfredo Martínez de Hoz during the military regime, the new program also had its own special features. Moreover, ideas that earlier had not been implemented fully now were carried out thoroughly and more coherently. In this sense, this was a new economic strategy that assigned a new role to the state and represented a real break with the past.

The foundations on which this program was based included convertibility of the Argentine currency, reduction of the fiscal deficit both by cutting expenditure and by increasing tax revenues, and deregulation of markets. Its ultimate objectives were modernization and the growth of savings, investment, and productivity. Trade liberalization was perceived mainly as a stabilization device, but one that would eventually serve to increase productivity and the competitiveness of Argentine manufactures. Although wages were not controlled directly by the state, wage policy encouraged decentralization of wage bargaining and subordinated wage increases to productivity increases.

The *Plan de Convertibilidad* (Convertibility Plan) of early 1991 was the centerpiece of the government's economic program to curb inflation. Its main characteristics were strict control of monetary emission, a fixed exchange rate with the U.S. dollar (1 to 1), and a monetary base backed by international reserves (gold and foreign exchange); indexation was prohibited. This plan, enacted by law, helped reestablish confidence in the Argentine currency, totally shaken by the hyperinflation of 1989 and the failure of previous stabilization packages. Although certain prices (e.g., of private services) continued to rise visibly, inflation gradually subsided; first wholesale prices and later the consumer price index showed the favorable impact of this program: between December 1992 and December 1993 consumer prices rose by only 7.4%.

Partly in the framework of the Southern Cone Common Market (MERCOSUR) signed in 1991 and partly as a result of generalized rebates of import duties, the opening up of Argentina to manufactures from abroad broke the long-established pattern of manufacturing protection that had been challenged only at the end of the 1970s by means of similar, albeit short-lived, measures. The result of the trade liberalization, together with the "cheap" dollar fixed by the convertibility law and maintained by the inflow of foreign capital that responded to high interest rates, was a dramatic surge of imports that more than trebled between 1990 and 1993, generating a growing trade balance deficit ($2.64 billion in 1992 and $3.70 billion in 1993).[6]

The fiscal deficit was to be tackled by curtailing expenditure and increasing tax revenues. To both reduce government expenditure and increase revenues, a vast privatization program was envisaged, and measures were taken to reorganize and modernize the state structure and reduce public sector employment. The latter was to be helped by ad hoc international loans. The GNP share of public expenditure, including the service on the public debt, averaged 32.6% in 1980–1983, 31.1% in 1984–1988, 27.7% in 1989, and 26.8% in 1993 (Vargas de Flood and Harriague, 1993).

Starting with the Argentine airline and the telephone system, privatization proceeded quickly. By 1993 a large number of formerly state-owned enterprises were in private hands, often owned jointly by domestic and foreign capital: water and sewage, electricity, oil, gas, telephones, railways and the underground transit system, roads, and steel works as well as many others. The Argentine state continued to share ownership in some of them; others were leased on a long-term basis.

Tax reforms were devised with a view to generating genuine resources for the state. They were based on changes in the structure of taxation, a reorganization of the system so as to foster registration (centralization and simplification of procedures), and a vast campaign among the population against the overwhelmingly widespread tax evasion.[7] One of the most important tax reforms was the generalization and increase of the value-added tax on the grounds of ease of collection. The government's effort met with some success; registration (tax filings) rose substantially, and tax revenues increased from 15.1% of GNP in 1989 to 18.1% in 1992.[8]

The privatization of the retirement pension scheme was intended not only to reduce public expenditure but also to contribute to an increase in domestic savings, to develop the capital market, and to foster investment. This reform, according to which the private system coexists with the public scheme and workers have the right to opt between them, came into operation in late 1994. In addition, by the end of 1993 an official decree reduced or eliminated (depending on the firm's location) payroll taxes of manufacturing enterprises for the social security system (retirement, health care, and family allowances); the alleged rationale was to increase investment and employment.[9] Apart from the privatization of the retirement scheme and the reduction of payroll taxes, the system of *obras sociales* (social services) has been under discussion. This system provides health and other services (such as tourism, consumption cooperatives, and sports) to workers. It rests on the compulsory contributions of workers and employers to each economic activity's *obra,* which is managed by the corresponding trade union; state centralization of the system ensures, however, redistribution of funds among the obras if necessary. As a large source of revenues (worker and employer taxes constitute 9% of the wage bill), it is the traditional stronghold of trade unions, and as such it was repeatedly attacked by governments since the 1960s. Official projects proposed the elimination of forced affiliation to the obra of the industry of employment in order to facilitate free election of coverage. Liberalization would give workers the right to choose among obras and, eventually, to opt for private insurance schemes for health care, helping undermine the main source of economic power of the trade unions.

The controversial national employment law approved by the end of 1991 after lengthy discussions[10] was expected to encourage employment growth and reduce youth unemployment through "promoted" temporary contractual modalities; it was also designed to reduce clandestine employment and stipulated a limited unemployment insurance scheme. Because this law failed to stimulate employment creation, the several official projects of a new labor code included a wide-ranging variety of deregulating measures involving the employment contract, dismissal, working time, and so on[11] that were supposed to foster investment and employment growth by satisfying employers' demands. In 1991, to ensure stabilization and to reduce labor costs, restrictions were placed on wage increments set through collective bargaining, which were permissible only if backed by effective or expected productivity increases ("productivity agreements").[12] With similar aims, the decentralization of collective bargaining was promoted through a decree in 1993.

The Labor Market

Labor Supply

Social and economic policies, together with those that were exerted through changes in labor demand, had impacts on the volume and structure of the supply of labor. In particular, state-administered wage levels affected female labor-force participation rates, state-controlled retirement pensions influenced the labor-market participation of older age groups, housing policy modified internal and international migration trends, and the exchange rate fixed by the government had an impact on the volume of immigration from neighboring countries.[13] These policies affected the composition of the labor force by gender, age, and place of origin; their effects were superimposed on underlying structural trends. Obviously, labor-force participation rates and migration trends are also influenced by other socioeconomic factors and labor-market conditions, and in practice it may be difficult to isolate the specific impact of those policies.

During the 1970s, labor-force participation rates tended to decline.[14] Male participation continued its longer-term downward trend,[15] and that of females stagnated after substantial growth in the previous decade. Lack of employment opportunities intensified the labor-market exit of male workers, as reflected in the fall in the activity rate of adult male household heads of working age (Cortés, 1985). As we will see, this exit from the labor force contributed to keeping official unemployment rates low. The stagnation of the overall female participation rate was the outcome of offsetting trends between the youngest and oldest segments, for which labor market participation dropped, and adult women aged 25–54, whose participation increased, helping to compensate for the job and income losses of the household head.

In the 1980s and early 1990s women continued to enter the labor market in larger numbers (see Table 3.1). In part, this happened because many women from low-income households, mainly spouses, faced with low wages and the unemployment of adult male household heads, entered the labor market to supplement family income.[16] Overall labor-force participation tended to rise (see Table 3.2) owing to the renewed growth of female participation. As a result, in Buenos Aires, the share of women and, after 1990, of household members other than the main breadwinner in the economically active population (EAP) increased (see Table 3.3).

Table 3.1 Wage Share, Labor-Force Participation, and Unemployment Rates: Greater Buenos Aires, 1970–1994 (percentage)

Year	Wage Share[a]		LFPR[b]			Unemployment		
	(1)	(2)	Total	Women	Men	Total	Women	Men
1970	43	43	—	—	—	—	—	—
1971	43	44	—	—	—	—	—	—
1972	40	41	—	—	—	—	—	—
1973	43	44	—	—	—	—	—	—
1974	45	45	40.5	24.8	58.0	2.4	4.1	1.6
1975	43	40	40.2	23.8	58.2	2.8	4.4	2.1
1976	30	25	39.1	23.7	56.5	4.0	7.3	2.5
1977	25	26	38.9	23.8	55.6	2.3	4.4	1.4
1978	28	33	39.9	25.7	55.6	1.9	3.0	1.3
1979	31	34	39.4	25.1	55.0	2.1	2.7	1.7
1980	35	39	39.3 (61.1)	24.7 (38.4)	55.2 (84.8)	2.3	3.4	1.8
1981	33	38	39.1 (59.8)	25.0 (38.1)	54.4 (83.9)	5.0	5.3	4.9
1982	22	26	39.2 (59.8)	25.3 (38.7)	54.5 (83.9)	3.7	4.5	3.3
1983	29	34	37.5 (58.4)	23.0 (36.2)	53.2 (82.4)	3.1	4.0	2.7
1984	36	40	38.4 (59.9)	24.4 (38.1)	53.4 (83.5)	3.6	4.4	3.2
1985	32	38	38.8 (60.3)	25.5 (39.5)	52.9 (83.0)	4.9	4.6	5.0
1986	35	44	40.0 (62.0)	27.5 (42.7)	53.7 (83.8)	4.5	5.0	4.2
1987	33	37	40.0 (62.1)	27.5 (42.7)	53.8 (83.6)	5.2	6.4	4.5
1988	29	32	40.5 (62.8)	28.4 (44.2)	53.7 (83.3)	5.7	6.4	5.3
1989	24	28	40.8 (63.0)	27.9 (44.1)	54.2 (83.5)	7.0	7.2	6.9
1990	—	—	40.3 (63.9)	27.9 (45.2)	53.4 (84.1)	6.0	6.5	5.7
1991	—	—	40.8 (63.3)	28.0 (44.3)	55.1 (83.6)	5.3	5.9	4.9
1992	—	—	41.7 (64.4)	29.3 (45.9)	55.2 (84.5)	6.7	6.3	6.9
1993	—	—	43.3 (65.6)	31.9 (48.5)	55.6 (84.1)	9.6	12.4	7.9
1994c	—	—	43.4 (66.0)	31.8 (48.7)	56.0 (84.5)	11.1	13.3	9.7

Source: INDEC-EPH (October), 1970–1994.

Notes: a. Estimates by FIDE (1) and Beccaria and Orsatti (2) on the share of wages (i.e., excluding payroll taxes) in GDP, cited in Beccaria (1991).

b. Labor force participation rate of total population compared to population aged 15–64 in parentheses.

c. May.

Table 3.2   **Urban Rates of Labor-Force Participation, Employment, and Unemployment: Greater Buenos Aires, 1974–1994**

Year	LFPR (1983=100) Urban[a]	GBA[b]	Employment[c] (1983=100) Urban[a]	GBA[b]	Unemployment[d] (%) Urban[a]	GBA[b]
1974	107.5	108.3	—	108.8	3.4	2.4
1975	106.4	107.2	—	107.7	3.8	2.8
1976	103.7	104.3	—	103.3	4.4	4.0
1977	103.5	103.7	—	104.7	2.7	2.3
1978	104.6	106.4	—	107.7	2.3	1.9
1979	102.9	105.1	—	106.3	2.4	2.1
1980	103.2	104.8	—	105.8	2.5	2.3
1981	102.7	104.3	—	102.5	5.3	5.0
1982	103.2	104.5	—	103.9	4.6	3.7
1983	100.0	100.0	100.0	100.0	3.9	3.1
1984	101.6	102.4	101.1	101.9	4.4	3.6
1985	102.4	103.5	100.3	101.6	5.9	4.9
1986	103.7	106.7	102.5	105.2	5.2	4.5
1987	104.3	106.7	102.5	104.4	5.7	5.2
1988	105.6	108.0	103.3	105.2	6.1	5.7
1989	105.4	108.8	102.0	104.4	7.1	7.0
1990	104.6	107.5	102.0	104.4	6.3	6.0
1991	105.9	108.8	103.6	106.3	6.0	5.3
1992	107.8	111.2	104.5	107.2	7.0	6.7
1993	109.9	115.5	103.6	107.7	9.3	9.6
1994	109.4	114.9	100.0	103.0	12.2	13.1

Source: INDEC-EPH (October), 1974–1994.
Notes: a. Refers to all twenty-five urban areas covered by the survey, including greater Buenos Aires (GBA).
   b. Greater Buenos Aires area.
   c. Rate of employment relative to population.
   d. Unemployment rate relative to EAP.

Table 3.3   **Selected Characteristics of the Labor Force: Greater Buenos Aires, 1984–1993**

	1984	1985	1988	1990	1992	1993
% 15–19 in EAP[a]	7.0	6.7	7.1	7.0	7.9	7.2
% 20–24 in EAP	14.3	12.6	13.7	12.1	13.2	13.9
% women in EAP	33.7	34.1	36.7	36.4	36.7	38.5
Employed	33.5	34.2	36.5	36.2	36.8	37.3
Wage earners	—	—	37.5	36.8	38.0	38.6
% not household heads in EAP	48.3	47.8	48.2	47.9	50.0	51.5[a]
Employed	47.7	46.9	46.9	46.7	48.9	49.1
Wage earners	50.0	49.8	50.0	50.2	52.6	53.1

Source: INDEC-EPH (October), 1970–1994.
Note: a. May.

The share of women in employment also rose in varying degrees in five of six important provincial urban centers.[17] In Córdoba and Rosario, the two largest and most industrialized areas after Buenos Aires, trends are similar to those found in this latter city: the growth of women's employment mirrors the decline of manufacturing, where male employment had dominated. Women's presence increased also in Neuquén (where one should take into account the substantial presence of women among the internal migrants to a province that shows a positive net in-migration) and Tucumán; in both cities the large fall in construction employment, a traditional absorber of male workers, might have contributed to the increase in women's employment share. Overall, the growth in female participation rates moved parallel to the shift of labor demand to trade and service-sector activities, prone to employ women, a shift that is examined in what follows.

At the end of the 1980s, the participation rate of persons aged 60 and over, many of whom were formally retired and receiving pension benefits, increased as a result of the sharp fall in the real value of retirement pay.[18] The opposite had happened in the late 1970s when some wage earners of retirement age had left economic activity because pension benefits had deteriorated somewhat less than wages (Marshall, 1988a).

Immigration from neighboring countries tended to fluctuate with economic conditions in Argentina and with variations in the exchange rate. Up to the mid-1970s, comparatively more extensive employment opportunities and better wage levels had attracted immigrants to Argentina, and better conditions in its more dynamic areas had been an inducement for internal migration. Settlement had been facilitated by a lax policy concerning use of empty state-owned urban spaces that resulted in the expansion of shantytowns.

After 1976, apart from directly discouraging immigration so as to check the growth of unemployment, the military government was intent on eradicating those shantytowns in Buenos Aires and impeding new settlements. It took several actions to deter immigrants, already less inclined to enter Argentina due to the fall in wages and employment, from staying (Marshall and Orlansky, 1983). The deregulation of rent also made housing more expensive. By contrast, the overvalued domestic currency in 1979–1981 provided an incentive for temporary immigration. Internal migrants also ceased to come to Buenos Aires as employment opportunities decreased and housing became more costly. The result was some decrease in the immigrant share in the area's workforce.[19] At the same time, the emigration of Argentines increased (Marshall, 1988b).

In spite of the more permissive attitude toward shantytowns of the post-1983 civilian government, the adverse economic conditions prevented any increase in migration. Economic decline seemed sufficient to discourage in-migration from the provinces to the earlier industrial poles of absorption, although migration to the relatively unpopulated Patagonian provinces, which had more employment opportunities, continued.[20] In Buenos Aires, the share of internal migrants fell from 27% in 1982 to 23% in 1994 (INDEC-EPH).[21] By contrast, immigrants from neighboring countries maintained their share. Although in the late 1970s immigration trends had contributed to reducing unemployment rates, their impact in the 1980s is not clear. But in 1992–1994, immigration from bordering countries seemed to be on the increase again, further enlarging labor supplies. It was now due to the comparative overvaluation of the Argentinean peso—immigrants were prepared to accept low wages in the host country that were high in terms of their national currencies.[22]

Labor Requirements

As was the case with the supply of labor, economic policies undoubtedly affected labor requirements on the demand side; again, their impacts intermingled with and are difficult to separate from those factors that determine long-term changes in the volume and composition of employment. Among the labor-market effects most obviously associated with economic policies implemented after 1976 were the contraction of manufacturing employment as a result of the overvalued currency; the opening up of the economy at the end of the 1970s; and the employment effects of cuts to state expenditure, downsizing of public enterprises, and privatizations.[23] And, of course, state management of macroeconomic variables and the level of economic activity systematically affected overall employment rates.

In spite of its comparatively small labor surplus (by Latin American standards), at each of the successive phases of the industrialization process Argentina's economy had operated as if it had unlimited labor supplies, in the sense that migration made labor continuously available to the more dynamic economic centers without rapidly increasing wages. Rural stagnation in some provinces and agricultural transformation in others generated excess labor. Further, from the 1950s on, labor requirements in some sectors tended gradually to fall, and workers were expelled from traditional manufacturing industries; together with internal and international migrants, these sources were more than enough to satisfy the labor needs of the expanding sectors (Marshall, 1980). In any case, unemployment showed marked fluctuations and reached fairly high levels during economic downturns. The unemployment rate in large cities (Buenos Aires, Córdoba, and Rosario) averaged 6% in the 1960s.

During the 1970s, unemployment tended to decrease (see Table 3.2).[24] At first, in 1973–1975, this was due to employment growth. But later, during a period when employment was falling in the private and public sectors, unemployment paradoxically attained very low levels as a result of the previously described withdrawal of certain groups from the labor market (discouraged workers, more people retiring), reduction of immigration from neighboring countries and of internal migration to industrial centers, and the growth of self-employment (Marshall, 1988a). In the initial years of the military regime the government had been keen to keep unemployment low so as to avoid providing further motive for social unrest. To this end, it not only took measures to restrict immigration from bordering countries but also advised employers not to reduce employment too much. Whatever the causes, unemployment rates in this period were moderate in Buenos Aires and the rest of the urban areas; they increased again only with the 1981–1982 recession.[25]

In the 1980s, in contrast to the growing labor-force participation rates noted above, the rate of employment relative to the urban population increased only slightly. In 1994 the urban employment rate was below the 1988 level (see Table 3.2). The oscillations of unemployment to some extent reflected GNP declines in 1981–1983 and 1985 as well as the 1986 and 1992 economic improvements. Because labor demand did not rise as much as the labor force grew, unemployment and underemployment rose (see Table 3.4). Unemployment rates tended to exceed the levels of the 1970s, and even the relatively high figures reached in 1989 and 1992 were well below the unprecedented rates of 1994 (see Table 3.2). In the 1980s, the growth of surplus labor had resulted from economic stagnation and the recurrent crises, the persistent lack of investment, the decline of construction and manufacturing activities, as well as other changes in the employment structure. In the 1990s, at a time when the workforce continued to expand, unemployment reflected, by contrast, the dampening impacts on manufacturing of the penetration of imports and the improvement in productivity ensuing from a trade liberalization that was concomitant to the appreciation of the domestic currency; to this were added the consequences of large-scale privatization.

Table 3.4   Economically Active Employed, Unemployed, and Self-employed Population of Working Age as a Percentage of Population Ages 15 or Over: Greater Buenos Aires, 1984–1994

	1984	1988	1993	1994
EAP	53.0	55.5	57.9	57.5
Employed	51.1	52.4	52.4	50.0
Unemployed	1.9	3.1	5.5	7.5
Self-employed[a]	10.7	11.3	12.7	11.7

Source: INDEC-EPH (October), 1970–1994.
Note: a. Included in "employed."

After having reached a peak of almost 75% in 1974–1975, the share of wage employment in total employment in Buenos Aires tended to fall in the 1980s, accompanying the process of economic retrogression (see Table 3.A2) and fluctuating with the rate of economic activity. In five out of the six provincial urban centers examined here, the share of wage employment also decreased, in some cases remarkably. For reasons I discuss later, the improved economic performance that followed the 1991 policy package was not accompanied by growing labor requirements; the share of wage employment in Buenos Aires, after a slight recovery in 1991–1992, dropped again (see Table 3.A2).

Since the late 1970s, many of those unable to get or keep stable wage employment had sought refuge in so-called informal activities and self-employment. Self-employment performed some role in the absorption of potential unemployment.[26] In Buenos Aires it has accounted for a steady 23% of the labor force since 1980, with peaks in 1989–1990 and 1993–1994, a figure that exceeds the usual level of the preceding decade. Self-employment, traditionally a relatively prosperous category, now incorporated a sizable segment with characteristics similar to the precarious, low-income, informal sector self-employment widespread in other Latin American countries.

During the 1980s the level of wage employment increased only slightly. The increase was explained entirely by the service sector (social and personal services and finance), which more than compensated for the contraction of employment in manufacturing, mining, and construction. Manufacturing employment in medium-sized and large firms declined throughout the 1980s, and this trend continued in the early 1990s.[27] This process was associated with the long-term restructuring of manufacturing—the growing industries were not absorbing labor—but it was exacerbated by Martínez de Hoz's trade liberalization and exchange rate policy and by the crises and continued investment decline of the 1980s. Starting in the late 1970s, the largest manufacturing establishments (with more than five hundred workers) reduced employment due to plant closures, concentration, rationalization, and productivity increases. Were it not for some expansion in the number of small and medium-sized establishments that generally absorbed labor under more precarious employment conditions, manufacturing employment would have fallen more sharply.[28] Deindustrialization intensified the "tertiarization" of the employment structure that had begun in the 1960s. The opening up of the economy since 1991, combined with the fixed and low exchange rate, with efforts to raise productivity and efficiency by using more modern, labor-saving technologies and work methods, and with the deepening of economic concentration, shrank manufacturing employment. The rapid growth of manufacturing exports since the late 1980s did not generate sufficient employment to offset those negative effects.[29]

In Buenos Aires, the main industrial center, the share of manufacturing in wage employment plummeted from 41% in 1974 to 32% in 1984; 28% in 1990; and, despite overall economic recovery, to 25.4% in 1994. Increasing shares were found in trade and social and personal services and to a lesser extent in transportation and finance, real estate, and business services (see Table 3.5). Construction failed to absorb more workers despite occasional recoveries in building activities. In Córdoba and Rosario, where manufacturing had been relatively important, its employment share also declined. In all six provincial cities, the weight of social and personal services increased, but the behavior of the remaining economic activities was determined by each province's specific features (e.g., extent of state employment, importance of tourism, availability of resources such as oil, access to industrial promotion schemes, etc.).[30]

Promotion of temporary employment under the 1991 employment law did not succeed in stimulating employment creation; according to official estimates, only 12,000 contracts were made in 1992 in the framework of that law (*"Argentina en Crecimiento,"* Ministerio de Economía y Obras y

Table 3.5   **Distribution of Wage Employment by Economic Sector:
Greater Buenos Aires (percentage)**

	1984	1988	1990	1992	1993[a]	1994
Panel A: Selected Years, 1984–1993						
Manufacturing	32.5	29.9	28.0	27.0	27.0	
Construction	4.3	5.0	3.4	4.0	4.0	
Trade, hotels, restaurants	12.9	15.1	14.5	16.5	15.9	
Transportation, communication	7.1	7.3	7.6	7.5	8.1	
Finance, real estate, insurance, business services	7.1	8.8	7.7	7.9	7.3	
Social and personal services	33.5	32.6	36.7	35.3	35.7	

Panel B: Revised classification of industries, 1993–1994	1993[a]	1994[a]
Manufacturing	27.2	25.4
Construction	4.1	4.3
Trade	14.8	15.6
Finance	8.4	10.2
Social and personal services[b]	32.8	32.1
Other[c]	12.7	12.4

Source: INDEC-EPH (October), 1970–1994.
Notes: a. May.
b. Public administration, domestic services, and social and personal services.
c. Transportation, communication, electricity, and hotels and restaurants.

Servicios Públicos, nd: 27). In Buenos Aires, the unemployment rate in manufacturing, which had been 3% in 1984, jumped to about 9% in the 1989–1990 recession and exceeded 10% in 1994 (INDEC-EPH, 1993 and 1994) at a time when manufacturing activity was relatively buoyant. Unemployment in construction traditionally explained fluctuations in the overall unemployment rate. Since 1982, it has been at double digits; it surpassed 20% in May 1994. Unemployment in commerce also practically doubled between 1992 and 1993. The dramatic increase (3.7% in 1991; 15.3% in 1994) in unemployment in household services is worth noting, because it paralleled the growth of women's labor-force participation at a time when, according to anecdotal evidence, middle-income households seemed to be reducing their demand for domestic services.[31] The deterioration of the labor-market situation was reflected also by the sharp increase in the proportion of unemployed workers who have been out of work for more than three months: 27% in 1992 and 43% in 1994 (INDEC-EPH, 1994). In 1991–1994 unemployment increased slightly faster among women than among men, but although it doubled among the youth (ages 15–19) from 15.4% in 1991 to a spectacular 30.5% in 1994, it doubled also in the case of other age groups and of household heads (see Table 3.6). Further, the growth of involuntary part-time work in major urban areas, above 10% in 1994 (as against 6% in 1983; INDEC-EPH), shows the poor quality and precariousness of available jobs.

State employment decreased after 1990, mainly because of employment losses that ensued from privatization of large, state-owned enterprises.[32] In the five years from 1989 to 1993, employment in public enterprises decreased from almost 350,000 to just 67,000, mostly as a result of privatizations.[33] In certain areas of the public sector such as public administration, voluntary resignation, advance retirement, and elimination of temporary contracts, among other measures, contributed to reduce personnel, but at the same time there were a number of new recruits (Orlansky, 1993).[34] Privatizations contracted not only the volume of state employment

Table 3.6   Unemployment Rates by Sex, Age Group, and Position in the Household: Greater Buenos Aires, 1991–1994 (percentage)

Year	Total	Household Heads	Men	Women	Ages 15–19	Ages 20–34	Ages 35–49	Ages 50–64
1991	6.3	4.3	6.3	6.5	15.4	7.6	4.0	5.1
1992	6.6	3.8	6.0	7.8	16.5	8.1	4.7	3.4
1993	10.6	7.4	9.1	13.0	24.5	10.5	7.4	10.9
1994	11.1	7.8	9.7	13.3	30.5	10.1	8.1	9.4

Source: INDEC-EPH (May).

but also that of total wage employment because privatized firms employed fewer workers than the former state enterprises.[35] Further, in certain smaller cities that had been wholly dependent on consumption of workers formerly employed by the state enterprise, the effects of privatization spread throughout the community.

Additional factors may have played a minor role in explaining, in some urban areas, the jump in open unemployment rates after 1993. Intensified control of compliance with employment registration and labor obligations might have been followed by dismissal of clandestine employees in certain "visible" sectors, as their employment became more expensive. At the same time, enforcement of tax obligations may have curtailed further the already low profitability of certain low-income own-account activities; these self-employed workers may have started to look for wage employment, thus joining the ranks of the unemployed.

The potential dampening effects of unemployment on wages and working conditions were not really cushioned by income protection schemes. Unemployment compensation, created in 1991, covered only a small segment of the unemployed at the national level (10% in 1993),[36] owing probably to the rather restrictive criteria to qualify for compensation.[37] This notwithstanding, between 1992 and 1993, the number of subsidies granted increased by more than 500%, as unemployment expanded and as increasing awareness of the existence of the compensation scheme led more people to apply.

Wages and the Distribution of Income

Institutional factors, namely state intervention, have played a major role in the determination of the growth of inequality in Argentina. The massive upward redistribution of income that occurred from 1976 to 1978 was implemented through wage and labor policy and determined a pattern of income distribution that still prevailed eighteen years later, in 1994. This upward redistribution did not lead to sustained economic growth but rather to stagnation, the labor-market impact of which (falling labor demand, growing unemployment, weak trade unions), together with the wage policies of later governments, preserved and even intensified the degree of inequality achieved during 1976–1982. The new upsurge of high inflation after mid-1987 aggravated income concentration and explains the inequality peak of 1989. From 1987 onward, state control of retirement pensions further lowered the share of the poorest 30%, in which the retired persons are concentrated.[38]

Despite oscillations partially associated with trends in GNP and in real wages,[39] the period between 1977 and 1994 has seen the establishment of a more uneven pattern of income distribution among income earners than that which had prevailed at the end of the 1960s and in the early 1970s (see Table 3.7).[40] The inequality peak of 1989 is an outlier in an otherwise rather stable pattern. Even though, in the supposedly better times of 1991–1994, inequality was less than in 1989, the share of the bottom 30% had by 1993–1994 fallen to its lowest level ever (with the sole exception of 1989), and overall distribution was clearly worse than in the mid-1980s.[41] In the early 1990s, wage and fiscal policies and the unfavorable labor-market trends once again combined to maintain the inequality pattern. The distribution of income of the *employed* population also remained quite stable between 1980 and 1994 (see Table 3.8).[42]

Table 3.7   **GNP Per Capita and Manufacturing Real Wages in Argentina: Distribution of Individual Income[a] in Greater Buenos Aires, 1974–1994**

Year	GNP Per Capita % Change	Real Hourly Wages Manufacturing 1983=100	Gini Coefficient[b]	Income Share (%) Deciles 1–3	Income Share (%) Deciles 4–6	Income Share (%) Deciles 7–9	Income Share (%) Decile 10
1974	3.6	132.4	0.36	11.3	22.4	38.2	28.1
1975	−2.2	134.3	0.36	11.4	22.4	38.6	27.6
1976	−1.6	94.9	—	12.1[c]	—	—	28.0[c]
1977	4.7	81.2	—	10.9	18.9	36.4	33.7
1978	−4.8	77.0	0.44	10.2	17.9	35.8	36.1
1979	5.3	88.9	—	—	—	—	—
1980	−0.1	99.0	—	10.5	19.2	37.2	33.1
1981	−8.2	92.8	—	10.5	18.7	35.8	35.0
1982	−6.5	80.6	0.42	10.8	19.6	36.0	33.6
1983	1.3	100.0	—	10.2	19.9	37.0	32.8
1984	1.0	127.1	0.41	10.2	20.3	36.3	33.2
1985	−5.7	111.6	—	10.0	19.4	37.3	33.3
1986	4.7	105.2/116.2[d]	—	9.6	18.9	36.8	34.6
1987	0.8	97.2/104.8[d]	—	9.1	18.5	36.3	36.0
1988	−4.0	93.3/101.4[d]	0.45	9.3	17.9	36.9	35.9
1989	−5.8	80.6/82.0[d]	—	7.9	15.7	34.8	41.6
1990	−1.4	78.7/85.8[d]	0.43	9.7	19.1	36.0	35.2
1991	4.1	—/87.0[d]	—	9.5	18.4	35.7	36.3
1992	—	—/88.1[d]	0.43	9.0	19.4	37.2	34.4
1993	—	—/86.9[d,e]	0.44	8.9	19.4	37.1	34.6
1994	—	—/—	—	8.9	19.3	37.0	34.8

Sources: CEPAL, 1995a and 1995b (GNP per capita and real wages); INDEC-EPH, October (income distribution); distributions for 1975, 1977–1978 and 1981–1985 were kindly made available by L. Beccaria.

Notes: a. Refers to all income earners, whether employed or not.

b. Own estimates on the basis of INDEC-EPH (October).

c. Data presented in Beccaria (1991).

d. This series, among other changes, refers to monthly wages deflated by the average of CPIs of same and next months, whereas the 1974–1990 series refers to wages deflated by the CPI of the same month.

e. Average three first quarters.

Table 3.8 **Distribution of Income Among the Employed Population: Greater Buenos Aires, 1974–1994**

Year	Percent of Income Accruing to:			
	Deciles 1–3	Deciles 4–6	Deciles 7–9	Decile 10
1974	13.0	23.6	38.1	25.4
1980	11.5	20.2	36.9	31.4
1986	11.1	20.4	35.9	32.6
1988	9.5	19.6	37.6	33.3
1990	10.5	20.5	35.9	33.0
1991	11.2	20.4	35.8	32.5
1992	11.4	20.3	36.2	32.1
1993	11.0	20.3	36.2	32.4
1994	11.1	20.3	36.5	32.2

Source: INDEC-EPH (October), 1970–1994.

Between 1950 and 1975, real wages had remained at an approximately constant level. The relatively strong trade unions had been generally able to preserve the purchasing power of wages, but the pressure of surplus labor prevented them from raising wages pari passu with growing manufacturing productivity. The decreed wage freeze of 1976 resulted in a decline of about 30% in real wages, and despite some occasional improvements, this loss was not to be recovered. Real wages improved in 1984 when, in its first year, the constitutional government implemented redistributive measures, and again in 1985–1986 with the favorable impact of the Austral Plan on the inflation rate, but later, even though free-wage bargaining had been allowed since 1988, wages receded as rapid inflation contributed to growing unemployment and weaker trade unions (see Table 3.7). Labor's share in GNP also fell after 1986 (see Table 3.1). The 1991 stabilization plan's success in arresting inflation contributed to some recovery in wage earners' purchasing capacity over that of the immediately preceding years. Free-wage bargaining helped, although trade union subordination to the state through cooptation of the main trade union leaders favored a passive attitude in relation to lost income. This notwithstanding, in a longer-term perspective, and also in comparison with mid-1980s rates, real wages remained at a very low level (see Table 3.7). Still, whereas between 1976 and 1990 labor costs had lagged behind productivity growth,[43] the opposite occurred in 1990–1992; even though real wages remained low, manufacturing wholesale prices rose more slowly than the consumer price index since 1990, and wage costs increased faster than productivity.[44]

From the mid-1970s wages fell, but earnings out of profits did not. This is evidenced by the rise in the income share of the richest decile of income earners in 1977 to a higher level (34–36%), around which it stabilized in the longer term (see Table 3.7). Those in the top decile were the recipients of either nonwage or salary income—managers, executives, or professionals in banking and finance (strongly overrepresented in this income class), manufacturing, and certain services[45]—38.6% of wage/salary earners in this income class and 34% of nonwage/salary earners had completed university education.

The foregoing describes the evolution of income distribution in Buenos Aires and its metropolitan area. Income distribution patterns in other cities were similar to those found in Buenos Aires, although there are some differences in trends over the 1984–1993 period that reflect diversity in local economic and political contexts.[46] In the early 1990s, for instance, the flow of funds with political aims (Corrientes), the growth of public sector employment (La Rioja), and the closing down of large factories (Córdoba, Rosario) are all likely to have affected distribution patterns.

The growth of income concentration after 1976 reflected not only the reduction of wages vis-à-vis earnings from profits but also the increase in inequality in the distributions of both wage income and the income of the self-employed (see Beccaria, 1991). Given the importance of wage labor in the employment structure, the changes in the distribution of wage income should have had a substantial effect on the overall distribution of individual income.[47] In the late 1970s, the earnings differential between manual workers and low-skilled employees and professional and highly skilled nonmanual personnel, managers, and executives widened sharply (Marshall, 1985; Beccaria, 1991). The wage gap between comparable jobs in different types of firms also increased.[48] Further, owing to attempts to reduce public expenditure, public sector wages after 1988 increasingly lagged behind those in the private sector, and salaries in banking continued to improve vis-à-vis the rest. This greater differentiation surely helps to explain the growth of inequality, but on the whole the long-term increase in wage dispersion across manufacturing industries and economic sectors was not spectacular (Marshall, 1994).

Distributional Effects of Fiscal Policy

The tax reforms (i.e., tax exemptions for distributed profits, increase and generalization of the value-added tax, social security financing reform) undertaken by the military government furthered income concentration and curtailed workers' disposable income. Social expenditure was no longer used as a mechanism of downward income redistribution. Even though real social expenditure (on education, health, and housing) and its share of GNP did not decline, the latter averaging 7% in both 1970–1975 and 1976–1983,[49] this did not halt the growing deterioration of the social infrastructure and services (Marshall, 1988a).

Tax policies that followed the return to democratic government, designed to augment fiscal revenues and to ease the deficit of the retirement pension system, did not alter the regressive structure of government revenues or moderate the growth of inequality. The slight increase in state social expenditure (education, health, and housing)[50] to an average of 8.3% of GNP in 1984–1988 (Vargas de Flood and Harriague, 1993) similarly failed to improve the provision and quality of social services. In addition, the erosion of the social security system (particularly the retirement scheme and family allowances) was notorious. Revenues of the public retirement scheme declined with wages and employment,[51] and in 1983–1989 the level of pensions fell faster than any other remuneration. The coverage of the obras sociales did not decrease (in Buenos Aires, it was only 27% in 1970, rose to 61% in 1980, and was 64% in the capital city and 58% in its metropolitan district in 1989), but the system's deficit expanded considerably to the detriment of the quality of health services.[52]

The changes introduced in the tax system after 1991 and the tougher policy against evasion increased tax revenues. But, although elimination of the so-called inflationary tax had a progressive effect,[53] the tax reforms themselves intensified regressiveness as a result of the generalization and increase of the value-added tax. Subsequently, the weight of indirect taxation in total tax revenues (including payroll taxes), which was already very substantial (59.4% in 1990), rose to 64.3% in 1993.[54] Between 1986 and the 1993, the two years for which we have information on tax incidence by income strata, average tax pressure on household income increased, but the increase was highest for the lowest-income groups and lowest for high-income families (CEB, 1994). Trends in state social spending in 1990–1993 reflected the tight policy in relation to public expenditure. Although the GNP share of social security expenditure increased in 1990–1992 from 6.1% to 7.6%, expenditure on education, health, and housing altogether was 7.6% in 1989 and 7.5% in 1990–1992 (Vargas de Flood and Harriague, 1993). Figures from the state budget of 1993 envisaged an increase to 8.3% in social security but only 7.4% for education, health, and housing. The reform of the public retirement pension scheme approved in 1993 had the objective of reducing its scope and increasing the privatization of social security, as described previously. Despite the increase in social security expenditure, the level of the minimum benefit, received by 59% of the retired (56% of whom had been self-employed workers), fell even further and was the pervasive object of social demands;[55] in 1992 minimum benefits reached their lowest level since 1980. In the light of the foregoing, 1990–1993 trends in state social expenditure and taxation at best did not alter, and at worst may have intensified, the degree of inequality in income distribution.

Conclusion

As in other Latin American economies, in Argentina wages fell and inequality increased in the 1980s; but these trends started well before the
debt crisis and subsequent so-called adjustment policies. In fact, the initial
large upward income transfer took place in the late 1970s and was the outcome of the views and deliberate policies of the military government of
that period. This new distribution pattern was to prevail from then onward
and was little changed as of 1994.

The initial worsening of income distribution as well as the long-term
persistence of a more unequal income distribution pattern can be explained, first and foremost, by state wage restraints and fiscal policies;
second, by the growth of a labor surplus and the weakening of trade
unions; and third, by spiraling inflation that in certain periods exacerbated
income concentration.

State income and labor policies, derived mainly from the successive
governments' conceptions of the economic role of wages, had a direct impact on the shape of income distribution. This was particularly the case
over the period 1976–1982, but to an important extent explains also distributional outcomes in 1985–1987 as well as in 1991–1994. During the
military government, the reduction of labor costs had been perceived as a
precondition for growth. In 1985–1987 (with the Radical Party in government), wage policy was based on the notion that increased consumption
out of wages would overheat the economy, unleashing inflationary pressures and leading to balance-of-payments difficulties. Finally, in 1991–
1994, once the Plan de Convertibilidad was launched by Menem's government, the notion again prevailed that a wage increase would trigger rapid
price increases and that higher labor costs would erode further the already
barely competitive position of Argentine manufactures in the world market. In this period, central aspects of the economic program seem to have
restricted the options for reversing income distribution patterns. Taking
other conditions as given, trade liberalization *and* the fixed, low exchange
rate precluded wage increases in the private sector; fiscal control limited
growth of public sector wages and of pensions; and the adoption of a more
regressive taxation structure tended to reinforce inequality.

It has been possible for the state to implement wage restraints not
only, as in 1976–1982, by repressing trade union activity, but also because
in the 1980s and early 1990s labor-market trends were unfavorable to
workers. In 1987–1990 in particular, only those who could rapidly adjust
their prices were able to avoid or minimize income loss; wage earners and
pensioners, with relatively "fixed" incomes, were among the main losers
in the hyperinflationary period. Trade unions, weakened by mounting unemployment and underemployment, were unable to obtain wage increases

that kept pace with the hectic evolution of the consumer price index. From 1991, with the new program that succeeded in checking price growth, unemployment nonetheless continued to expand; again, weak and divided trade unions (and coopted trade union leaders) were not able to really challenge the real wage status quo.

Labor-market trends themselves were affected by economic policies. In the years 1991–1994, for instance, the negative labor-market effects seem to have been imbedded in the economic strategy: although certain components of the policy package contributed to check the growth of labor demand (e.g., the adverse impacts of trade liberalization and convertibility on manufacturing employment, or employment cuts coming with the "state reform"), at the same time some measures tended to stimulate the increase of the supply of labor (i.e., low wages and unemployment of adult males intensified the labor-force participation rates of women; the overvalued exchange rate fostered immigration).

The years 1991–1994 were a transitional period between the structural crisis and the expected strengthening of a new growth model. This period witnessed fast economic reconversion fostered by drastic policy change; GDP grew at an average of about 8% per year. It is uncertain how long this transitional period will last; whether it will effectively lead to sustained economic growth; and whether, in this case, labor-market conditions and the pattern of income distribution will improve or, instead, an ample labor surplus and strong inequality will crystallize into permanent features of Argentine society. The economy suffered a recession in 1995 with negative growth of 4.4% and very high unemployment. Early 1996 saw a modest revival.

Appendix

Table 3.A1 Gross Domestic Product and Selected Macroeconomic Variables: Argentina, 1980–1994

Year	GDP[a] $	Mfg. GDP $	(1)	(2)	(3)	(4)	(5)	(6)	(7)	(8)	CPI
1980	10,331.2	2,890.4	78.3	22.5	4.1	26.6	2.3	−4.9	−1.5	7.5	5.4
1981	9,737.8	2,544.1	80.2	19.2	4.4	23.6	3.1	−3.8	−3.7	13.3	7.2
1982	9,431.2	2,475.8	78.1	17.9	2.5	20.4	1.2	1.5	−5.2	15.1	9.9
1983	9,783.3	2,658.3	78.4	16.9	2.6	19.5	1.4	2.1	−6.1	15.1	15.0
1984	9,962.2	2,728.6	79.9	15.9	2.6	18.5	2.2	1.6	−6.4	11.9	18.8
1985	9,303.3	2,458.4	79.8	15.2	1.1	16.3	1.3	3.9	−6.2	5.4	14.1
1986	9,984.1	2,737.6	80.7	14.7	2.7	17.5	0.0	1.8	−4.6	4.1	5.1
1987	10,241.8	2,785.7	79.7	15.8	3.8	19.5	−0.3	0.7	−4.2	5.0	8.8
1988	10,049.1	2,650.1	77.5	18.5	1.1	19.5	0.7	3.0	−4.7	6.0	14.1
1989	9,424.3	2,461.2	79.3	16.0	−0.3	15.7	1.6	5.0	−6.2	3.8	38.6
1990	9,430.4	2,511.5	78.9	17.7	−3.5	14.2	1.0	6.9	−4.5	3.8	24.9
1991	10,270.0	2,810.8	81.6	15.7	0.6	16.3	1.4	2.1	−4.1	1.6[b]	5.2
1992	11,158.7	3,017.0	83.2	14.6	5.1	19.6	1.5	−3.2	−3.3	0.1[b]	1.4
1993	11,832.0	3,152.8	82.9	16.0	5.0	21.0	1.6	−3.9	−2.7	0.1[b]	0.6
1994	12,672.0	3,282.0	81.9	17.1	6.1	23.2	1.9	−5.1	−2.9	0.4[b]	0.3

Source: CEPAL,1991, 1995.
Notes: Rates (%), relative to GDP, of:
(1) Consumption
(2) Domestic savings
(3) Foreign savings
(4) Gross investment
(5) Effect of terms of trade; base year 1986
(6) Trade balance (goods and services)
(7) Net external payments; deflated by price index of imports
(8) Fiscal deficit (from 1985, national public sector).
CPI: Consumer price index (monthly % rate of change).
a. GDP at 1986 market prices, in thousands of Argentine pesos; 1986 prices; revised estimates by the Central Bank (BCRA), published April 1993.
b. Estimated on the basis of budget laws; this does not always coincide with the real fiscal deficit.

Table 3.A2 Wage Employment and Employment Rate: Greater Buenos Aires, 1974–1994

Year	Wage Employment as a % of Total Employment	Employment Rate		
		All Ages	Ages 15–64	Women Ages 15–64
1974	74.9	—	—	—
1975	74.6	—	—	—
1976	73.3	—	—	—
1977	71.9	—	—	—
1978	70.7	—	—	—

(continues)

Table 3.A2 continued

Year	Wage Employment as a % of Total Employment	Employment Rate		
		All Ages	Ages 15–64	Women Ages 15–64
1979	71.6	—	—	—
1980	70.3	38.4	59.3	37.1
1981	71.3	37.2	56.8	36.1
1982	70.3	37.7	57.8	36.9
1983	70.9	36.3	56.5	34.7
1984	70.9	37.0[a]	59.5	36.4
1985	70.8	36.9[b]	57.5[b]	37.7[b]
1986	71.4	38.2[b]	59.2[b]	40.5[b]
1987	71.1	37.9	59.0	40.1
1988	70.6	38.2	59.3	41.3
1989	69.1	37.9	60.6	40.9
1990	69.2	37.9	60.0	42.3
1991	70.2	38.6	59.9	41.7
1992	70.0	38.9	60.1	42.9
1993	68.7	39.1	59.1	42.4
1994	70.2	38.6[c]	58.7[c]	42.1[c]

Source: INDEC-EPH (October), 1970–1994.
Notes: a. April.
b. November.
c. May.

Notes

Adriana Marshall is on the National Research Council (CONICET), Buenos Aires. A preliminary version of this chapter was presented at the Conference on the Impact of Structural Adjustment on Labor Markets and Income Distribution in Latin America, San José, Costa Rica, September 8–9, 1994. She wishes to thank Albert Berry and Gustavo Indart for their valuable comments.

1. See Table 3.A1, Appendix. Investment also increased, but although in the 1980s machinery had taken up about 31% of gross fixed investment (with the exception of 1982–1983, when it fell to 27–28%; in CEPAL, 1991: 1988–1990 preliminary figures), a 1994 study made by the union of manufacturing employers holds that only 19.4% of fixed investment in 1992 can be assigned to machinery and that only a segment of this latter portion is machinery for production (*Página 12,* Economic Supplement, January 30, 1994).

2. Wage workers, protected by the labor code, accounted for over 70% of the Argentinean labor force—a very high figure by Latin American or LDC standards.

3. Taxes on income and profits dropped from 9.6% of tax revenues in 1972 to 5.4% in 1981; figures for industrialized countries were, respectively, 41.4% and 38.7%, and for Latin America and the Caribbean, 21.7% and 19.4% (data from Petrei, 1984).

4. See, inter alia, Canitrot (1992) on factors behind the failures of the 1976–1983 and 1984–1989 programs. In relation to the latter, Canitrot emphasizes

the combination of structural vulnerability (the ways in which the fiscal deficit had to be financed) with political events.

5. Figures are from Carciofi (1990). In 1986 the impact of taxation on family income (26.1%), although quite similar in all income classes, was not completely neutral but was highest on the poorest decile (29.3%), followed by the second lowest and the top deciles (27%) (Santiere, 1989; see this study for further details as well as for a note of caution on tax incidence on the poorest decile).

6. These data are from Instituto Nacional de Estadística y Censos (INDEC), 1994; the figures for 1993 are preliminary.

7. Government efforts to control evasion have no earlier precedent: advertising through the media, a campaign of denunciation, more inspections, benefits to compliers, lotteries, stronger penalties to evaders, etc.

8. Ministerio de Economía y Obras y Servicios Públicos (nd: Table 4). The number of persons registered on the tax files increased in 1989–1992 by 78% in the case of taxes on profits and by 327% in the case of the VAT, and the amount collected rose concomitantly (nd: 12).

9. In the words of the secretary of economic programming, "with the very low wage levels in some provinces and a 60% discount in payroll taxes, labor costs in some areas of Argentina are today similar to Chile's"; this, added to reduction in energy costs for manufacturing, "will make investment attractive" (in *Página 12,* February 1, 1994; my translation).

10. Trade union and labor lawyers argued that it would legitimize precarious forms of employment and foster temporary employment at the expense of indefinite contracts. Employers found this law insufficient because it did not satisfy their demands for greater deregulation of the employment contract, and too complicated because of many regulations that required trade union approval.

11. This list is not exhaustive; among other changes in labor legislation, limitations on the right to strike in essential services were decreed in 1990; the law on work injuries was modified to reduce costs; and collective bargaining in the public sector was allowed.

12. At the time of writing, there is still an ongoing controversy on how productivity increases should be estimated.

13. Naturally, education policy should be expected to affect the educational structure of the labor force. In this case, the growing deterioration of the public education system was not reflected by the usual educational indicators, as these show rising schooling rates, the educational upgrading of the population, and declining dropout rates (INDEC, 1981 and 1993).

14. Participation rates were 53.6% in 1960, 53.2% in 1970, and 50.3% in 1980 (INDEC, 1965, 1970, 1981; data refer to population aged 14 and over). In the 1970s, participation rates fell in all age groups except for those aged 35–44 (whose participation increased) and 45–54 (whose participation did not change).

15. The downward trend in male participation in 1960–1970 was explained mainly by the lower participation of the youngest (14–24), particularly of those aged 14–19, and oldest (65 and over) age groups. As occurred in other countries, the former was associated with increasing education (the impact of which was evidenced also by the falling participation of women aged 14–19) and the latter with the expanding coverage of the retirement pension scheme. But in 1970–1980, male participation decreased in all age groups (population censuses).

16. Cortés (1994) concludes that this is what happened during the 1980s: women who are part of the poorest half of all families increased their participation most, the participation of female spouses rose markedly (from 24.3% in 1980

to 33.4% in 1991), and spouses' contribution to household income increased (on the basis of INDEC-EPH, 1980 and 1991, for Buenos Aires). Further, jumps in the participation rate of women in both 1986 and 1992–1993 in Buenos Aires were due more to women aged 35 and over getting jobs than to younger groups (data in INDEC, 1993). Berger (1995), on the basis of EPH data, found that in 1980–1991 the labor force participation rate of spouses (women) in households headed by employers/professionals and by nonmanual employees and the self-employed increased more than in those headed by skilled and unskilled manual workers. The contribution of spouses to total household income, which expanded from 13.7% in 1980 to 19.4% in 1991, increased the most in households headed by nonmanual employees and the self-employed and the least among households headed by unskilled workers.

17. The household survey (INDEC-EPH) covers, apart from Buenos Aires, twenty-four urban centers, most of which are provincial capitals. The largest centers include their surrounding metropolitan area. From here on, observations on the provinces refer exclusively to Córdoba, Rosario, Corrientes, La Rioja, Neuquén, and Tucumán. These regions vary in their economic and social structure; their role in the overall economy; their economic dynamism; and, in some cases, their political leadership.

18. In Buenos Aires, for instance, participation was higher for both men and women in 1988–1993 than in 1984–1985. Retirement pay declined steadily from 1984 on, and in 1992 minimum pensions were half of what they had been in 1983 (data in FIDE, 1993). In Buenos Aires, the labor force participation rate of persons aged 60–69 had been 23.4% and 24.2% in 1984 and 1985, respectively; the figures rose to 28.9% (1988), 28.7% (1990), 32.8% (1992), and 29.1% (1993). Those aged 70 and over increased their labor force participation only in 1993, from the usual 5–6% to 8.5% (data from INDEC-EPH). The same happened in Córdoba but not in Rosario. It does not seem to have taken place in the other four provincial cities examined here either, but the small number of cases in each category casts some doubt on the results (data from INDEC-EPH).

19. According to EPH data in Cortés (1985), internal migrants as a share of the economically active population (EAP) fell from 39% in 1974 to 35% in 1981 and 1982.

20. Data on migration, based on the population censuses, are from Lattes and Sana (1992).

21. Data from the 1980 and 1991 population censuses show the same trend.

22. No data on international migration are readily available. In 1991, immigrants from border countries represented almost 4% of Buenos Aires city's population and 3.5% of Buenos Aires metropolitan area's population (INDEC, 1993c). In early 1994, facilitated by an "amnesty," some 260,000 immigrants from bordering countries regularized their situation, but there are still many more illegal residents.

23. Rationalization of state enterprises took place not only in the 1991–1994 period but also before then (e.g., employment in state enterprises fell by more than 25% in the late 1970s).

24. The unemployment rate is estimated by the household survey (see above) taken twice a year in twenty-five urban centers. Following the usual international definition, those who did not work in the week of the survey, had no job, and were actively seeking employment are classified as unemployed.

25. Limited coverage of the unemployed due to relocation of part of the population to the fringe of Buenos Aires may have contributed also to downplaying the real magnitude of overt unemployment in this city (Marshall, 1988a).

26. According to the population censuses, the share of self-employment in the country as a whole increased the most in the 1960s and continued to increase thereafter at a slower rhythm. See also Table 3.4.

27. Manufacturing employment: 1970 = 100, 1980 = 88.2, 1990 = 62.6, 1990 = 100, 1992 = 94.9, 1994 = 89.4 (INDEC, various years, preliminary figures).

28. In this period, the number of manufacturing establishments with 6 to 100 employees increased, whereas those with over 100 workers fell. Employment increased in establishments of all sizes within the range 6 to 500 employees but declined in those with more than 500 workers; the highest rates of increase were in those with 6 to 25 workers, whereas employment growth in establishments with 101 to 500 workers was very slight. Net manufacturing employment creation between 1973 and 1984 was only of some 40,000 jobs (INDEC, 1980, 1989). Productivity growth was associated more with organizational rationalization than with technological change (Kosacoff, 1989). There was some decentralization of manufacturing employment away from the traditional industrial centers as a result of state industrial promotion schemes.

29. The incidence of import penetration and negative trade balances on the employment levels of different manufacturing industries during 1991–1994 deserves investigation. Preliminary assessment of data for 1991–1993 suggested that some were adversely affected by import penetration (their output declined), but others were not, and even in some of the cases where output was maintained or increased, employment fell as a result of internal reorganization and/or improved efficiency. The largest employment losses were found in the industrial groups "textiles, clothing, and leather" and particularly in "basic metals" (data from INDEC, Encuesta Industrial, unpublished).

30. Trends in the economic structure of the self-employed (i.e., their distribution by economic activity) are similar to those described for wage employment.

31. Sectoral unemployment rates are based on last job held by workers with previous employment. Although some of these unemployed workers might have quit their jobs voluntarily or might have been dismissed long before the time of the survey, these rates provide some estimate of layoff rates.

32. Between 1960 and 1980, the employment share of the public sector gradually declined, principally but not exclusively as the result of employment cuts in public enterprises (see Orlansky, 1990, for more details). According to the population censuses, state employment (all levels of government) maintained an invariant proportion of wage employment between 1980 and 1991 (31.3%; domestic service excluded from estimates), with 2.065 million employees in 1980 and 2.221 million in 1991. But its employment share fell after 1991: the proportion of public sector employment in total nonagricultural employment decreased from 19.3% in 1990 to 16.8% in 1993 (according to estimates in OIT, 1994: 1).

33. Data from an official report cited in *Página 12,* October 16, 1994.

34. In Buenos Aires, the unemployment rate in public administration more than doubled between 1991 and 1992, and after decreasing in 1993, it rose again in 1994 (INDEC, 1993b, 1994).

35. No global estimates on these employment changes are available, but numerous journalistic articles have discussed specific cases.

36. The proportion varied by province between a maximum of 19% and a minimum of 3% (FIEL, 1993).

37. Inter alia, rural, household, and public administration workers were not entitled to compensation; construction workers qualified for a different scheme; to qualify, workers had to have been dismissed unfairly or, due to force majeure,

contributed to the fund during twelve months in the three latest years (with specific conditions for agency labor) and been registered by their employers. Also, length of compensation was linked to the duration of contributions to the fund.

38. The retired and other noneconomically active income recipients are included in overall individual income distributions because these refer to all income earners. According to FIDE (1989), in 1985 the noneconomically active earning some income (about 80% of whom were retired or pensioners) accounted for 51.2% of the population in the 40% poorest income class, and 47.2% in 1988 (INDEC-EPH data, 1988).

39. Trends in manufacturing wages are fairly representative of trends in the average wage (see Marshall, 1994, on the evolution of wage differentials). Falling wages in 1977–1978 and again in 1987–1989 affected the second poorest 30% more than the next 30% (wage workers are somewhat more concentrated in these two strata), but both lost some of their income share.

40. Table 3.7 refers to the distribution of individual income, but the distributions of total household income and per capita household income follow the same trend (data from INDEC-EPH, 1974–1990). For 1974–1990 see also Beccaria (1991).

41. From 1974 to 1994, inequality in the distribution of income among the employed population of Buenos Aires (Table 3.8) rose somewhat less (particularly in 1980–1994) than that among all income earners (Table 3.7), and that among families ranked by per capita income rose somewhat more than that among income earners (INDEC and Table 3.7).

42. Income distributions of employed individuals (considering earnings from their main job only) exclude nonworking income recipients (such as the retired), who are included in the overall individual income distributions.

43. Real manufacturing wages (deflated by the consumer price index; at that time trends in consumer and wholesale prices resembled each other) fell annually –1.6% in 1976–1989, and manufacturing productivity (per hour) increased by 2.8% (see Marshall, 1993). Labor costs in manufacturing had fallen –5.1% annually in 1981–1985 and increased 1% per year in 1986–1990, and in the same periods productivity (per worker) had declined –3.2% and risen 1.4%, respectively (unpublished estimates from Ministerio de Trabajo y Seguridad Social).

44. Notoriously, the price of commercial and private services increased much more than manufacturing prices, and this is reflected by the consumer price index, which is the standard of reference for wage change. Between 1990 and 1992 manufacturing labor costs per unit rose by 9% (on the basis of productivity per worker; Ministerio de Trabajo y Seguridad Social, unpublished estimates). Owing to the fixed exchange rate, in the same period unit labor costs in dollars increased even more, eroding the competitiveness of Argentine manufactures. The 1993 decreed rebates of payroll taxes in manufacturing firms were expected to offset at least partially such increases in labor costs (payroll taxes represented 33% of the manufacturing wage bill).

45. INDEC-EPH, October 1988. There is consensus on the fact that income concentration is underestimated by EPH data because underdeclaration by highest-income classes is widespread.

46. Comparable data for cities other than Buenos Aires were made available from 1984, but there are no grounds to doubt that income distribution in the provinces also worsened in the longer term (for 1975–1980, see Altimir, 1986, who points out that inequality increased in Buenos Aires and in other important cities).

47. It is worth noting that wage earners represented 71.3% of the three poorest employed population deciles, 78.8% of the following 30%, 76.3% of the next 30%, and 62.4% of the richest 10% (data are from Buenos Aires, 1988; INDEC-EPH).

48. According to Beccaria (1991), the latter was the most important factor in accounting for the increase of inequality in the distribution of wage income.

49. Data on the consolidated public sector from Secretaría de Hacienda. Other, minor, welfare programs are not considered here.

50. Other, comparatively minor, social programs, among which are the national food plan created in 1984 and the nutritional programs for schoolchildren, were not counted here.

51. In 1985–1990, revenues from personal and employer taxes for the state retirement pension scheme (once employer payroll taxes had been reinstated) were lower than in 1980 at constant prices (CEPAL, 1991).

52. Data from Ministerio de Salud Pública, 1982.

53. According to official estimates, in 1990 the inflationary tax "pressure" on the poorest 20% of the population was three times its impact on the richest 20% ("Argentina en Crecimiento," op. cit.: Table 5).

54. On the basis of data in Ministerio de Trabajo y Seguridad Social (1991), and FIDE (1993).

55. Data from Anuario Estadístico de la República Argentina, Buenos Aires, 1993.

4

Chile's Structural Adjustment: Relevant Policy Lessons for Latin America

Luis A. Riveros

During the world recession of the early 1990s, Chile was among the most dynamic economies in the world and a very noticeable exception to the rule in Latin America. Twenty years before, however, Chile was a less-developed country (LDC) characterized by a record of poor growth, frequent and substantial macroeconomic imbalances, low investment rates, and a large and inefficient public sector, as well as by protective policies in specific industries and markets, which produced a highly distorted resource allocation pattern. The average per capita annual growth rate in the period 1900–1989 was approximately 1.3% (Ferraro and Riveros, 1994), and inflation went from an average of more than 25% per year in the 1960s to hyperinflation in the early 1970s. In contrast, during the past eight years (1988–1995), the average annual per capita growth rate has been almost 5.5%, with yearly inflation rates averaging less than 15% and declining notably during the 1990s. Meanwhile, the investment rate in the 1990s has reached 25% of gross domestic product (GDP) and more (27% in 1995), a level substantially above historical averages; and from 1988 to 1995 the fiscal deficit turned into a surplus, export growth was solid, and the balance-of-payments situation appeared quite sustainable. After being a typical inward-looking economy, Chile has become one of the most aggressive new exporting economies, has resisted well the recent negative financial developments after the Mexican devaluation in late 1994, and has become especially attractive to foreign investors in natural resources-based industries as well as manufacturing. With low unemployment and notable macroeconomic stability, Chile enjoys a solid base from which to confront the challenge of improving social conditions.

Latin American countries seeking stabilization and adjustment may be able to draw some central lessons from Chile's experience. Replication of the Chilean experiment must, however, be viewed with caution, particularly considering the timing and political conditions that prevailed during

111

the Chilean reforms. In some respects, replication would for most countries be infeasible; the significant social and political costs involved in Chile's pursuit of sustainable structural adjustment would normally demand broad political consensus. In other respects, replication would be undesirable; for example, Chile's experience was unnecessarily costly because reforms to make the labor market function more smoothly and to improve the effectiveness and efficiency of social policy were postponed too long.

Overall, the Chilean experience reveals crucial lessons regarding the phasing and strategy of economic reforms. Two phases need to be distinguished, involving different emphases on macro- and microeconomic policies. First, in order to reduce inflation and improve the market's allocative efficiency, it is necessary to stabilize the inflation rate, eliminate the most distorting trade restrictions, and reduce the economic size of the state. Second should come additional adjustment measures, particularly stronger privatization strategies, adoption of labor-market reforms, export promotion, and measures aimed at reinforcing macroeconomic equilibria. High and persistent unemployment together with increasing poverty in Chile resulted from the lack of appropriate labor-market and social policies during the 1970s reform phase. The reform phase of the post-1985 period, on the contrary, was effectively accompanied by measures aimed at making the functioning of the labor market smoother and at building up more efficient social services. As a result of these measures, economic growth in the late 1980s and early 1990s has led to substantially lower unemployment, increasing real wages and labor productivity, and falling poverty levels.

In this chapter I review the major stylized facts of the Chilean economic transformation occurring over the past two decades and examine the three major phases of that transformation: the stabilization phase (1974–1982), the financial crisis, and the post-1985 structural adjustment phase. I discuss the implications of the Chilean experience for countries in need of stabilization and structural adjustment, especially with regard to the sequencing and coordination of economic policies. I conclude that a possible replication of the Chilean experience needs to be carefully considered in the light of the prevailing internal and external conditions in any given country.

The Economic Scenario of the 1970s

The Socialist Experiment (1970–1973)

The government of Salvador Allende pursued radical changes aimed at attaining lower inflation, a better income distribution, and higher growth. Against the backdrop of the import-substituting industrialization (ISI) strategy Chile had followed since the 1940s, the chief elements of policy were a high level of state intervention in production activities and expansionary wage, fiscal, and monetary policies. For instance, during 1971 the fiscal deficit increased from 2.7% to 10.7% of the GDP, and credit from the Central Bank to the public sector increased by more than 110% (see Table 4.1). On the external front and partly as a result of a sharp drop in

Table 4.1   Macroeconomic Indicators: Chile, 1970–1995

Year	GDP Growth (1)	Output Growth (T) (2)	Output Growth (NT) (3)	CPI Infl. (4)	M1 Growth (5)	Gross Inv. (% GDP) (6)	Fiscal Def. (% GDP) (7)	C. Acc. Def. (% GDP) (8)	Real Exch. Rate (9)
1970	2.1	1.4	2.9	32.5	66.2	16.4	2.7	–1.2	38.5
1971	9.0	9.2	8.8	22.1	113.4	14.5	10.7	–1.9	35.3
1972	–1.2	–0.8	–1.1	260.5	151.8	12.2	13.0	–4.0	36.7
1973	–5.6	–7.3	–3.7	605.1	362.9	7.8	24.7	–2.7	56.7
1974	1.0	6.6	–0.4	369.2	231.2	21.2	10.5	–2.6	83.8
1975	–12.9	–16.6	–8.4	343.3	257.2	13.1	2.6	–6.8	100.0
1976	3.5	5.3	1.6	197.9	189.4	12.8	2.3	1.5	91.5
1977	9.9	7.8	9.4	84.2	113.5	14.4	1.8	–4.1	83.5
1978	8.2	4.5	9.6	37.2	65.0	17.8	0.8	–7.1	101.6
1979	8.3	7.0	10.0	38.9	57.8	17.8	–1.7	–5.7	105.9
1980	7.8	5.5	10.0	31.2	64.0	21.0	–3.1	–7.1	94.0
1981	5.5	3.8	5.4	9.5	–3.8	22.7	–1.7	–14.5	74.8
1982	–14.1	–11.2	–10.8	20.7	7.3	11.3	2.3	–9.5	81.1
1983	–0.7	0.5	–6.1	23.1	27.7	9.8	3.8	–5.6	98.1
1984	6.3	7.9	5.3	23.0	12.1	13.6	4.0	–10.7	100.8
1985	2.4	2.5	2.4	26.4	11.3	13.7	6.3	–8.3	123.0
1986	5.7	6.7	5.0	17.4	41.4	14.6	2.8	–6.5	139.9
1987	5.7	3.5	6.6	21.5	9.8	16.9	–0.1	–4.6	143.5
1988	7.4	6.9	7.7	12.7	17.7	17.0	–1.7	3.0	149.9
1989	10.0	8.4	11.0	21.4	13.2	23.5	–1.8	–2.1	146.4
1990	2.1	0.7	3.0	27.3	17.5	23.1	–0.8	–1.9	151.9
1991	6.1	5.0	6.7	18.7	54.0	21.1	–1.6	–1.7	147.2
1992	10.3	7.1	12.0	12.7	16.8	23.9	–2.3	–2.0	132.1
1993	6.0	2.3	7.9	12.2	26.4	26.5	–2.0	–5.0	131.0
1994	4.2	3.4	4.7	8.9	19.7	26.3	–1.2	–2.0	111.8
1995	8.2	6.0	8.5	8.1	24.0	26.5	–1.6	0.0	110.6

Sources: (1), (2), (3), (5), (6), and (7), Banco Central de Chile (1987), IBRD (1990), Ministry of Finance, and ECLA (several issues of *Panorama Económico*); (4), Cortazar and Marshall (1989); (6) and (8), Corbo (1985b), IMF, and Mujica and Basch (1994); (9), Cottani (1987) and IDB; the data for 1995 are estimates provided by the Economics Department, University of Chile.

Notes: T = tradable; NT = nontradable; Inv. = investment; C. Acc. = current account; Def = deficit.

Tradables includes agriculture, fishing, mining, and manufacturing. Nontradables includes construction and services. CPI inflation and M1 growth correspond to the December to December change in the variable.

The real effective exchange rate is the real multilateral exchange rate in terms of the wholesale prices of trading partners and Chile's CPI. For 1991–1995, the index used ECLA data.

The average ratio investment to GDP during 1960–1969 was 14.9%.

world copper prices—Chile's major export at that time—international reserves dropped dramatically (from $390 million in 1970 to $161 million in 1971), and a trade balance surplus of $156 million in 1970 became a deficit of $16 million in 1971. The policy response to these external shocks fostered further distortions: for instance, significant quantity controls on imports were added to traditionally high tariffs rates and real wages were allowed to grow by about 22% in one year[1] at the same time that real interest rates were rising. The need to transfer resources to a growing number of public enterprises—working in a scheme of low fixed nominal prices—in combination with a sharp drop in tax collection and growing inefficiency throughout the entire public sector, created additional pressures on fiscal accounts. The fiscal deficit expanded dramatically to almost 25% in 1973 (see Table 4.1, col. 7). The productive sector—in which the government intervened heavily and that suffered from distorted input and output prices—soon included a soaring black market. Real GDP fell at rates of 1.2% and 5.6% respectively in 1972 and 1973, a drop accompanied by a steady decline in investment from 16% to 8% of the GDP in 1970–1973 (see Table 4.1, col. 6). Paralleling these developments on the output side was a further decline in average real wages, by 11.3% in 1972 and 38.6% in 1973 (see Table 4.3, col. 2). Facing active opposition from conservative parties, and having lost the cooperation of key political and social forces that had supported the administration in the beginning, Allende's overthrow can be seen as the tragic conclusion of a generalized crisis.

The Economic Reforms of the 1970s

The economic scenario created in the 1970–1973 period was not atypical of many Latin American countries in different periods during the post–World War II era. Though not accompanied by the heavy political emphasis of the socialist government of Allende, excessive fiscal expansion, distorted trade regimes, excessively controlled financial markets, growing state intervention in production, misaligned relative prices, a relatively high level of hidden unemployment, and fixed nominal wages were common. Although they were designed to improve the income distribution and to achieve better resource allocation by means of greater government intervention, these policies instead resulted in high inflation, recession, and political unrest. The condition of the Chilean economy in 1973 can thus be seen as a classic example of an economy in profound need of both stabilization and adjustment.

The post-1973 military government embarked upon intense economic reforms aimed at improving efficiency in the framework of an open economy.[2] The adoption of fiscal restraint and the privatization of public firms were the main policy instruments in this regard; loosening of traditional wage and employment controls—both legal and administrative—and deregulation of product markets were other key reforms. Assuming that the reallocation of productive resources could not proceed successfully on the basis of misaligned prices, the government's emphasis during the immediate post-1973 period was on reducing the presence of high inflation and restoring the allocative role of relative prices; structural reforms to allow for higher productive efficiency were left for later. With no previous adjustment events of the magnitude then contemplated, economic policy design could not rely on any former experience and was therefore in practice guided by general prescriptions of economic theory and the neoclassical paradigm.

The Stabilization Program to Reduce Inflationary Pressures

The Chilean economic reforms began in earnest with a sharp stabilization effort in 1975–1976, following 1974 measures aimed at reforming central government institutions and privatizing firms previously taken over under the Allende regime. By 1975, annual inflation was still above 300 percent (see Table 4.1, col. 4). To combat it, a dramatic cut in the fiscal deficit was achieved—from 24.7% of GDP in 1973 to 10.5% in 1974 and 2.6% in 1975—basically through reduction in public sector expenditures; this stringent fiscal policy was accompanied by a tighter monetary policy. Inflation was significantly curbed between 1975 and 1978, and it continued dropping until 1981 thanks to the implementation of a nominally fixed exchange rate that, however, fostered serious investment allocation problems.

The inflation stabilization program produced a severe drop in aggregate demand, leading to a real GDP decline of almost 13% in 1975 (see Table 4.1, col. 1) with high associated social costs. The across-the-board reduction in aggregate demand contributed importantly to open unemployment's surge to over 20% in 1976 (see Table 4.3). A drop in real wages was another key outcome of the 1975–1976 stabilization effort; although the real minimum wage doubled between 1973 and 1975–1976 (see Table 4.3, col. 1), all other wage indicators (average, manufacturing, and unskilled labor) showed a marked drop during this stabilization period (see Table 4.3). In addition, the stabilization effort seriously affected long-run growth because of its negative effects on investment and wealth (Edwards, 1985).

Trade Reforms

Chile, like most Latin American countries, pursued industrialization mainly via the creation of a sizable import-substituting industrial sector. High trade barriers, considerable inefficiency, discrimination against agriculture, and growing government intervention in economic affairs were major outcomes of that policy (Corbo, 1985a). Paradoxically, employment growth in manufacturing was negatively affected by this policy approach (Corbo and Meller, 1984), and labor-market segmentation was accentuated by labor protection and strong unionization. Moreover, the failure to achieve an efficient industrial sector demanded progressively higher protective barriers, leading to an average tariff rate as high as 105% by 1973 (Torres, 1982).[3]

The post-1973 reform aimed at sharply reversing the closed import-substitution process by means of a far-reaching opening of the economy to international trade. At the time, the measure was chiefly inspired by the need to curtail inflation. But the opening was expected to bring more investment and employment in the longer run and to focus economic activity in those sectors with international comparative advantage. The failure to actually achieve higher exports and more rapid growth of labor-intensive industries from 1974 to 1982 can be traced to two drawbacks: (1) the tariff reduction program did not start with a very precise target—the final tariff being pursued was shifted several times, which created uncertainty among investors[4] (Riveros, 1986); and (2) the exchange rate was used as a stabilization device, particularly after 1978, producing a notable overvaluation that affected expectations and export industries negatively (Corbo, 1985b; Edwards and Edwards, 1987).[5] In fact, the exchange rate was nominally fixed between 1979 and 1982, with the basic aim of reducing the inflation rate that, despite the fiscal and monetary discipline already in place, was still around 40% in 1979. At the same time, amid high domestic interest rates and a growing peso appreciation, the economic authorities decided to further open the capital account; in a period of rapidly expanding international credit flows, the immediate result was a heavy external indebtedness.[6] In addition to the macro imbalances generated by the debt problem (Edwards and Edwards, 1987), this policy allowed large firms to adopt more capital-intensive techniques, thereby limiting employment growth in the expanding activities.

Privatization and Public Sector Reforms

Another key set of reforms aimed at reducing the economic size of the state by cutting real government expenditures and by privatizing parastatal firms. The share of these firms in GDP, 14% in 1965, reached as high as 39% in 1973 (Hachette and Luders, 1987). Total public sector employment (civil service, local governments, and public firms) grew by 38% between 1970 and 1973, rising from 10% to about 14% of total employment (or 36% of total formal employment). This latter share declined to 7% by 1980 and to about 5% in 1988 (Hachette and Luders, 1987). Together with the downsizing of public employment came a major privatization program and a set of policies aimed at achieving more efficient services. Firms expropriated during Allende's socialist experiment were immediately privatized; by the end of 1974, 202 out of 259 firms had been returned to their owners (Larrain, 1988). Most were operating at substantial losses; a condition for their return to their original owners was that they assume all accumulated debts and waive any possible damage claim against the government. Additionally, a sale of other assets owned by the state was quickly implemented, with most bank shares (U.S.$171 million) and a significant part of the industrial property (U.S.$58 million) being sold by 1975; since this was a year of unprecedented economic decline (GDP fell by 12.9%), many of the sales were unprofitable in the sense that the price received by the state was below book value although still typically above stock market value (Larrain, 1988). By 1981, however, the parastatals' share in GDP had dropped only to a still-high 24%, and the state still controlled all of the top ten enterprises in the country (copper, steel, telephones, energy, coal mining, etc.). This fact cast some doubts on the sustainability of the adjustment effort, and a further privatization effort was undertaken that coincided with the crisis of the 1980s.

Market Deregulation

A top priority of the post-1973 reform program was the improvement of resource allocation through a more efficient market system. Accordingly, price regulation by government was almost completely eliminated in one blow,[7] reversing a strong historical pattern that included control of interest rates and several quantitative constraints on capital market operations. The increased market competition prodded the private sector into improving productive efficiency, and it caused several bankruptcies during the transitional period.

The wave of deregulation also reached the labor market, which was considered a crucial area after a period of extensive government intervention and union activism. A partial liberalization in wage-setting schemes was achieved, and adjustment measures aimed at eliminating overemployment were also encouraged by the government, particularly in the case of public firms. Policy aimed mainly at simply dismantling the existing institutions of the labor market, not at replacing them with a structure providing for more flexibility. Thus, collective bargaining was eliminated, as were job security regulations aimed at making labor dismissals more expensive: after 1973 massive labor dismissal required only a simple administrative authorization from the government. Unions were de facto eliminated, their new leaders being handpicked by the government itself. The private sector was thus given full power to implement its preferred employment-wages strategy.

The absence of a legal framework for the labor market during most of the 1970s was, nonetheless, a factor that fostered uncertainty in the private sector. During the entire period 1973–1979, no new legal provisions governed labor relations, inter alia, in connection with procedures for wage bargaining, job security, the right to strike, negotiation of working conditions, and union activities. After a long history of labor-market intervention and as private employers may have envisaged a return to an environment characterized by confrontations with the unions, the legal vacuum of 1973–1979 did not favor a more labor-intensive production technology. Minimum wages and nonwage cost regulations were upheld by the military regime, and a wage indexation system was implemented, although with little real effect, given a lack of enforcement (Edwards and Edwards, 1987; Riveros, 1986). Apparently, however, these particular interventions were enough to foster segmentation of the labor market, making wage adjustment and interindustry labor mobility far more difficult (Riveros and Paredes, 1990).

The social costs of the structural adjustment were very high, as indicated by a rising incidence of poverty, high unemployment, a drop in real wages, and a deteriorating income distribution. During this first phase of the adjustment, too few proactive or reactive labor and social policies were implemented; the only important one was the creation of an unemployment subsidy that operated through public works. No special training or retraining programs were put in place, nor was there an employment information system to facilitate greater labor mobility. Meanwhile, the fiscal limits imposed by the stabilization target put a squeeze on social sector spending, which in the absence of specific measures aimed at improved targeting of such spending did not constitute an efficient reactive program. In the presence of such high social costs, the continued implementation of an adjustment program without policy reversals was possible primarily because the military government had the power to repress dissent.

The 1982 Financial Crisis and the Policy Response

The 1982–1984 financial crisis produced another sharp economic decline in Chile amid serious balance-of-payments problems. Afterward, because of sharp devaluations in the exchange rate combined with expenditure reductions and other policies aimed at affecting expectations, increasing savings, and promoting exports, the economy experienced a notable export-led economic expansion. The situation of the Chilean economy after this financial crisis resembled the circumstances of many other Latin American countries that, either after stabilization or in the absence of inflationary episodes, need structural adjustment to correct resource misallocation and improve the balance of payments. Domestic economic policies introduced at the end of the 1970s had created macroeconomic disequilibria, which in turn led to unsustainably high expectations and, ultimately, to a disruption in the economic recovery initiated in 1976. The combination of a fixed nominal exchange rate, used as in Uruguay and Argentina to curb inflation, and the full opening of the capital account produced large capital inflows and heavy external indebtedness; in this context the binding full indexation of wages to past inflation (introduced in the 1979 labor law) resulted in increasing production costs for exporters. With economic policy fostering the production of nontradables, the large capital inflows financed an otherwise unsustainable expansion of private consumption and investment.

Optimism about future trends was based on the stable growth path of the economy since 1976, the balanced public budget, the sustained improvement in real wages after 1975, and the opening of the economy. But such optimism was unrealistic. The financial boom of 1979–1981 was basically financed with foreign credit provided in an expansionary period of world financial markets, and few of the resources transferred were allocated to productive investment, such as export-oriented activities. The magnitude of the financial crisis into which Chile was plunged in 1982–1984 is revealed by the explosion of the external debt from 40% of GDP in 1979 to 100% in 1983 (see Table 4.2); yearly interest payments increased from 3% to 10% of GDP. At the same time and because of an early policy reaction to the crisis, the value of imports in real terms declined by more than 40% in 1982 (see Table 4.2), triggering a GDP drop of more than 14% (see Table 4.1), which was accompanied by an equally dramatic decline in aggregate investment. The magnitude of the external shock is seen in the drop in terms of trade (from 119 in 1979 to 88 in 1983) and the increase in real (London inter-bank offered rate) interest rates from 1.1% in 1978 to 6.1% in 1984 (Corbo and Sturzenegger, 1988). The sharp curtailment of capital inflows in early 1982 amplified the problem and pushed the economy into a deep recession.

The First Phase of the 1980s Structural Adjustment

During 1979–1981, the authorities shifted their attention from stabilization policies toward structural adjustment. A series of reforms addressed traditional social policies with the aim of decentralizing administration and targeting social expenditures more effectively to the poor. A major concern raised by the adjustment already experienced in 1976–1981 was the social dimension. The most telling criticism of the economic program was that it lay behind the deteriorating income distribution and the increasing poverty problem. The Gini coefficient of the greater Santiago family income distribution had reached about 0.47 in the mid-1960s and remained above

Table 4.2　External Sector: Chile, 1979–1993

	1979	1980	1981	1982	1983	1984	1985	1986	1987	1988	1989	1990	1991	1992	1993
External debt															
Total	8.49	11.80	15.50	17.10	17.40	18.90	19.30	19.40	19.10	17.60	16.30	17.40	16.40	18.30	19.20
Interest	0.67	0.93	1.46	1.92	1.75	2.02	1.90	1.89	1.70	1.60	1.70	1.92	1.81	1.86	1.50
Debt/exports (%)	2.70	2.40	4.10	4.60	4.60	5.20	5.10	4.60	3.70	2.51	2.00	2.09	1.84	1.83	2.08
Debt/GNP (%)	0.40	0.40	0.50	0.80	1.00	1.10	1.40	1.30	1.20	1.10	0.90	0.64	0.52	0.47	0.47
Exports (FOB)															
Traditional	2.16	2.62	2.18	2.12	2.34	1.96	2.12	2.10	2.60	3.85	4.82	4.59	4.39	4.22	3.98
Nontraditional	1.68	2.09	1.66	1.58	1.50	1.69	1.68	2.10	2.62	3.20	3.26	3.72	4.54	5.27	5.22
Total	3.84	4.61	3.84	3.71	3.83	3.65	3.80	4.20	5.22	7.05	8.08	8.31	8.93	9.99	9.20
Imports (CIF)															
Consumer goods	1.33	2.07	2.73	1.48	1.02	1.04	0.75	0.75	0.90	1.01	1.49	0.80	1.13	1.69	1.90
Capital goods	0.95	1.27	1.45	0.70	0.39	0.60	0.65	0.74	1.10	1.37	1.95	2.13	1.84	2.57	3.04
Total	4.71	6.15	7.32	3.69	2.85	3.29	2.96	3.10	3.99	4.83	6.50	7.02	7.45	9.46	10.54
Terms of trade (1980=100)	118.50	100.00	84.30	80.40	87.50	83.20	78.50	82.00	77.00	93.30	92.10	82.56	82.09	81.31	74.21

Sources: Boletin Mensual, Banco Central de Chile, various issues, 1979–1993; and International Financial Statistics Yearbook, IMF, 1994; Corbo and Sturzenegger (1988).

Notes: Figures are expressed in billions of current U.S. dollars. Traditional exports include copper and mining. Nontradiitional exports are agricultural and industrial products.

0.51 in the period of economic recovery in 1978–1982; the income share of the poorest two quintiles fell from almost 13% (1960s) to less than 11% in 1980 (see Table 4.4),[8] and fiscal expenditure plummeted and the efficiency of the social services was wanting. Unemployment had not returned to its more normal 1960s levels, despite the recovery of most other economic indicators by the end of the 1970s. It was thus clear that a social strategy was needed to attain political sustainability for the structural adjustment phase. Also, as the labor market had thus far performed poorly in reallocating labor from contracting to expanding industries, reforms aimed at making its role more dynamic and flexible were of paramount importance in order to cut unemployment.

In 1981 a key change transformed social security from a pay-as-you-go system to one in which benefits depended only on individual contributions to a privately managed savings account system. This change was vital to a successful privatization program because of the significant potential of the social security system to accumulate savings and mobilize financial resources. A health care reform was also implemented in 1981; it increased the participation of the private sector by allowing the formation of private insurance companies providing free health care. At the same time, public sector social services (health and education) were being decentralized; the central ministries retained responsibility for policy formulation but not for direct administration of personnel and the budget. Hence, both education and health units were transferred to local governments, which became directly responsible for their administration and performance. Similarly, systems of targeted assistance programs, in the form of monetary subsidies for the poor, the elderly, and the unemployed, were put into operation or improved. They were important during the stage of recovery from the world recession because they allowed a better targeting of social expenditures toward the poor. Later, it would be realized that local governments were unprepared to effectively manage education and health, especially because their participation in budgetary programming was inadequate.

With a view to making the labor market more flexible and responsive, a labor law was enacted in 1979 that established new guidelines for unionization and collective bargaining procedures, broadly modeled on the U.S. system. It allowed more than one union in a given enterprise, countering a long Chilean tradition, and limited wage bargaining to the company level (reversing the tradition of industry-level wage bargaining); the right to strike was curtailed by granting firms the right to hire temporaries. In addition, the law established the principle of voluntary affiliation to unions and banned strikes by public employees. Finally, the law substantially reduced job security payments and instituted 100% wage indexation to past inflation as a floor for any wage negotiation. As I noted previously, this

	1980	1981	1982	1983	1984	1985
Box 4.1 **Results of the 1984–1985 Adjustment: Chile**						
Public expenditures	3,158	3,602	3,528	3,485	3,766	4,343
Public revenue	3,579	3,842	3,239	3,025	3,241	3,504
International reserves	4,074	3,775	2,578	2,023	2,056	1,867
IMF credits	123	49	6	606	781	1,086

Source: Banco Central de Chile (1987). Public expenditures and revenues are expressed in millions of 1976 U.S. dollars. International Reserves and IMF credits are expressed in current U.S. dollars.
Note: IMF = International Monetary Fund.

last measure was singularly problematic in the presence of the fixed nominal exchange rate regime prevailing in 1979–1982.

In 1984–1985 a so-called adjustment-without-recession approach was used to confront the financial and external crises. This approach—widely used in the region at different times by countries trying to get out of economic chaos—consisted of fostering aggregate demand to encourage output growth, based on expanding fiscal outlays and a higher external indebtedness.

Continuously declining terms of trade contributed to a rather modest increase in exports of 7%, and imports were rising by 16%; the current account deficit doubled, leading to extensive use of IMF credits (Box 4.1). Increasing public expenditures and declining revenues (Box 4.1) pushed the fiscal deficit up from 4.0% to 6.3% of GDP, the highest figure in the post-1974 period, and guaranteed strong inflationary pressures in 1985 (see Table 4.1). Although the economy grew by 6.3% in 1984, the inability to draw on external resources placed a tough constraint on the planned expansion of aggregate expenditures, making the recessionary effect even worse after that year.

Nonetheless, the use of expansionary policies was deemed necessary on political grounds because of the extremely weak condition of the economy in 1984. To counteract the recessionary shock, policies were designed to encourage exports and continue the structural reforms initiated in the late 1970s. After the traditional policy approach to get the economy out of the recession and back to a sustainable growth path failed, in 1985 the government reverted to the earlier strategy of restricting fiscal and monetary policies, increasing roles for the market and the private sector in resource allocation, and fostering sectors with a comparative advantage in production. The government realized that the exchange rate should play a key role in the development of a more dynamic export base and that healthy investment, both domestic and external, required adequate signals to investors on the institutional character of the economy and its expected evolution.

The Second Phase of the Structural Adjustment

After 1985, the adjustment program maintained a high real exchange rate, continued the privatization of public firms and the control of fiscal expenditures, created mechanisms to convert external debt into domestic investment,[9] gave specific incentives to exports, and strengthened a system to target social expenditures to the poor. The economy resumed strong growth (more than 5.5% per year from 1986 to 1988), led by a large expansion of nontraditional exports and a significant increase in private investment. Systematic real exchange rate devaluation (see Table 4.1) accompanied by other standard export promotion policies was a key factor in this strong growth and the resulting fall in unemployment and rises in real wages (see Table 4.3). The latter outcome was strongly linked to the increase in labor productivity associated with the expansion of new export industries. Fiscal and monetary discipline—further safeguarded at the end of the decade by the transformation of the Central Bank into an autonomous institution—resulted in falling inflation (see Table 4.1), at least until 1988, though there was another increase over 1989–1991.[10]

A key element in promoting exports was the large devaluation of the real exchange rate (see Table 4.1). The associated increase in the relative price of tradables to nontradables produced a substantial movement of factors into export and import-substituting industries and contributed to a positive trade balance. The increasing capital inflow and expanding domestic investment, jointly with a growing and more efficient financial sector, enabled a satisfactory flow of capital into productive activities. Labor-market reforms facilitated the labor reallocation needed after the recessionary shocks by fostering greater interindustry labor mobility and higher flexibility; the new job security norms made the hiring and firing processes less expensive, allowing for effective reentry of the unemployed into the market, which is reflected in the notable drop in unemployment between 1986 and 1990 (see Table 4.3, col. 6). As R. Paredes and L. Riveros (1993) have shown, the employment-output elasticity was shifted upward by these reforms.

The reaction of wages to falling unemployment was sluggish, however; average wages first dropped between 1986–1987, increasing afterward at 4% per year (see Table 4.3, col. 2). The real minimum wage grew

Table 4.3   Real Wages, Labor Cost Indices, and the Unemployment Rate:
Santiago, 1970–1993 (indices: 1980=100)

Year	Minimum Wage (1)	Average Wage (2)	Manufacturing Wage (3)	Informal Sector Wage (4)	Labor Cost (U.S.$) (5)	Unemployment Rate (6)	Skilled Wage (7)
1970	81.0	109.7	97.1	124.1	0.69	5.7	116.1
1971	106.8	134.1	106.6	133.7	1.09	3.8	136.7
1972	101.7	119.0	101.2	138.4	1.06	3.1	113.4
1973	46.2	73.1	68.4	99.0	0.58	4.8	95.0
1974	90.6	70.2	62.2	94.5	0.53	9.4	83.0
1975	105.1	62.5	58.3	77.3	0.43	15.5	86.3
1976	100.1	78.9	78.6	77.0	0.60	20.6	101.1
1977	84.6	79.9	78.6	80.3	0.88	19.2	111.7
1978	97.4	85.0	87.4	82.4	1.06	18.0	119.4
1979	98.3	92.0	94.2	102.6	1.28	17.2	101.2
1980	100.0	100.0	100.0	100.0	1.45	16.5	100.0
1981	111.0	108.8	115.5	120.4	2.42	15.1	98.6
1982	122.2	108.6	110.7	126.6	2.08	25.7	105.3
1983	93.2	97.0	102.9	80.9	1.30	30.1	118.5
1984	82.1	97.1	99.0	77.8	1.13	22.9	115.0
1985	74.3	93.0	97.1	75.6	0.77	20.9	98.1
1986	78.8	95.0	101.9	64.4	0.78	18.0	103.4
1987	66.9	93.1	103.2	63.1	0.81	15.2	103.3
1988	74.2	98.6	109.8	64.3	0.92	13.1	104.0
1989	80.1	100.4	111.8	65.5	0.98	10.1	109.3
1990	87.9	104.7	116.1	89.4	1.11	9.0	110.3
1991	101.0	109.9	123.8	88.4	1.28	6.5*	93.0
1992	108.1	118.4	129.7	108.4	1.33	4.9*	88.0
1993	119.6	119.0	133.1	129.5	1.42	4.6*	92.6

Sources: (1), (2), and (3): INE; (4) Paredes (1987) and University of Chile-Labor Force Survey, May of each year, unpublished data; (5) Riveros (1988); (6) University of Chile; (7) Paredes (1987). All the wage data have been deflated by the average corrected CPI based on INE, Yáñez (1979), and Cortazar and Marshall (1989).

Notes: (1) Two legal minimums existed in 1970, for white- and blue-collar workers. The latter is used here.

(2) Average wages. National yearly averages for all skills.

(3) Manufacturing sector wages. Yearly average for all skills.

(4) Urban informal sector wage, proxied by the average hourly income of self-employed workers with less than eight years of formal schooling; it has also been reported as "unskilled wage" in the free sector of the economy (informal sector). Figures correspond to May of each year.

(5) Labor cost corresponds to the wage of unskilled labor in the manufacturing sector, plus fringe benefits, expressed in hourly (nominal) U.S. dollars.

(6) * indicates that the source is the National Bureau of Statistics (INE).

(7) The skilled wage correspond to blue- and white-collar workers employed in the formal sector, with eight or more years of schooling. The unskilled wage corresponds to that reported in (4).

at 9.5% per year after 1987, and the wage of unskilled labor—after falling by half between 1982 and 1987—increased at 12% per year thereafter. Total labor costs also increased at 11% per year after 1987.

The privatization strategy fulfilled a key role during this second phase. As a result of the debt crisis of 1982–1984, the financial system was highly indebted and had very little public credibility. Most of the banks were unable to produce the capital resources needed to contribute to a meaningful recovery. A pure market solution, which would have implied the bankruptcy of important banks indebted beyond their capital, would have produced a clear negative impact on the credibility and viability of the Chilean economic model as a whole. Finding a less extreme solution for the debt problem of the banking system and, in several cases, the solvency of financial institutions, was considered a top priority. The scheme chosen involved issuing bank shares to be sold on an open market to small investors, with the Central Bank providing the credit to the purchasers of the new shares. This capitalization strategy—literally, a "rescue" operation—created a huge long-term debt owed by most of the beneficiary banks to the Central Bank. This exercise in "popular capitalism" restored the solvency of the heavily indebted banks while avoiding the politically unpalatable option of subsidizing the large private interest groups in the process.

		Box 4.2			
		Structure of Chile's Social Spending			
	Health	Education	Housing	Social Security	Other
1970	18.0	41.5	9.6	26.9	3.9
	(1.6)	(3.8)	(0.9)	(2.5)	(0.4)
1975	16.3	34.8	8.6	25.9	14.4
	(1.7)	(3.6)	(0.9)	(2.7)	(1.5)
1980	14.0	33.5	5.5	29.5	17.5
	(1.4)	(3.4)	(0.6)	(3.0)	(1.8)
1985	7.1	24.6	4.4	41.3	22.5
	(1.1)	(3.8)	(0.7)	(6.3)	(3.4)
1989	7.5	27.7	6.0	49.4	9.4
	(2.2)	(2.8)	(1.1)	(6.7)	(1.1)
1990	7.5	27.7	6.6	52.4	5.8
	(2.1)	(2.7)	(1.1)	(6.9)	(1.1)
1991	8.5	25.0	7.7	49.8	9.0
	(2.4)	(3.1)	(1.3)	(6.7)	(1.2)
1992	9.3	25.4	8.5	47.2	9.6
	(2.6)	(3.1)	(1.3)	(6.6)	(1.2)

Sources: Banco Central de Chile (1994); Yañez (1993).
Notes: The series are not directly comparable after 1989. Figures are expressed as a proportion of the social fiscal expenditure. Parentheses indicate a proportion of the GDP.

Meanwhile, many large nonfinancial enterprises remained in state hands as of 1985. The decision to transfer most of them to private hands was based on the need to reduce the fiscal drain they constituted and the need to raise their productive efficiency and thereby to emphasize clearly to foreign creditors the private sector's indisputably leading role in the economic strategy. Large public enterprises (including telephone, steel, coal mining, and other secondary industries) were sold either through open stock market operations or by means of direct allocation of shares (as in the case of the Energy Company [ENDESA] employees using their severance funds to acquire shares). Energy was one of the sectors privatized through direct sale of shares to small investors facilitated by a longer-term credit line set up by the government.

Debt-equity swap operations allowing the transformation of external debt into foreign investment in Chile were among the policies designed to attract foreign capital. In sum, the Chilean government introduced changes in the areas of privatization and external debt management, which facilitated continued implementation of a macro framework aimed at encouraging growth and exports while at the same time giving a more prominent role to the private sector in resource allocation.

The Distribution Effects of the Adjustment Program

The economic reforms of the 1970s had major effects on the labor market. Open unemployment increased from an average of about 6% in the 1960s to more than 16% during 1974–1981 (see Table 4.3),[11] in the wake of combined shocks from the stabilization program of 1975–1976 and the initial phase of the opening of the economy. The reduction in public sector employment and the higher growth in labor-force participation have also been cited as contributing factors (Riveros, 1985). The government reacted by creating emergency employment programs in 1976, designed both to provide modest monetary subsidies for the urban unemployed, thereby reducing the social impact of open unemployment, and to boost participation of the secondary labor force (married women, children).

Even in the presence of the strong economic recovery of 1976–1981, open unemployment remained high (see Table 4.3); this persistence reflected substantial shifts in production patterns caused by the more open trade regime. Both transitional and skill-mismatch unemployment were high, and there were no institutional mechanisms to help adjust supply to the new structure of demand (Riveros, 1986). Simultaneously contributing to a structurally higher level of open unemployment was an intense shift toward capital-intensive production techniques, particularly in manufacturing and services, which was due in part to a lack of correct market signals as to future labor costs—a failure due in turn to ambiguity about the labor-market institutions that would prevail in the future. The previous institutions had been virtually suspended but not replaced by an alternative set. During the financial and macroeconomic crises of 1982–1984, unemployment rates skyrocketed, reaching 30% in 1983 (see Table 4.3), a demand-driven result, since participation rates did not notably change during the recession. Later, with a strong economic recovery and a more fluid labor market, unemployment dropped sharply after 1985; by the early 1990s its level was close to the natural rate of 4–5%.

The adjustment process also severely affected real wages in the 1970s and early 1980s. They declined by about 50% from 1972 to 1975 (see Table 4.1, col. 2), bounced back quickly until 1981 in spite of the higher unemployment level (see Table 4.3), then declined markedly between 1982 and 1983, partly as a result of the recession and growing unemployment but also due to the elimination of the legal wage indexation system in 1979. A further decline between 1982 and 1985 coincided with falling unemployment. After 1985, average real wages increased slightly, more notably in the case of manufacturing, as real wages mirrored the observed behavior of labor productivity. The informal sector real wage (see Table 4.3, col. 4) had fallen dramatically during 1972–1975 but also showed a much more marked recovery than did average wages between 1975 and 1982. Afterward, the two series (average wages and informal sector wages) behaved quite differently: average wages dropped by 4% over 1982–1987, whereas informal sector wages declined by almost 50%. Then during 1987–1990, informal sector wages increased by 42%, whereas average wages rose by just 12%. The informal sector is mostly made up of the self-employed, whose earnings are clearly more sensitive to open unemployment than that of other workers.[12]

The distributive situation worsened markedly during the adjustment, at least judging by a comparison of the Gini coefficients and the share of the poorest 40% in 1980 vis-à-vis 1960–1965 (Table 4.4, col. 3). There was some improvement in the distribution of family income in the late 1980s, which was more noticeable for Chile as a whole (see Table 4.5, p. 129) than for Santiago (see Table 4.4), reflecting the fact that the nonmetropolitan regions of the country were undergoing important economic progress by that time, and more noticeable for the bottom quintile than in the overall distribution. The trajectory of the Gini coefficient coincided rather closely with the path of open unemployment; it increased notably in 1974–1976, then declined only slightly between 1976 and 1979 and remained high throughout the 1980s (see Table 4.4).[13] Nonetheless, the situation of the poorest 40% recovered somewhat during the 1980s; given that public social expenditure declined between 1984 and 1990 as a share of GDP (see Table 4.4, col. 5), that recovery may suggest higher efficiency and a greater equity impact of public expenditures after the 1980s' social reforms.

Table 4.4   Selected Social Indicators in Santiago and Chile, 1960–1992

	Santiago			Chile	
Year	Gini Coefficient (1)	(2)	Income Share of 40% Poorest (3)	Fiscal Social Expenditure (% of GDP) (4)	Per Capita GDP (1976 U.S.$) (5)
1960	0.459	0.401	13.59	n.a.	n.a.
1965	0.475	n.a.	12.87	n.a.	n.a.
1968	0.498	n.a.	11.70	n.a.	1,114
1970	0.501	0.434	11.50	n.a.	1,137
1974	0.450	0.423	n.a.	11.08	1,090
1975	0.471	0.413	12.78	10.30	933
1976	0.538	0.489	n.a.	9.99	950
1977	0.526	0.476	n.a.	10.56	1,026
1978	0.520	0.466	n.a.	10.16	1,091
1979	0.518	n.a.	n.a.	9.25	1,162
1980	0.526	n.a.	10.88	10.29	1,231
1981	0.522	0.479	11.24	12.80	1,277
1982	0.539	n.a.	9.95	15.76	1,078
1983	0.542	n.a.	10.07	15.10	1,052
1984	0.555	0.515	9.33	15.40	1,100
1985	0.532	0.501	10.13	15.12	1,108
1986	0.539	0.500	10.00	14.30	1,230
1987	0.531	0.495	10.22	13.97	1,271
1988	0.543	0.501	10.91	14.01	1,312
1989	0.552	0.500	11.61	14.03	1,442
1990	0.542	0.499	11.72	14.02	1,516
1991	0.539	0.497	11.84	14.46	1,538
1992	0.534	0.495	12.01	14.70	1,599

Sources: (1), (2), and (3): Riveros and Weber (1987); (4): Torche (1985) and unpublished data; (5): *World Tables,* World Bank, 1980 and 1995.
Notes: (1) Estimates based on total family income, representing the greater Santiago area.
(2) Estimates based on per capita family income, representing the greater Santiago area.

During the 1980s, an increasing array of monetary and nonmonetary subsidies were targeted at the poor (including not only the unemployed but also the elderly, women, children attending public schools, etc.); the fact that their effects are not necessarily reflected in labor incomes makes the interpretation of many distributive indicators controversial. As Riveros and Weber (1987) have shown, including the various subsidies in the definition of income makes a notable difference in the measurement of poverty. Overall, however, the negative distributional effects of the adjustment of the 1970s and the crisis of the early 1980s were clearly severe. To a large extent, this was due to the absence of an adequate social safety net to alleviate the condition of the unemployed and the poor and the absence of proactive policies aimed at facilitating labor reallocation. This combination created unnecessary social friction; it reduced the credibility and sustainability of

Table 4.5 Quintile Distribution of Income Among Families: Chile, 1980–1991 (percentage)

Quintiles	1980	1981	1982	1983	1984	1985	1986	1987	1988	1989	1990	1991
1	4.6	4.2	3.2	3.4	3.8	4.1	4.0	4.2	4.6	4.7	4.5	4.7
2	9.0	8.5	8.2	8.3	7.7	8.3	8.0	7.8	8.2	8.9	8.5	8.3
3	12.7	12.7	12.0	11.8	11.7	11.9	11.6	11.5	12.6	12.8	12.2	12.3
4	18.7	19.4	19.3	19.1	18.1	18.6	18.3	18.2	19.1	19.6	18.8	17.8
5	55.0	55.1	57.3	57.5	58.7	57.1	58.1	58.4	55.5	53.9	56.0	56.9

Source: Unpublished data processed by M. Basch and J.Yañez (University of Chile, Department of Economics).
Note: Figures correspond to the percent share of each quintile of families in total family income. The quintile distribution was based on a ranking of families by per capita family income. Data are from the national household survey taken by the University of Chile.

policy and may thereby have delayed the completion of the adjustment process. The lack of appropriate social policies is probably attributable to the perception that the adjustment process would be short enough to make significant social reform unnecessary, a view that can be traced in part to the lack of precedents for an adjustment of the magnitude of Chile's.

In 1976–1979, the need for lower inflation and fiscal discipline led to a severe decline in social outlays, particularly in health and education (see Box 4.2); this apparently magnified the impact of the adjustment cost on poverty. After 1980, the increase in social outlays (see Table 4.4, col. 4) is associated with the privatization of the social security system, which brought a significant increase in social security payments as a proportion of the state's social spending and of GDP (see Box 4.2).[14] The increase is also linked with unemployment subsidies,[15] but it does not necessarily imply that more resources were devoted to redressal of structural poverty. The decline in the GDP share of social outlays after 1985 is associated with fiscal restraint and with improvement in some labor-market outcomes, particularly the decline in open unemployment.[16] This decrease coincided with better targeting toward the poorest groups. In general, however, access to and financing of the health and education systems are still paramount problems in Chile, challenging policymakers with the need to make the economic program distributionally more equitable and politically more sustainable. At the end of the 1980s, the proportion of poor households was estimated to be as high as 40%. This indicator, although open to the usual methodological concerns, does no doubt reflect the severity of the productive shock of the early 1980s combined with stubborn labor-market disequilibria. The latest measures of the absolute poverty level in Chile do show significant declines, as the economy continues on a high-growth path and social policy further refines its targeting methods (Pardo et al., 1993).[17] Although there has been a clear improvement in poverty (to which the rising income share of the lowest quintile has contributed [see Table 4.5]), the highest quintile has also done unusually well during the 1980s and particularly up to 1987. The adjustment experience has led to a fall in the income shares of quintiles 2, 3, and 4, which gives support to the claim that the middle class has been most affected by the process, and is consistent with its having lost access to the complex and bountiful system of subsidies that existed prior to the economic reforms and with the shift to the targeting of social expenditures to the truly needy.

The Democratic Aftermaths: 1990–1995

Chile returned to a democratic political system in 1990. Contrary to the expectations of many, the two administrations that have been in power since that time (Patricio Alwyn and Eduardo Frei) have not changed any fundamental aspects of the economic model. The economy continues to be open, with orderly macroeconomic management and fiscal restraint. In spite of contractionary policies aimed at reducing persistent inflationary pressures, growth has continued at an average of more than 6% (including an expected 8.2% for 1995), and inflation has systematically declined from 12% to about 8% in 1995. In the distributional context, a real increase of more than 70% in social fiscal expenditures took place over 1990–1994, partly because of a tax reform implemented at the beginning of the period, and there has been a notable drop in poverty incidence from 40% to 29%. Real wages have grown systematically in the period at an average rate of more than 4% per year, and open unemployment has remained around the frictional level (ie., the level that would result from normal mobility between jobs).

Three important challenges must be met if Chile is to enter the next century with a rapidly expanding economy and with a stable and sustainable economic system: an inflation rate similar to those of its main trading partners (4–5% per year), since this is a paramount condition for successful trade agreements; modernization to achieve the productivity gains needed for continued growth with limited labor supply, which will require a reform of the state and an upgrading of the Chilean labor force through better education and training; and new or better policy instruments to improve the social indicators by effectively reaching the poor in a sustainable manner.

Lessons of the Chilean Adjustment Experience

Though elements of the Chilean experience are relevant and applicable to other countries of the region in need of stabilization and adjustment, the idea of simple replication is clearly inappropriate. Country-specific factors must be taken into account before considering any direct application of the Chilean experience. In addition, four general qualifications are worth noting. First, the Chilean reforms were undertaken very early on, when trade protectionism was still the norm and government intervention was considered indispensable to the attainment of growth and equity. The present wave of economic globalization and the almost undisputed leading role given to the private sector in economic strategy have totally changed that scenario, making feasible a higher level of political support and a more sustainable economic program than that applied in Chile in the 1970s and early 1980s. Second, the full battery of lending programs and financial assistance from industrial countries and international agencies, which are now supporting the implementation of neoconservative structural changes in most LDCs, were not available to finance the transition in Chile;

reforms were implemented in the absence of a lending program for the introduction of adjustment policies, particularly during the stabilization phase of the 1970s. Third, the unavailability at the time of a suitable social sector lending program and its practical irrelevance after the financial crisis, even if one had existed, made the attainment of specific adjustment targets more difficult and probably more costly from a social viewpoint. Finally, the absence of any precedent for the Chilean experience made it more difficult to avoid mistakes, policy reversals, and unnecessary prolongation of the process, with these adding up to higher adjustment costs. Countries currently undergoing economic reforms have the advantage of familiarity with the Chilean experience and that of other countries that have had different degrees of success in their reform experience.

However, the basic problems confronting the Chilean economy at the beginning of the 1970s and at the outset of the 1980s are still characteristic of other Latin American countries. Some, like Brazil, suffer from persistent inflationary pressures and fiscal/monetary mismanagement and require profound stabilization programs first. This is also the case in countries with middle-level inflation such as Ecuador and Uruguay. For them, the lesson of the Chilean experience—ratifying direct implications of economic theory—is the unavoidable need for inflationary stabilization based upon standard fiscal and monetary policies to precede the adoption of structural adjustment measures. Today it is an accepted fact that before any productive restructuring led by the private sector can take place, a reduction in state intervention and the alignment of relative prices is indispensable. This principle also recognizes the fact that only in a more open market environment would it be possible to attain an adequate supply response to policies seeking a resource reallocation toward expanding economic sectors.

In other countries, such as Costa Rica, El Salvador, and Peru, a comprehensive agenda of structural changes is under way, including public sector reform and privatization of public enterprises; financial sector reform; and the adoption of export promotion policies, particularly through measures regarding the exchange rate and the fiscal side. In this connection, the Chilean experience provides useful guidelines regarding the sequencing of policy measures and the priorities in designing a reform agenda. Keeping in mind other adjustment experiences of more modern fashion, such as those from Argentina and Mexico, four fundamental policy lessons consistent with the Chilean stabilization/adjustment experience are applicable to countries in either pre- or poststabilization situations.

1. There are usually two phases in adopting adjustment packages. A proper sequencing of stabilization and structural adjustment policies requires different instruments at different points in time. During the first

(stabilization) phase, standard fiscal and monetary policies are the key. Measures aimed at attaining a trade opening and at reducing the size of the public sector are normally important in order to complement the agenda and also constitute key signals for the private sector and a necessary preparation for the structural change phase. During the second phase (adjustment), privatization of public firms is one of the most important policy actions, requiring a financial sector reform to allow the capital market to allocate resources effectively among alternative projects. Along with the consolidation of the trade and financial reforms, decentralizing the social sectors, promoting exports, and introducing labor market flexibility are essential to achieving a structural change in relative prices, production, employment, and property.

2. The adjustment process takes a long time. It involves a learning process for the population as a whole and for the new entrepreneurial groups that will arise as a result of a more deregulated and competitive economic environment, and this process is necessarily time-intensive. A transition toward more modern trade unions is needed on the labor side to facilitate negotiations on more technical grounds; and labor reallocation from contracting to expanding industries—normally affected by a process involving significant skill mismatching—must take place, raising questions about the effectiveness of the program in the meantime. The new regulatory policies needed by a market economy also require a substantial learning process. It is also important to realize that making mistakes and suffering policy reversals is unavoidable in any adjustment experience. These lengthen the process and make it more difficult to attain the desirable political sustainability.

3. Apart from obvious equity considerations, social policies are paramount to gain political credibility and to achieve sustainable economic reforms. Targeting the poor, improving the efficiency of traditional social services, and devolving services to local governments and specific groups are important aspects of reducing social costs in the presence of significant fiscal constraints. This improvement is especially important in light of the fact that the middle class will necessarily be the major loser during the adjustment, particularly because of the greater fiscal stringency. This was not a key concern in 1970s Chile, it being assumed that adjustment would be attained more rapidly than it actually was; the resulting dissatisfaction could be managed only in the type of political nondemocratic environment prevailing in Chile from 1973 to 1990, but it still notably reduced the political credibility needed to foster a significant increase in private investment.

4. Labor-market reforms are indispensable early in the program. Absence of appropriate reform lengthens the period during which the economy suffers from high unemployment. At the same time, deregulating the labor market is crucial to attaining more flexibility, this being a crucial

factor in Latin America, given the tradition of heavy government intervention in labor markets. However, as the Chilean experience suggests, it is wrong to pursue the virtual elimination of such typical policies and institutions as job security, fringe benefits, the right to unionize, and so on. Such actions do not raise program credibility, but they do seriously reduce any possibility of attracting union support. In this sense, it may be highly desirable to organize coalitions aimed at transforming traditional labor-market policies in a way consistent with a modern adjusting economy.

Conclusion

A series of stabilization policies, which included reduction of the size of the state, deregulation of product and factor markets, and opening the economy to foreign trade in addition to adoption of standard macroeconomic policies, were undertaken in Chile during the 1970s. After the financial crisis of the 1980s, the Chilean economy underwent another wave of significant structural adjustment policies, the success of which was partly expedited by the economic reforms carried out in the late 1970s and early 1980s. The postcrisis policy was characterized by significant real devaluations, a far-reaching privatization program, significant reforms in the social arena, the promotion of nontraditional exports, and financial policies that dealt with both the external debt problem and the need to raise investment. The results of the adjustment process in terms of the labor market were dramatic: open unemployment and real wages deteriorated severely during the 1970s and 1980s because of both the stabilization phase and the financial crisis. The adjustment involved substantial social costs, which were relatively well cushioned in the late 1980s by the targeting of fiscal social expenditures to the poor but could have been further reduced had more proactive and reactive social policies been used more extensively and earlier.

Notes

Luis A. Riveros is a professor of economics at the University of Chile. Comments on earlier drafts by Oscar Altimir, Albert Berry, Akio Hosono, Armando Pinheiro, Susumu Sambommatsu, the participants at the Economic Cooperation Workshop organized by the Economic Planning Agency of the Japanese Government (Tokyo), the participants at the Seminar on Labor Markets and Income Distribution (San José), and my colleagues at the Department of Economics at the University of Chile are deeply acknowledged. Luis Figueroa and Claudio Soto provided efficient research assistance.

1. See the series presented in Table 4.3, col. 2, corresponding to INE's (National Bureau of Statistics) Real Average Wage Index. In the case of manufacturing (col. 3), this real increase was close to 10%, similar to that of the hourly labor

incomes for the urban informal sector (col. 4). The series in col. 5, Table 4.3, corresponds to the hourly labor cost expressed in U.S. dollars; hence, the real increase of almost 60% in this indicator between 1970 and 1971 could be partly explained by the increase in the nominal exchange rate (broker's market) of 50% in that period.

2. See Edwards and Edwards (1987), Walton (1985), and Corbo (1985a).

3. Ad valorem tariff rates ranged from 0% to 750%, import prohibitions applied to 187 tariff classifications, a ninety-day import deposit requirement was in effect for 2,800 others, and 2,300 categories required special approval from the Central Bank.

4. Initially, tariffs were planned to reach an average of 60% by 1977. By 1975, average tariffs had reached 57%, and almost all quantitative restrictions were eliminated. In a second stage, a new structure, with tariffs ranging from 10% to 35%, was achieved during the third quarter of 1977. Finally, a more radical reform allowed the average nominal tariff rate to reach a uniform 10% by late 1977.

5. After unification of the exchange rate in 1973, an initial 300% devaluation, and a series of minidevaluations, the real exchange rate (pesos per dollar) reached a peak in late 1975. Subsequently, the real exchange rate declined sharply, topped off by a 10% appreciation in June 1976. Real peso appreciation continued to be used as a stabilization device through a system of devaluations that allowed for certain real appreciation. However, inflation did not drop as expected. From June 1979, a nominally fixed exchange rate was implemented and maintained until mid-1982, when dramatic peso devaluations took place in the wake of world recession.

6. The total external debt increased from U.S.$8.5 billion to U.S.$17.1 billion in the period 1979–1982.

7. After an era in which more than 3,000 prices were set and controlled by the authorities, only thirty-three commodities remained under control, most of them utilities.

8. In this connection, see also Table 4.5, which shows that the share of the poorest quintile of the national family income distribution fell dramatically between 1980 and 1982 and that a noticeable improvement did not occur until 1988.

9. This has yielded a drop in the total external debt of more than 10%.

10. A factor underlying the persistence of the inflationary record is the existence of widespread indexation mechanisms, which encompass all financial obligations and rental prices, thereby introducing downward inflexibility in output prices. Until recently and in spite of the conservative macro and fiscal framework in place, Chilean inflation has remained well above international levels, as is the case in most Latin American nations.

11. This average includes unemployed individuals participating in Emergency Employment Programs (EEG). Average unemployment in 1974–1981, excluding EEG members, was about 13%.

12. As explained in Table 4.3, the informal sector wage is proxied by the hourly labor income of those self-employed with low skill levels.

13. In Table 4.4, we include two alternative Gini coefficients for the family income distribution. In calculating the first (col. 1), households are ranked by total income, but for the second (col. 2) they are ranked by per capita income (Riveros and Weber, 1987). The trajectories of the two series are similar. The information used corresponds to the Santiago Labor Force Survey (University of Chile).

14. The privatization of the social security system implied a significant increase in fiscal spending because of the honoring of commitments accumulated under the former system. The importance of social security outlays, as a proportion of the GDP, jumped from 2.5% in 1970 to 6.6% in 1992 (Box 4.2).

15. Unemployment subsidies are included in Box 4.2 in the category "Other." The figures indicate an important decline since the mid-1980s, as a consequence of the elimination of massive unemployment.

16. In this connection, see the column "Other" in Box 4.2. This includes unemployment compensation outlays, which dropped from 3.4% of GDP in 1985 to only 1.2% in 1992.

17. The CASEN (Chilean Socioeconomic Survey) permits estimates of total poverty, including access to monetary subsidies. In 1987 38.2% of households were poor; by 1990 and 1992 that number had declined notably to 34.5% and 27.7%, respectively. Critical poverty (also referred to as "structural poverty" in the literature), defined as those whose income is below the poverty line and who also have unsatisfied basic needs, was at 16.8%, 13.8%, and 9.0%, respectively, in those three years.

5

Increasing Wage Inequality and Trade Liberalization in Mexico

Diana Alarcón and Terry McKinley

The Macroeconomic Performance of the Mexican Economy

The performance of the Mexican economy through the 1980s and 1990s has been weak. After rapid growth, averaging 6.4% per year between 1950 and 1980, and reasonable price stability, Mexico's moratorium on its foreign debt in 1982 signaled not only the "official" start of the international debt crisis, but also a period of severe economic retrenchment and adjustment for Mexico. In contrast to Brazil, whose balance of payments was negatively affected by the oil price hikes, Mexico eventually benefited from the high prices of oil but by the latter 1970s was attempting to maintain a level of expenditures inconsistent with its tax effort and turned to heavy foreign borrowing to make up the difference. From 1982 to 1986, the debt crisis brought an output decline of about 8%, a serious bout of inflation, and a sharp decline in real wages of about 30%.

Policies of stabilization were successful in bringing inflation under control and attracting capital inflows. On other counts, however, the economy performed poorly. GDP fell by 4.5% over 1981–1983 and only recovered the previous peak in 1987. From then through 1993, average yearly growth of GNP was a modest 2.5% (see Table 5.1). Gross national product (GNP) per capita was growing at an average rate of only 0.8% a year.

One of the explicit objectives of structural adjustment is to alter the composition of output by increasing the share of tradable goods. During the wrenching adjustment of 1981–1987 the ratio of exports to GDP (in constant prices) rose sharply from 12% to nearly 20%, reflecting a rapid growth of export volume. The corresponding import ratio fell from an atypically high 25% (related to the serious overvaluation during the years just before the crash) to 13%. This period thus saw a sharp increase in the

Table 5.1 Indicators of Mexico's Macroeconomic, Employment, and Wage Performance, 1980 and 1987–1994

	1980	1987	1988	1989	1990	1991	1992	1993	1994
GNP at 1980 prices (growth rates)	9.2	1.9	1.3	3.3	4.5	3.6	2.8	0.4	2.4
GNP per capita (growth rates)	5.4	-0.1	-0.6	1.5	2.7	1.9	1.2	-1.0	1.0
Share of manufacturing exports in total exports (%)	19.5	47.6	56.0	55.2	52.0	58.7	60.8	80.3	81.8
Share of manufacturing exports in nonoil exports (%)	59.8	82.1	83.2	84.2	83.4	84.4	87.2	93.7	93.2
Share of manufacturing imports in total imports (%)	87.2	89.1	89.6	89.8	91.0	94.0	93.7	94.2	94.1
Trade deficit (millions of dollars)	-3,058	8,433	1,667	-645	-4,433	-11,063	-15,934	-13,480	-18,990
Share of tradables in total output (%)[a]	NA	33.6	33.6	33.8	34.2	34.0	33.6	33.1	31.7
Share of manufacturing in total output (%)	NA	21.3	21.7	22.5	22.8	22.9	22.8	22.3	22.7
Index of manufacturing employment (1980 = 100)	100	87.0	86.8	88.8	88.8	87.3	84.0	77.9	74.5[b]
Share of maquiladora employment in total manufacturing employment	100	69.0	68.7	74.8	77.5	82.2	89.4	93.3	93.2[b]
Index of mean earnings in manufacturing (1980 = 100)[c]	4.9	12.6	16.0	17.5	NA	NA	NA	16.8	NA
Share of wages in disposable personal income	40.6	32.1	30.6	29.5	28.1	29.0	NA	NA	NA

Source: Instituto Nacional de Estadística, Geografía e Informática (INEGI). Electronic database (BINEGI), Mexico; Nacional Financiera (1994); Presidencia de la Republica (1994).

Notes: Tradables include agriculture, mining, and manufacturing production. Share figures are based on current price data. NA: Not available.

a. Since 1991 manufacturing exports include exports from the maquiladora sector.

b. To July 1994.

c. Includes both blue and white collar workers.

ratio of real exports to real imports. During the halting growth since 1987, this shift has been reversed as the constant-price export ratio has fluctuated without trend, whereas the import ratio skyrocketed to over 30% in 1992–1993. In current-price terms, however, the export ratio fell and the import ratio rose only modestly. For 1981–1993 as a whole, export volume grew at a healthy 5.5% per year and imports somewhat less rapidly. The balance of trade did not improve more than this because of a reversal of the terms of trade associated mainly with the fall in oil prices.

Thus far, however, there is little to suggest that significant resource reallocation between tradables and nontradables has accompanied these changes in export and import levels during the postcrisis years after 1987; the share of primary and manufactured products has remained relatively unchanged at about one-third of total production. Performance has, however, varied among the tradable goods sectors. Agriculture has stagnated; its average yearly rate of growth was a mere 0.5% between 1987 and 1993. The manufacturing sector has had a more dynamic average growth of 3.5% per year. Within manufacturing, exports of machinery and equipment became a leading sector, and this industry's share of total manufacturing output increased from 17.3% in 1987 to 23.1% in 1993. Manufacturing exports as a whole increased from half of total exports of goods in 1991 to three-quarters in 1993 (ECLAC, 1995b: 111).

Unfortunately, the rapid growth of manufactured exports has not led to increased employment. In fact, by March 1994, employment in manufacturing was only about two-thirds of its 1980 level. Moreover, it is precisely the most dynamic exporting sectors within manufacturing that have shown the largest loss of employment. By March 1994, employment in the machinery and equipment sector, for example, was only 68% of its 1980 level.

Maquiladora activities have been one of the few sectors of rapid employment growth. By March 1994, maquiladoras employed 557,658 workers, or about 17% of the manufacturing labor force, most of them concentrated in the northern border states. However, since less than 2% of their inputs are produced in Mexico, these enterprises have weak multiplier effects on the rest of the country. Thus, their job creation effects throughout the economy have been minimal.

In the wake of the economic crisis flowing from the debt crisis, Mexico's economic policy gave high priority to combating inflation through exchange rate and income policies. Political pacts were negotiated with labor and business to restrain wage and price increases.[1] The government allowed the exchange rate to become overvalued as a means to moderate inflation. These efforts were successful in lowering inflation, but they hampered the process of economic restructuring.

Trade liberalization combined with an overvalued exchange rate led to a rapid increase in imports and a sharp drop in production of importables for the domestic market, as well as a slowing in the growth of exports. The government maintained a policy of high interest rates in order to attract capital inflows to finance the large current account deficit, but these high rates throttled domestic productive investment by raising the cost of credit. Most of the capital flowing into the country was used to purchase short-term government securities rather than to finance the desired long-term productive investment. Eventually, macroeconomic mismanagement proved disastrous for the Mexican economy.

Mexico's policies of trade liberalization—within the context of generalized contraction of the economy—have in fact led to a distorted process of economic restructuring and a pattern of trade specialization that does not reflect the country's endowment of abundant labor. Most of the growth of manufactured exports in the 1980s was the result of intrafirm or intra-industry trade in a few sectors already highly internationalized, rather than any broad-based reorientation of domestic producers toward exporting.

It is now widely recognized, especially since the financial crisis of December 1994, that the government's macroeconomic policies contributed to the poor performance of the economy: lack of per capita income growth, widespread bankruptcies and job losses, the sharp contraction in the agricultural sector, the persistence of high levels of poverty, and rising inequality in the distribution of income.[2]

Changes in the Distribution
of Total Income and Its Components

The distribution of income in Mexico became substantially more unequal during the period 1984 to 1992. The Gini coefficient rose sharply from 0.429 in 1984 to 0.469 in 1989, then rose more slowly to 0.475 in 1992—overall a 10.7% increase (see Table 5.2).[3] The income components most clearly contributing to greater inequality were profits, both industrial and commercial, and income from personal services; their share of total income increased and their disequalizing impact on its distribution was intensified. Meanwhile, income from agriculture and livestock had the opposite effect: its share of total income was cut by more than half, and it became more concentrated among the lower-income deciles.

The great majority of workers have suffered net losses over the period of structural adjustment and trade liberalization. These have resulted from economic stagnation; modest job creation from such growth as has occurred; and, for some workers, the government policy of wage repression. Nonetheless, wages (including those of the highly paid) remained the largest single component of reported income during the period from 1984 to 1992, their share dropping only marginally from 46.9% to 45.4%. The

Table 5.2   Gini and Pseudo-Gini Coefficients of Total Current Household Income and Its Components: Mexico, 1984, 1989, and 1992

Income Components	1984		1989		1992	
	Share of Total Income	Gini and Pseudo-Gini Coefficients	Share of Total Income	Gini and Pseudo-Gini Coefficients	Share of Total Income	Gini and Pseudo-Gini Coefficients
Total	100	0.429	100	0.469	100	0.475
Wages	46.9	0.443	46.4	0.430	45.4	0.466
Profits	7.1	0.468	10.2	0.634	8.4	0.613
Services	4.7	0.427	6.5	0.623	7.3	0.635
Agriculture	10.4	0.395	4.9	0.257	4.5	0.328
Rent	2.8	0.671	2.8	0.758	1.1	0.566
Cooperatives	0.2	0.445	0.3	0.432	0.1	0.407
Transfers	6.5	0.350	6.0	0.397	5.8	0.383
Other	0.3	0.823	0.5	0.816	1.1	0.794
Nonmonetary	21.2	0.389	22.6	0.455	26.1	0.429

Source: Own calculations based on INEGI (1984, 1989, 1992).
Notes: Calculations are based on group data. Households are ranked by total household income.

distributional impact of wages underwent a U-shaped pattern of change. Wages first became more concentrated among lower-income deciles between 1984 and 1989—while the distribution of total income was becoming markedly more unequal—and then ended up being more concentrated among higher-income deciles in 1992 than they had been in 1984.[4]

This dramatic change in the distribution of wage income in the latter years was the major factor contributing to increased inequality in the distribution of total income during the early years of the liberalization process begun in the late 1980s. Although wage income's share of total income marginally contracted, it became more unequally distributed in 1992 than it had been in 1984. In this chapter we attempt to explain these important changes in the distribution of wages.

Changes in Wage Dispersion Among Major Groups of Workers

To help identify the changes in the distribution of wage income from 1984 to 1992,[5] we divide wage earners into seven pair comparisons of groups of employees: (1) urban and rural employees; and within urban employees, we divide the sample into (2) male and female workers, (3) union and nonunion workers, (4) workers in the tradable-goods sector and in the non-tradable-goods sector, (5) workers in border states and nonborder states, (6) workers in poor states and in the rest of the country; and within the manufacturing sector itself, we divide the sample into (7) workers in the export sector and in the nonexport sector. These comparisons were chosen to help identify the effect of trade liberalization on specific groups of workers.

Substantial wage differentials existed between these various paired groups of employees in 1984 (see Table 5.3). The largest gap was between urban and rural workers, with the mean ratio of the latter reaching only about 56% of the former. Within manufacturing, wages in the nonexport sector were a surprisingly low 69% of those in the export sector. Substantial gaps also separated wages of union and nonunion workers and of male and female workers.

At the level of these broad categories, two main trends in these differentials between 1984 and 1992 are worthy of special note for their possible relations to structural adjustment and trade liberalization:

1. Wage differentials increased somewhat between males and females;[6] between workers in poor states and those in the rest of the country; and between urban and rural workers, the last two of these reflecting the overall decline of the agricultural sector.

2. There was a contrasting tendency toward equalization of wages across certain groups of workers, as evidenced by the narrowing wage differentials between export and nonexport workers and, most notably, between tradable-goods workers and nontradable-goods workers and between union and nonunion workers. Although in 1984 workers in the nontradable-goods sector earned wages only 86% of those of tradable-goods workers, by 1992 they earned wages that were 8% higher. Whereas in 1984 nonunion workers earned wages only about three-quarters the level of union workers, by 1992 that disadvantage had virtually vanished.[7] The narrowing union-nonunion gap was at least partly a result of the wage policies of the Mexican government, one of whose main instruments in fighting inflation was wage-price agreements between labor and business. These mainly affected workers adversely in the lower wage brackets.

Paradoxically, while wages were being equalized across broad groups of workers, wage inequality within many of these groups worsened appreciably, a point to which we now turn.

The Rise of Within-Group Inequality

Much of rising inequality in the distribution of wage income from 1984 to 1992 is attributable to within-group inequality rather than changing differences in mean wages between these groups. Increases in within-group inequality must thus be related to factors other than those identified in the geographical, sector, gender, and other distinctions just cited.

Table 5.3   Wage Differentials Among Groups of Workers: Mexico, 1984, 1989, and 1992

Groups of Workers	1984 Monthly Wages	1984 Ratio (%)	1989 Monthly Wages	1989 Ratio (%)	1992 Monthly Wages	1992 Ratio (%)
Female	25.14		25.88		21.19	
Male	32.78		36.17		28.38	
Female/male		76.7		71.6		74.7
Nontraded	30.68		32.95		27.14	
Traded	35.74		33.85		25.21	
Nontraded/traded		85.8		97.3		107.7
Nonexport	29.55		29.94		22.74	
Export	42.79		35.94		27.50	
Nonexport/export		69.1		83.3		82.7
Nonunion	27.93		31.35		25.85	
Union	37.17		36.42		26.70	
Nonunion/union		75.1		86.1		96.8
Poor	28.13		27.24		22.74	
Nonpoor	30.65		33.15		26.28	
Poor/nonpoor		91.8		82.2		86.5
Nonborder	30.12		31.25		25.93	
Border	32.18		39.48		27.24	
Nonborder/border		93.6		79.1		95.2
Rural	16.94		14.97		14.38	
Urban	30.49		32.79		26.09	
Rural/urban		55.6		45.6		55.1

Source: Own calculations based on INEGI (1984, 1989, 1992).

Notes: Wages are given at constant new pesos. August 1984 = 100. One new peso = 1,000 old pesos. Pair comparisons, except for urban and rural workers, are calculated for urban wage earners. The tradable-goods sector includes mining and manufacturing activities only, and the nontradable goods sector includes utilities, construction, commerce, transport and communication, financial services, and social and community services. Exporting and nonexporting sectors include manufacturing activities only. Exporting sectors are those that export an above-average percentage of their total production. They include chemicals, basic metals, metallic products, machinery, and equipment. Poor states are Oaxaca, Guerrero, Chiapas, and Hidalgo. Border states include the five states along the U.S. border: Baja California, Sonora, Chihuahua, Coahuila, and Tamaulipas.

Judged by the standard deviation of log variance (SDLV), inequality among all wage earners was significant in 1984, at 1.04 (see Table 5.4); that for urban wage earners was 0.91, for urban manufacturing workers only 0.77, and for rural workers significantly greater at 1.14.[8] There was unusual equality among union workers, for whom the SDLV of 0.47 was considerably below that of any other group, reflecting the tendency for unions to compress the range of wage income among their members. Note also that inequality among workers producing nontradables is significantly greater than among those producing tradables.

Table 5.4   Standard Deviation of Log Variance of Monthly Wages and the
Percentage of the Variance Explained by Human Capital (R^2):
Mexico, 1984, 1989, and 1992

Pair Comparisons	1984		1989		1992	
	Standard Deviation	R^2	Standard Deviation	R^2	Standard Deviation	R^2
All wage earners	1.036	0.42	0.978	0.36	1.299	0.22
Rural	1.144	0.35	1.024	0.24	1.145	0.20
Urban	0.912	0.39	0.841	0.32	1.331	0.20
Male	0.850	0.40	0.815	0.34	1.288	0.22
Female	1.009	0.40	0.856	0.30	1.391	0.17
Union	0.467	0.26	0.621	0.26	1.530	0.14
Nonunion	0.989	0.40	0.899	0.32	1.245	0.23
Poor	0.744	0.39	0.778	0.38	1.191	0.10
Nonpoor	0.922	0.39	0.845	0.32	1.339	0.21
Border	0.901	0.31	0.897	0.26	1.457	0.24
Nonborder	0.914	0.41	0.823	0.35	1.312	0.20
Trade	0.776	0.34	0.838	0.32	1.321	0.27
Nontrade	0.870	0.37	0.830	0.32	1.338	0.18
Urban manufacturing						
Wage earners	0.770	0.33	0.835	0.31	1.320	0.27
Export	0.734	0.46	0.811	0.29	1.455	0.30
Nonexport	0.761	0.24	0.842	0.32	1.218	0.24

Source: Own calculations based on INEGI (1984, 1989, 1992).
Note: R^2 is from regression with monthly wages as dependent variable. Categories of workers are as defined in Table 5.3, p. 143.

A significant proportion of intragroup inequality was explained by variations in human capital (levels of education and work experience) among wage earners. For all wage earners the share was 42%, for urban employees 39%, and for manufacturing workers 33%. Among manufacturing workers in the export sector, however, this share was the highest of any group at 46%. Among union workers the opposite was the case; only 26% of wage variation was explained by our indicators of human capital.

According to the SDLV measure, inequality among all wage earners and for most categories had declined marginally by 1989. The major exceptions were manufacturing workers and union workers, for whom the variance increased during this period. The proportion of the variance among wages that is explained by human capital also fell between 1984 and 1989—from 42% to 36%; for urban workers it dropped in a similar manner to 32%. For workers in the export sector the share plummeted from 46% to 29%. Already in 1989, we can see the signs of incipient divergence between human capital and earnings.

Although wage inequality did not change significantly between 1984 and 1989, the short period from 1989 to 1992 witnessed an extraordinary leap in inequality among all wage earners and across all subgroups of wage earners. The SDLV for all wage earners jumped from 0.98 to 1.30. Inequality among urban employees now surpassed that for rural employees, reversing the situation that had prevailed in 1984 and 1989. The principal source of rising inequality among all wage earners was now inequality among urban workers. Astonishingly, SDLV among union workers, who composed 27% of all urban employees, exploded to 1.53, the highest among any subgroup of urban wage earners (see Table 5.4);[9] that among border workers also surged to reach 1.46, and that among employees in export manufacturing rose substantially. The proportion of wage variation explained by human capital declined precipitously over this short period, from 36% in 1989 to just 22% in 1992, after falling moderately from 42% in 1984.

The combination of the generalized stagnation of the Mexican economy and a more pronounced outward orientation was thus associated with rising inequality among wage earners. Though quite general, the tendency toward greater inequality was more pronounced in some of the groups most closely tied to the process of integration with the global economy, such as those in the border region and in export manufacturing.

Inequality rose dramatically because of factors apparently unrelated to differences in measured human capital. Labor markets were channeling higher rewards to workers according to criteria other than education and experience. One factor in the increasing wage dispersion has probably been the differential impact of government wage policy on various groups of workers. Since December 1987, minimum wages were not allowed to increase beyond the target rate of inflation, and this set the pattern for workers with relatively low wages. In contrast, the wages and salaries of white-collar workers, technicians, supervisors, and higher-educated workers were not bound by such wage restraint. Also, compared to manufacturing sectors producing for a depressed domestic market, exporting sectors were in a better position to offer higher wages, especially to workers with higher levels of skill and education, who were in demand.

The Decomposition of Wage Inequality by Theil Indices

In order to further probe the factors associated with the dramatic increase in observed wage inequality, we utilize Theil's population-weighted L index to decompose total inequality into the respective contributions of inequality within groups of employees and inequality between groups. Between-group inequality is the inequality associated with specified factors used to divide the sample, such as level of organization or education; within-group inequality, conversely, is the inequality unexplained by those specified factors.

Inequality between groups of workers distinguished by broad trade-related sectors (specifically nontradables; export manufacturing; nonexport manufacturing; and mining, which includes the all-important petroleum export sector) does not contribute much to total inequality. It explains only 2.9% of all inequality among urban wage earners in 1984, 1% in 1989, and a mere 0.5% in 1992. The decline illustrates a general tendency toward greater homogenization of wage and salary payments across broad sectors of the Mexican economy between 1984 and 1992.

Geographical dispersion equally explains little of the inequality among urban wage earners. The distinction among wage earners in poor states, in border states, in the large established industrial centers in the Federal District and Nuevo León, and in the rest of the country explained 2.4% of total wage inequality in 1984 but only 0.9% in 1992.

Distinctions based on level of organization, education, and occupation do explain important, albeit falling, proportions of inequality (see Table 5.5). Four groups of urban wage earners were distinguished according to their level of organization: those with a union, those without a union but having a labor contract of indeterminate duration, those without a union but having a labor contract of determinate duration, and those with neither union nor labor contract. Nonunion members without a labor contract had the lowest wages (see Table 5.6). As of 1984, those with at least a temporary contract

Table 5.5 **Theil L Indices of Inequality of Monthly Wages of Mexican Urban Wage Earners: Within-Group and Between-Group Inequality, 1984, 1989, and 1992**

Group	1984	1989	1992
Organization			
No contract	0.392	0.365	0.409
Nonunion determinate contract	0.243	0.300	0.694
Nonunion indeterminate contract	0.223	0.328	0.483
Union contract	0.104	0.198	0.744
Between-group %	18.8	8.5	5.4
Education			
No education	0.308	0.291	0.380
Primary	0.262	0.259	0.457
Secondary	0.256	0.276	0.581
Tertiary	0.244	0.261	0.747
Between-group %	16.7	16.2	12.1
Occupation			
Elite	0.244	0.313	0.793
Technical	0.144	0.183	0.593
"Ordinary" workers	0.207	0.258	0.511
Low-income workers	0.399	0.364	0.423
Between-group %	24.5	17.7	13.5

Source: Own calculations based on INEGI (1984, 1989, 1992).

Note: Theil L indices are not comparable over time because their maximum value varies with the logarithm of average monthly wages.

Table 5.6   Relative Wages Among Selected Groups of Mexican Urban Wage Earners: 1984, 1989, and 1992

Group	1984		1989		1992	
	Actual Wage	Wage Index	Actual Wage	Wage Index	Actual Wage	Wage Index
Organization						
No contract	18.63	100	22.70	100	17.69	100
Nonunion temporary	26.66	143	28.65	126	26.03	147
Nonunion permanent	41.77	224	39.96	176	33.98	192
Union	37.17	200	36.34	160	26.68	151
Education						
No education	15.84	100	18.33	100	13.95	100
Primary	21.14	133	25.00	136	18.78	135
Secondary	29.48	186	30.36	165	23.34	167
Tertiary	50.50	318	57.84	315	53.04	380
Occupation						
Low-income workers	14.89	100	18.95	100	15.09	100
"Ordinary" workers	28.99	195	28.47	150	21.72	144
Technical	36.16	243	37.43	198	31.61	209
Elite	71.30	479	67.92	358	61.34	406

Source: Own calculations based on INEGI (1984, 1989, 1992).
Note: Monthly wages at constant new pesos. August 1984 = 100.

earned 43% more, and those with a more permanent labor contract 124% more than nonunion workers without contracts. Unionized workers as a group earned a little less than this last group. Inequality between these groups explained a quite considerable 18.8% of all inequality among urban wage earners in 1984. Between 1984 and 1992, the wages of the top three groups fell relative to the bottom one. The wages of both union workers and workers with somewhat permanent nonunion contracts fell by roughly one-fifth relative to the wages of unorganized workers between 1984 and 1989. By 1989 the inequality "between" these four groups explained only 8.5% of all wage inequality—less than half the 1984 figure. From 1989 to 1992, employees with nonunion labor contracts of either determinate or indeterminate duration widened their advantage over unorganized workers, whereas that of union workers continued to decline. The latter's 1984 advantage over unorganized workers of 100% had by 1992 been cut in half. Mainly as a consequence of this decline in the relative wages of union members, plus the increased variance of wages within that group, the share of total inequality explained by between-group inequality fell to 5.4% and the share accounted for by wage variance among union members themselves increased dramatically from 9% in 1984 to 32% in 1992.

Level of education also explains a considerable share of wage variance among urban workers. A four-way distinction among those with no education, some or completed primary, some or completed secondary, and some or completed tertiary education explains 16.7% of all inequality among urban wage earners in 1984, 16.2% in 1989, and 12.1% by 1992. Relative wages among these four groups did not change appreciably from 1984 to 1989, the only noticeable change being an 11% decline for those with secondary education. This stability continued through 1992 with the striking exception of those with tertiary education, whose relative wages increased from 3.15 to 3.80 times those of workers with no education. In short, the recession and earlier phases of trade liberalization during the 1980s did not significantly alter the relative earnings of workers by level of education, but the recovery period, which coincided with the later phase of liberalization, saw a sharp relative increase for the most educated, an increase that contributed to overall widening of the variance of wage earnings. Note also that although in 1984 wage variance was greatest among uneducated workers, by 1992 it was greatest among workers with higher education. The contribution of the wage variance of employees with tertiary education to total inequality increased from 14.6% in 1984 to 18.3% in 1992. Economic restructuring and trade liberalization were rewarding the more elite, skilled sectors of the Mexican labor force.

These statistics support our hypothesis that government wage policy had a differential impact on the wages of various groups of workers. Although workers with primary education became a larger proportion of the total labor force—increasing their share from about 22% in 1984 to about 34% in 1992—their relative wages remained fairly stagnant. Workers with secondary education became a smaller proportion of the total labor force and actually saw their average wages drop relative to those of uneducated workers. Workers with tertiary education were not subject to the restraints imposed by government pacts with unions and businesses and, as a group, clearly gained. This differentiation of wages became most marked in 1992 after four years of economic growth.

A four-way distinction by type of occupation explains a significant share of total inequality among urban employees. The four occupation groups are elite employees (professionals; public officials; and private sector administrators, managers, and supervisors); employees with technical or specialized training (technicians, teachers, and equipment operators); ordinary workers (direct operators, workers, and artisans in industry; office workers; workers in commerce; and workers in personal services); and poor unskilled employees (domestic workers, helpers and unskilled laborers in industry, employed street vendors, and urban agricultural workers). This four-way distinction explains 24.5% of total inequality among urban wage earners in 1984, 17.7% in 1989, and 13.5% in 1992.

The urban wage hierarchy by occupational category narrowed between 1984 and 1989 (see Table 5.6); although the relation among the top three categories changed little, all fell vis-à-vis the "poor unskilled." This explains in part the drop in the share of inequality accounted for by occupation over that period. One reason between-group inequality declined relative to within-group inequality is the sharp increase in the variance of wages among both elite employees and technical workers between 1984 and 1992; from a low 0.244 in 1984, the figure for the former group jumped to a very high 0.793 in 1992 (see Table 5.5). Between 1989 and 1992, there was a partial reversal of narrowing wage gaps, as average wages of elite employees rose relative to those of all other groups; their wages were over four times those of poor, unskilled workers. However, the gap between "ordinary workers" and the poor unskilled continued to decline. The great majority of workers have been clear losers in relative terms throughout the period of structural adjustment and trade liberalization.

Pseudo-Gini Coefficients by Education and Occupation

To analyze in greater detail how the wages earned by each of the educational and occupational categories distinguished above affect the overall distribution of earnings among urban workers, we have calculated pseudo-Gini coefficients for the wage income earned by each of those categories of urban workers.

In 1984, urban wage income, separately considered, was relatively equally distributed, with a Gini coefficient of 0.384. The pseudo-Gini coefficient for the wage income of uneducated urban workers was –0.202;[10] over 66% of this wage income was received by the bottom 50% of urban wage earners. At the other extreme, the pseudo-Gini coefficient of the wage income of employees with a tertiary education was 0.765; two-thirds of that income was concentrated among the top 10% of urban wage earners. Between 1984 and 1989, total urban wage income became somewhat more unequally distributed. The rising pseudo-Gini coefficients for the uneducated employees and employees with some primary education indicate that these groups were contributing to that trend. The falling coefficients for the other two educational categories imply that their effect was working in the opposite direction. Between 1989 and 1992 when the distribution of urban wage income became dramatically more unequal (with the Gini coefficient rising to 0.514), all four categories contributed to the trend. By 1992, almost three-quarters of the wage income of persons with tertiary education, for instance, accrued to the richest decile of urban workers.

The trends in the distributional impacts of the occupational categories distinguished here are broadly consistent with those of the educational categories. The wage income of professionals and of managers was the most highly concentrated among the upper deciles of the distribution, with 81.3% and 89.6%, respectively, accruing to the richest decile of urban employees in 1992. Although the pseudo-Gini coefficients of both groups fell somewhat between 1984 and 1989, this trend was reversed from 1989 to 1992. During the whole period from 1984 to 1992, wage income of technicians and teachers became more concentrated at the top of the distribution of total income. This was true as well for ordinary workers and salespeople, although the income of both groups remained less concentrated among high-income employees than was true for wages as a whole.

Conclusion

During the period from 1984 to 1992, government policies to control wage increases, mainly through setting minimum wages, have supported greater equalization of wages between such broad economic divisions as tradable goods/nontradable goods and export manufacturing/nonexport manufacturing. Average wages of unionized workers have fallen to the level of wages of nonunion workers. Large regional wage differentials have not emerged between border and nonborder states or between poor and nonpoor states.

Despite the equalization of some wage differentials and the relative stability of others, this period of restructuring and policy reform of the Mexican economy saw wage income become tremendously more dispersed, especially since 1989, a shift that contributed to the overall increase in inequality of income distribution. Significant variance of wages across workers grouped according to educational level and occupation remain. Most strikingly, large unexplained variances have arisen among urban employees. Within border states and within export manufacturing and also among union members, great inequality of wage income has emerged. Those groups of workers most closely associated with the increasing export orientation of the Mexican economy are precisely those among whom wage differentiation has been most intense. Yet this differentiation is not positively correlated with differing productivity levels among workers, at least insofar as differences in endowments of human capital are concerned. One possible reason is that the functioning of the labor markets has become more subordinate to government-imposed wage restraint in order to combat inflation, with the associated restraint affecting mainly workers with lower wages. These differing mechanisms of wage determination, along with the concentration of growth in exporting sectors and in the border region, have had an increasingly arbitrary impact on the dispersion of wages among urban employees in Mexico.

Appendix

Table 5.A1 compares several measures of inequality—the standard deviation of log variance, the Theil population-weighted L index, the Gini coefficient, and the coefficient of variation—among all wage earners, rural wage earners, urban wage earners, and urban wage earners within the manufacturing sector. Each measure gives a somewhat different, and in some cases conflicting, picture of the changes in inequality from 1984 to 1989. Theil's population-weighted L index changes little. The normalized Theil index, which is the L index divided by the logarithm of mean monthly wages, suggests a decline in inequality.[11] However, both the Gini coefficient and the coefficient of variation of monthly wages indicate an increase in inequality for all wage earners and for urban employees. Both these latter measures avoid the weakness of the standard deviation of log variance in understating the degree of dispersion among higher-wage employees. All measures of inequality concur that inequality declined among rural wage earners.

Table 5.A1   Selected Measures of Wage Inequality in Mexico: Various Groups of Wage Earners, 1984, 1989, and 1992

	1984	1989	1992
All wage earners			
Standard deviation of log variance	1.036	0.978	1.299
Standardized Theil[a]	0.039	0.031	0.047
Gini coefficient	0.419	0.443	0.519
Coefficient of variation	0.930	1.092	1.319
Rural wage earners			
Standard deviation of log variance	1.144	1.024	1.145
Theil L index	0.492	0.403	0.404
Standardized Theil[a]	0.051	0.032	0.038
Gini coefficient	0.471	0.433	0.466
Coefficient of variation	0.964	0.908	1.064
Urban wage earners			
Standard deviation of log variance	0.912	0.841	1.331
Theil L index	0.319	0.320	0.632
Standardized Theil[a]	0.031	0.024	0.047
Gini coefficient	0.383	0.411	0.514
Coefficient of variation	0.870	1.020	1.288
Urban manufacturing wage earners			
Standard deviation of log variance	0.770	0.835	1.320
Theil L index	0.269	0.300	0.758
Standardized Theil[a]	0.026	0.024	0.048
Gini coefficient	0.369	0.411	0.528
Coefficient of variation	0.960	1.018	1.437

Source: Own calculations based on INEGI (1984, 1989, 1992).
Note: a. Standardized Theil is Theil's L index divided by the natural logarithm of mean monthly wages.

From 1989 to 1992, all measures of inequality are consistent in showing that there was a substantial rise in inequality among all wage earners and across all subgroups of wage earners.

Notes

Diana Alarcón works for the International Labour Organisation, and Terry McKinley is employed by the United Nations Development Programme. Research for this paper was carried out at the Centre for International Studies, University of Toronto. Alarcón and McKinley appreciate the comments by Albert Berry on a previous manuscript of this paper. All remaining errors and omissions are the responsibility of the authors.

1. The first *pacto* was signed in December 1987 between the government-controlled labor unions, business representatives, and the government. Thereafter, pactos were renewed several times—until February 1995, when the attempt to negotiate a new pacto failed to keep prices under control in the aftermath of a sharp devaluation of the peso in December 1994. Wage increases, however, are still restrained. Along with agreements by unions and business to restrict price and wage increases, the pactos included government commitments to maintain the exchange rate within certain limits.

2. For a discussion of the relationship between trade liberalization and changes in income distribution between 1984 and 1989, see Alarcón (1994).

3. These Gini coefficients should be regarded as rough approximations to the level of inequality since they are based on ranking households by total household income and on grouping data by deciles.

4. Table 5.2 allows us to assess the impact of each major income component on the distribution of total income by presenting each component's pseudo-Gini coefficient, or concentration ratio. (The pseudo-Gini coefficient measures not the inequality of distribuiton of a given source or type of income taken by itself but the degree to which that source contributes to the inequality of total income. Thus, a high pseudo-Gini means that the particular income in question [e.g., business income] is concentrated among persons who rank high in terms of total income. Since the ranking of each group of workers is by total income and not by the component under analysis, the pseudo-Gini coefficient for that component can vary from −1 to +1.) In 1984 wage income was a factor contributing to greater inequality in the distribution of total income, as reflected in the fact that its pseudo-Gini coefficient (0.444) was higher than the Gini coefficient for total income (0.429). In 1989, however, more wage income accrued to the lower-income deciles, the pseudo-Gini coefficient for wage income being 0.430 compared to the Gini coefficient of 0.469 for total income. By 1992, wage income's pseudo-Gini coefficient was only marginally lower, at 0.466, than the 0.475 Gini coefficient for total income.

5. The results presented in the following sections were obtained from analysis of the 1984, 1989, and 1992 income-expenditure surveys by Instituto Nacional de Estadistica, Geografia e Informatica (INEGI). The results are comparable because of the similarity of methodologies used in the design of the three surveys. Although the surveys are primarily intended to capture the income and expenditure patterns of households, they also include comprehensive reporting of the income earned by individuals, the sectors in which these individuals work, their job position, and their demographic characteristics.

6. An analysis of wage differentials by gender may be found in Alarcón and McKinley (1994a).

7. These differentials are examined in more detail in Alarcón and McKinley (1994b).

8. This measure can be directly related to standard regression analysis of the relationship between human capital and earnings. The dependent variable is the natural logarithm of monthly wages, and the independent variables specified for human capital characteristics of workers are used to explain the variance or "inequality" in the distribution of log monthly wages. The main drawback of such a measure is that it compresses the wages of higher-paid workers relative to the wages of lower-paid workers and thus understates inequality among workers in the upper range of the distribution. In Table 5.A1 of the Appendix, we compare the results for the standard deviation of log variance with the results for Theil's population-weighted L index, the Gini coefficient, and the coefficient of variation.

9. The within-group inequality among union wage earners alone accounted for well over a third of all inequality among urban employees.

10. For the definition of the pseudo-Gini coeffcient, see note 4. Recall that its value ranges from −1 to +1.

11. The Theil population-weighted L index varies from 0 to the log of the arithmetic mean. In order to normalize it for intertemporal comparisons, we divide each Theil index by the log of the arithmetic mean of monthly wages of each group for each year.

6

Trade Liberalization, Labor Reform, and Income Distribution in Colombia

Albert Berry and Jaime Tenjo G.

Colombia emerged from the 1980s in a much better economic state than most other countries of the region. Present export and overall growth prospects are favorable, given the oil/gas discoveries and the demonstrated export capacity in a range of other products. Trade liberalization, the major policy change in recent years, is also expected by its proponents to have a positive effect on growth. Related components of the market-oriented reforms have been privatization, financial market reform, and reform of labor legislation.

Colombia's experience during the 1970s and 1980s appears to have been unique within the region, since a good case can be made that income distribution showed some net improvement[1] while the country was also recording one of the few good growth records over that span. An important part of the story is the unusually marked decline in earnings differentials across educational levels and between genders, declines especially concentrated in the late 1970s while the economy was still growing rapidly and in the early 1980s when it was not (Tenjo, 1993). Rural earnings were also showing considerable improvement at this time (Ministerio de Agricultura, 1990: 228).

Differences in economic structure or in growth rates could be at the root of the contrast between Colombia's experience during the 1970s and 1980s and those of Argentina and Chile, for example. If the contrast was due more to differences in policy, the intriguing hypothesis would be that Colombia's positive experience was due to the absence of major shifts in trade or labor-market policy.

In this chapter we consider the possible labor-market effects of the economic policy reforms of the last decade in Colombia, in particular the *apertura,* or liberalization of trade, which began (or accelerated, depending on how one looks at it) in the early 1990s, and the labor-market reforms of the early 1990s. Although our concern is with labor-market

155

outcomes in general, including unemployment, wage levels, quality of work, stability of work, and so on, we focus on the distribution of income (especially labor income) as a key indicator of how well the economy is serving the interests of the majority of the population. A highly unequal distribution of income means that the share of jobs paying somewhere close to the economywide average income is low.

Predictions as to the distributive impact of the policy reforms have ranged from the positive to the quite negative.[2] That impact may be joined by Dutch disease effects of strong export growth in the mineral sector. Few countries have experienced the benefits of major oil booms without accompanying problems and costs, one of the major fears being a worsening of income distribution. Clearly, if both the mineral export boom[3] and the liberalization cum related policy reforms were to have negative impacts on Colombia's income distribution, the combined effect might be quite severe. Hence the importance of assessing the possible dimensions of these effects and the ways in which they might be avoided or offset.

It is interesting, inter alia, to consider whether the distributional effects of policy reforms and a mineral export boom would be more likely to reinforce each other or to offset each other. In one respect the latter should be the case: whereas the boom lowers the relative price of other tradables, the policy reforms (the trade reform, to be specific) have the opposite effect. At a more concrete level, one hope of the trade reform is to bring labor-intensive exports like clothing, leather goods, furniture, and some agricultural products more firmly into the export sphere. But, with the strong comparative advantage and the easy "rents" that it implies, Cusiana (the major oil find) brings the threat of Dutch disease effects on such relatively labor-intensive sectors.

Effects of the policy reforms initiated in the first years of this decade may still be appearing, while those of the gradual liberalization under way from the mid-1980s should have mainly played themselves out by now. The evidence available on the labor-market effects of the apertura and other policy reforms, though somewhat inconclusive (partly because it is impossible to judge which effects may be transitory and which permanent), is certainly worrisome. Of greatest concern is the relatively sharp reversal of the previous equalizing trend in the urban distribution of income. The story that the data tell is matched by a growing concern in Colombia that the new "model" is widening income gaps (Sarmiento, 1993). That concern should be less when overall growth is faster, and with the oil resources about to come onstream, Colombia is expecting a robust rate of growth. Also on the positive side, urban unemployment has remained low by Colombian standards.

Economic Policy and Macroeconomic Performance
Since the 1960s

Since the late 1960s, Colombia's macroeconomic performance has been among the best (or least bad) in Latin America. From 1970–1993, average gross domestic product (GDP) growth was 4.4%, placing the country second only to Brazil at 5.1% (Berry, Mendez, and Tenjo, 1994b: Table 1). Growth was also the least unstable among major countries in the region because the debt crisis and the accompanying recessions hit Colombia much less hard than most other countries. Growth in the early 1990s (through 1994) has been about average for the region, at around 3.5% per year.

This creditable record has been based on generally good exchange rate management since the switch to a flexible rate in 1967; a trade regime offering incentives both for import substitutes and for exports; and a relatively prudent fiscal and monetary policy, under which fiscal deficits were never long maintained at the unsustainable levels of several other countries of the region, and monetary growth was accordingly more modest. The administration of Lleras Restrepo marked an important turning point for the economy. The 1967 trade and exchange rate reforms ushered in one of the most successful periods of industrial and export growth in Colombia's history and put an end to a liberalization episode that had taken place since 1965 under severe pressures from the donor agencies (Diaz-Alejandro, 1976: Chap. 7). The Lleras government refused to devalue and instead adopted the crawling peg, stringent import and exchange controls, and a stable export promotion policy (Ocampo, 1994: 136). This process has been interrupted since the late 1970s by the Dutch disease effects of the coffee and foreign indebtedness booms between 1975 and 1982, reflected in the real appreciation of the peso and a mini-episode of import liberalization around 1980. As industrial and overall growth slackened to about zero in 1982–1983, export coefficients declined and structural change ceased. Since the mid-1980s, there has been renewed growth in the industrial sector, but the presumably falling returns from the import-substituting industrialization (ISI) elements of the model and the acute change in the external conditions facing the country led to a radical turnabout in policy in 1990–1991 and the adoption of a more explicitly outward-oriented strategy (Ocampo, 1994: 145). It is still too early to do more than guess at the growth effects of this strategy.

Protectionism, though well embedded in policies since the nineteenth century, played a somewhat secondary role during the first phase of import substitution, whereas real exchange rate fluctuations provided the most important price signals to industrial entrepreneurs (Ocampo, 1994: 134). J. A.

Ocampo sees the 1967 package as the consolidation and rationalization of the mixed strategy followed since the late 1950s. Over the years, a gradual import liberalization occurred. By the mid-1970s, inflation was a serious threat; the López government (1974–1978) addressed it via tight monetary and fiscal policy, which was reversed by the Turbay administration in favor of expansionary fiscal policy, tight monetary policy, and import liberalization. These, however, led to a consolidated public sector deficit of 7.1% by 1982 and massive public sector borrowing abroad. Real appreciation deepened in the early 1980s debt boom, and export promotion was downgraded, not as a result of an explicit decision but of short-term macroeconomic considerations. The deteriorating situation led the Betancur administration (1982–1986) to rapidly reverse more than a decade of import liberalization.[4] The liberalization during the rest of the decade was moderate (Ocampo, 1994).

During the early 1980s, then, the economy became more closed; from a high of 22% in 1982, the ratio of imports (constant 1975 prices) to GDP fell to 14.4% in 1984, then fluctuated in the 16–18% range through 1991 (see Table 6.1). The comparable current price series declined and rose more smoothly. The time profile on the export side is similar; after the lows of 1982–1983 of under 15% (constant prices) or 12% or less (current prices), the recovery brought the export share to around 19% over 1986–1989.

Industrial growth was unstable during the 1980s. Like the overall growth rate, it remained below the levels reached over 1967–1974. By the

Table 6.1   Exports and Imports as a Percentage of GDP: Colombia, 1980–1993

Year	Constant 1975 Prices					Current Price	
	GDP	Exports	Imports	Exports/GDP	Imports/GDP	Exports/GDP	Imports/GDP
1980	525.8	90.6	107.1	17.2	20.4	17.4	16.5
1981	537.7	81.6	111.2	15.5	21.3	13.0	16.2
1982	542.8	80.5	119.8	14.8	22.1	12.0	15.9
1983	551.4	77.3	112.3	14.0	20.4	11.1	14.3
1984	569.9	84.9	108.2	15.0	14.4	12.6	13.5
1985	587.6	95.9	101.2	16.3	17.2	14.4	13.6
1986	621.8	118.1	112.4	19.0	18.1	20.1	13.9
1987	655.1	126.6	118.1	19.3	18.0	18.0	14.9
1988	681.9	128.8	121.0	18.9	17.7	17.5	15.4
1989	705.1	161.6	116.6	19.3	16.5	18.9	15.2
1990	735.5	161.6	126.2	22.0	17.2	21.7	16.1
1991	750.7	167.2	120.9	22.3	16.1	22.3	15.0
1992	777.2	178.4	156.6	23.0	20.1	20.4	17.7
1993	—	—	—	24.0	28.0	20.0	—

Source: Departamento Administrivo Nacional de Estadistica (DANE), *Cuentas Nacionales de Colombia,* unpublished data.

end of the 1980s, slowing growth and accelerating inflation were increasingly interpreted as the result of a structural blockage based on two factors: stagnation in the growth of factor productivity and a lack of dynamism in investment, frequently blamed in turn on the inward-looking development model (Republica de Colombia, 1991: 7; Montenegro, 1991, cited by López, 1993: 19). This contributed to a perception that trade policy required a radical change toward an explicitly outward-oriented strategy, a perception that was consistent with a generally more market-friendly ideology in Latin America at this time.

The Gaviria administration (1990–1994) came to power facing a difficult inflation challenge (to which the need to devalue in the previous years had contributed) *and* having committed to continuing and accelerating the already initiated process of liberalization, which was accompanied by a partial freeing of exchange controls, more open access to foreign investment, and a liberalization of the labor market. The government was aware that distributional problems might result from the liberalization, a concern derived both from an understanding of the sorts of adjustments that would be involved in the process of apertura and related reforms and from the experience of other countries of the region, Europe, and elsewhere.

The apertura was carried out quickly, though its effects on imports were delayed.[5] In December 1989, 38.8% of tariff positions (product categories for which tariff levels were individually designated) were free, 60.1% required previous permission, and 1.1% were prohibited; by November 1990 these numbers were 96.7%, 3.3%, and 0%. The ratio of tariffs (including surcharges) collected to GDP fell sharply in 1992, though the decline was less than might be suggested by the data on tariff positions.[6] The crawl of the peso was accelerated to prepare the ground for the liberalization, and some external funding was arranged in expectation of an import surge, which, however, came much later than expected. The government's emphasis on curbing inflation pushed real interest rates quite high, and since the government opened the capital market at an early stage of the apertura, this helped to flood the economy with foreign exchange, rendering the tight domestic monetary policy unsuccessful. With inflation accelerating and imports not growing, and believing that the main factor in this situation was the expectation of further tariff cuts, the government decided to accelerate the program, dropping rates in 1991 to the levels previously planned for 1994 (Becerra et al., 1993: 123). When even this did not raise imports quickly, the government felt forced to appreciate the exchange rate, even though one of the arguments that had been put forward for the more hasty opening was to avoid a revaluation that would compromise the development of the export sector. At the beginning of 1992, the newly created Junta del Banco de la Republica decided to lower the anomalously high interest rate to a level consistent with the international market and accept that the money supply would be a passive variable. Imports finally jumped in 1992 (by 30%) and surged in 1993 (by over 50%). The export quantum rose sharply in 1990 (mainly due to coffee), since which time growth has been moderate. The ratio of current-price exports to GDP appears to have leveled off at around 20%.

Growth, which had recovered to average 4.5% over 1985–1990, fell to a low of under 2.5% in 1991, from which it gradually accelerated to around 5% in 1993–1995. The fixed investment ratio (current prices) fell from a recent high of 19.5% in 1988 to 14.2% in 1991, recovering to 15.5% in 1993.

The composition of exports has changed significantly since the early 1980s, when coffee accounted for about half of the total. Since then its absolute dollar value has fallen, while that of mining products rose sharply to about $2.2 billion of a total of $7.3 billion in 1992, with coffee at just $1.3 billion, other agriculture at $1.2 billion, and other items (essentially manufactures) at $2.6 billion. Manufactures rose from about 7% of the total in 1970 to 31% in 1991 (World Bank, 1993b: 268). The main manufactured export sectors have been foods, textiles, and chemicals (accounting for three-quarters of such exports in the 1980s). Three structural features seem to have been important. First, these exports are relatively natural resource–intensive and unskilled labor–intensive (Thoumi, 1979; Villar, 1983). Second, exporting firms are relatively larger and more capital-intensive than nonexporting firms in each sector (Echevarría and Perry, 1981; Villar, 1983). Third, a few capital- and human resource–intensive firms have been successful in combining import substitution with penetration of regional markets (Ocampo, 1994: 155). These regional markets are dominant in the cases of chemicals and machinery (70% in 1990), whereas the natural resource–based exports go mainly to developed countries. The 1980s and early 1990s may have seen some modification in these patterns, though the evidence is not yet conclusive: there has been some increase in more skill-intensive exports and also an apparent increase in the share of exports coming from small and medium-sized plants (Berry and Escandón, 1994).

The fairly rapid quantum growth of exports in the last few years (about 8% per year since 1988) and the considerable changes in their composition would suggest that some Heckscher-Ohlin effects might show up. On the import side this is even more evident, with the slow growth over the late 1980s followed by the dramatic increases in 1992 and 1993. Consumer goods fell to under 10% of total imports by value in 1984–1985, then gradually recovered to 13.4% in 1992, and intermediate goods fluctuated in the range 50–60% of the total. The big surge of imports in 1992 and 1993 saw consumer goods rise especially fast (by 82.3% in 1993 alone) to reach 18% of the total.

Trends in the Distribution of Income

It is generally believed that income inequality decreased in Colombia at some time between the early 1970s and the late 1980s, both in urban areas and for the nation as a whole and both for earners and for households. J. L. Londoño's detailed study suggests a decline in the Gini coefficient between 1971 and 1978, from 0.53 to 0.48, with essentially no change from then until 1988, for which his estimate is 0.475 (Londoño, 1989).[7] Our main concern here is with the period beginning in the late 1970s, during which the economy went through a brief period of liberalization (early 1980s), then a sharp reduction in openness, followed by a gradual reopening through the rest of the 1980s and the abrupt apertura of the early 1990s. Labor-market reforms occurred mainly around 1990, though union power was clearly weakened by the recession of the early 1980s.

Our estimates of income distribution in three of Colombia's largest four cities (Bogotá, Medellín, and Barranquilla) reveal a quite significant decline in inequality between 1976 and 1990—though it was concentrated in the first years of that interval and more striking among income earners (whose Gini coefficient fell from 0.50 to 0.41) than among persons ranked by per capita family income (where the decline was from 0.52 to 0.46; see Table 6.2).[8] Among earners, the relative income of the top decile fell from 28.6 times that of the bottom decile to 18.8 times. The distribution among earners is of interest because it reflects directly the way the economy determines the incomes of factory owners, but the distribution among persons (a variant of the distribution among families) is of ultimate concern since it is most revealing of the welfare distribution in the society. Inequality probably bottomed out in the late 1980s, after which it has increased sharply, especially among earners (where the Gini coefficient rose from 0.41 in 1990 to 0.47 in 1993), but significantly also among persons (from 0.46 to 0.51). Earner inequality thus returned to the 1980 level (with the ratio of the top decile to the bottom decile back up to 27.3), but remained below that of 1976, whereas inequality among persons now exceeded that of 1980 and was close to the 1976 level, when the Gini coefficient was 0.52. In each case, the largest deterioration was that between 1990 and 1991. Among earners, the 1990–1993 period saw significant declines in the income share of the first six deciles (30.8% to 27.7%); the only major gainer was the top decile (36.2% to 40.4%; see Table 6.3, p. 163).

In percentage terms, the biggest losers were the lowest deciles; the first saw its share fall by 23% from 1.93% to 1.48%, about the level of the late 1970s. Among persons, all deciles lost except the top one, whose share jumped from 37.3% to 42.5%, nearly recovering the 1976 level (Table 6.4, p. 163). Percentage share losses at the bottom were less than in the earner

Table 6.2   Income Distribution Trends in Colombia Since 1976, Gini Coefficients

Year	Persons Ranked by Per Capita Family Income, Three Cities,[a] March (1)	Earners, Three Cities[a] (2)	Earners, Seven Cities[b] (3)	Households, Seven Cities[b] (4)	Persons Ranked by Per Capita Family Income, Urban Areas,[c] September (5)
1976	0.520	0.500	—	0.496	—
1978	—	—	—	0.483	—
1980	0.492	0.464	—	0.461	0.46
1983	—	—	—	0.459	0.46
1984	0.475	0.442	—	—	—
1985	—	—	—	0.474	0.47
1986	—	—	—	—	0.48
1987	—	—	—	—	0.47
1988	—	—	—	—	0.49
1989	0.470	0.421	—	—	0.50
1990	0.459	0.413	0.433	—	0.49
1991	0.483	0.451	0.454	—	0.48
1992	0.494	0.468	0.470	—	0.45[d]
1993	0.507	0.467	0.476	—	—
1994	—	—	0.470	—	—
1995	—	0.467	0.472	—	—

Sources: Cols. (1) and (2) are calculations by the authors using unpublished data from the Departamento Administrativo Nacional de Estadistica's (DANE's) household surveys for March of each year. Income has been corrected for truncation problems but not for missing values, and live-in maids are excluded from the figures (see Appendix on methodology and the alternative estimates presented there, which make it clear that these last two adjustments do not change the trends in distribution, though they do change the estimated absolute level of inequality at each point of time). Col. (3) is from Reyes Posada et al. (1996: 15) and includes adjustment for the truncation bias and for missing values; in the latter correction missing values are not simply estimated by an earnings equation (a procedure that leads to an underestimate of variance), but are assumed to have a variance comparable to that of individuals with the same set of human capital characteristics. Col. (4) is from Reyes Posada (1987: 81). Col. (5) is from Sarmiento (1993: 73).

Notes: a. Bogotá, Medellín, and Barranquilla.

b. Bogotá, Medellín, Cali, Barranquilla, Bucaramanga, Manizales, and Pasto.

c. The data refer to the major urban centers of Colombia plus a few smaller centers; they thus include the seven cities listed under (b) plus several other small or intermediate-sized cities.

d. Refers to June; methodology not comparable to that for earlier observations (communication from L. Sarmiento).

distribution, with the first decile losing 17%, from 1.75% to 1.45%. Most of the bottom deciles still had a slightly higher share than in 1976, as reflected in the marginally lower Gini coefficient in that year.[9]

It is interesting that the trends in level of concentration of each of the major components of personal income parallel those of total income (see Table 6.5, p. 164). Note also that business income has become more important over time at the expense of labor income.[10] Since the latter is the

Table 6.3 Decile Distribution of Total Reported Income Among Income Earners: Bogotá, Medellín, and Barranquilla, 1976–1995 (March) (percentage)

Decile	1976	1980	1984	1989	1990	1991	1992	1993	1995
1	1.51	1.49	1.51	1.79	1.93	1.68	1.48	1.48	1.60
2	3.05	3.58	3.66	3.94	3.97	3.53	3.23	3.42	3.44
3	3.61	4.69	4.83	5.38	5.56	4.96	4.71	4.87	4.62
4	4.36	4.97	5.34	5.73	5.89	5.24	5.18	5.06	4.81
5	5.31	5.64	5.98	6.22	6.30	5.82	5.62	5.49	5.39
6	6.25	6.62	7.06	7.01	7.12	6.56	6.47	6.41	6.51
7	8.00	8.02	8.67	8.27	8.41	8.02	7.77	7.82	8.05
8	10.00	10.11	10.68	10.40	10.42	10.17	10.27	10.28	10.61
9	14.76	14.49	15.02	14.73	14.22	15.27	14.96	14.74	14.97
10	43.15	40.40	37.27	36.52	36.19	38.76	40.32	40.43	40.00
Top 5%	30.58	28.42	25.85	25.50	24.70	27.00	28.63	28.82	—
Top 1%	12.33	11.31	9.86	10.19	9.12	10.49	11.94	9.57	—
Gini	0.500	0.464	0.442	0.421	0.413	0.451	0.468	0.467	0.467

Source: Calculations based on DANE household surveys.

Table 6.4 Decile Distribution of All Reported Income Among Persons, Ranked by Total Family Income Per Capita: Bogotá, Medellín, and Barranquilla, 1976–1993 (March) (percentage)

Decile	1976	1980	1984	1989	1990	1991	1992	1993
1	1.40	1.49	1.57	1.76	1.75	1.73	1.55	1.45
2	2.46	2.74	2.83	2.97	2.99	2.80	2.70	2.62
3	3.25	3.65	3.73	3.86	3.94	3.67	3.62	3.45
4	4.11	4.51	4.68	4.74	4.88	4.51	4.46	4.27
5	5.03	5.42	5.77	5.78	6.01	5.62	5.43	5.25
6	6.20	6.56	7.03	6.94	7.20	6.81	6.61	6.44
7	7.84	8.30	8.68	8.56	8.99	8.40	8.22	7.97
8	10.46	10.88	11.25	11.06	11.21	10.81	10.77	10.47
9	16.01	16.06	15.98	15.64	15.70	15.66	15.47	15.55
10	43.24	40.40	38.48	38.68	37.33	40.00	41.17	42.53
Top 5%	30.58	28.07	26.38	26.77	23.34	28.20	29.44	29.73
Top 1%	12.87	11.29	10.06	10.28	7.31	10.67	11.68	11.22
Gini	0.520	0.492	0.475	0.470	0.459	0.483	0.494	0.507

Source: Calculations based on DANE household surveys.

most equally distributed of the components distinguished here, its falling share of total income probably contributes an upward push to the overall level of inequality. (Business income is in the middle with respect to the Gini coefficient, and "other" income, which includes rental income, interest income, dividends, pensions, and other transfers, is the most concentrated of the three.) Business income is most important in the lowest and the highest deciles, whereas labor income is predominant in the middle of the distribution. At lower levels of the distribution, however, "business income" probably comes from informal activities; to the extent that these involve very little capital, such income is primarily labor-based and its level is likely to be heavily influenced by the outcomes of the labor market. More generally, the very similar time patterns of the distributions of labor and of business incomes suggest close links between the markets in which the two types of income are determined.

The increase in the Gini coefficient of labor incomes occurred mainly between 1990 and 1991 (March of each year), whereas the concentration of business incomes, though also rising most sharply between 1990 and 1991, continued up over the next two years as well. Thus the overall worsening since 1991 has come from the distribution of business income; in 1993 its effect was offset by a decrease in concentration of "other" income.

Unfortunately, Colombia does not have systematic national household surveys allowing year-by-year analysis to be undertaken at the national level. Rural data available for 1988 and 1992 have not yet been subjected to a careful analysis that includes the adjustments undertaken by Reyes Posada et al. (1996) for urban areas in the 1990s. A best guess is that there

Table 6.5   Gini Coefficients of the Distribution of Total Reported Income Among Earners: Bogotá, Medellín, and Barranquilla, 1976–1993 (March)

| | Labor Income | | Business Income | | Other Income | | Total |
Year	Gini	Weight (%)	Gini	Weight (%)	Gini	Weight (%)	Gini
1976	0.439	67.27	0.577	26.13	0.829	6.60	0.500
1980	0.373	63.77	0.565	28.39	0.841	7.84	0.464
1984	0.360	58.25	0.510	27.35	0.644	14.40	0.442
1989	0.341	57.20	0.487	27.63	0.606	15.17	0.421
1990	0.346	58.89	0.466	28.74	0.688	12.37	0.423
1991	0.371	56.09	0.516	30.19	0.631	13.72	0.451
1992	0.370	55.04	0.533	29.47	0.694	15.49	0.468
1993	0.374	54.92	0.547	31.06	0.651	14.00	0.467

Source: Calculations based on DANE household surveys.

Notes: The Gini coefficients for total income, labor income, and business income are in each case calculated for that group of individuals receiving the type of income in question and on the basis only of that type of income. Thus a person with labor income and other income would appear in the labor income distribution as having only his/her labor income.

The surveys do not collect both labor and business income for anyone; i.e., they exclude this possible income combination from consideration and thus leave an unknown amount of income unreported.

At some point between 1980 and 1984, the surveys began to include information on the income of nonparticipants in the labor force. This accounts for the sudden increase in the share of income falling in the category "other" between those years. Since such income is more concentrated than either of the other two components, it might be expected that the increase in reporting of such income would produce a spurious increase in the overall level of concentration. In fact, the overall Gini coefficient continued to fall between those years, so if such an effect existed, the true decline in concentration was greater than the data show.

was not much change between those two years.[11] But a serious cause for concern is the evidence that although urban incomes rose by 18% between 1990 and 1993, rural incomes fell by at least 5% (Lora and Herrera, 1994). It would be natural to interpret such an outcome as due in part to the production problems of the agricultural sector in 1992 and in part to the price impact of the apertura. Together with the sharply increasing inequality in the urban areas and the roughly constant level in rural areas (at least over 1988–1992), this widening gap between the two distributions would suggest an even larger increase in inequality at the national level than for the urban areas;[12] it also suggests that, depending on where the poverty line is drawn, the percentage of the population in poverty was probably increasing over the early 1990s.[13]

Developments in the Labor Market

A number of significant changes that have taken place in Colombian labor markets since the late 1970s are part of the backdrop to the change in the direction of the trend in income inequality—which might, as noted above, be dated around the end of the 1980s or somewhat sooner, depending on the precise series on which one focuses. Possibly the most important are (1) a sharp increase in female participation rates; (2) increasing levels of education in the labor force, especially among women; (3) a marked equalization of incomes between men and women, partly as a result of changes in levels of education; (4) a reallocation of labor, again especially female labor, from low- to higher-paying occupations; and (5) toward the late 1980s and early 1990s, a change in hiring practices (more temporary or sporadic work) and the introduction of important labor-market reforms. These changes have no doubt had a variety of effects on income distribution, with the net impact hard to predict.

The increase in female participation rates has been one of the largest in Latin America. In Bogotá, for example, the participation rate of women age twelve and older rose from around 37% in 1976 to 51% in 1992 (Berry and Tenjo, 1994: Table 7), with the increase especially important for those aged 20–50 years and among women with secondary and university educations. The rate for men also increased until the mid-1980s, although much less sharply, and decreased afterward.

Since the mid-1950s human capital accumulation in the form of significant improvements in the level of education has proceeded rapidly, especially among women. As might be expected, this process generated an important decrease in the returns on investment in education from about 15.6% and 21% for wage-earning men and women, respectively, in 1976 to 11.3% and 13.9% in 1989.[14] Most of the decrease occurred between

1976 and 1984, especially in the case of men, whose rates during the late 1980s remained more or less stable, while those of women continued to decline, but at a slower pace than in the first part of the period. This decline was more important for those with primary or secondary education than those with a university education (see Table 6.6 and Table 6.7, also Tenjo, 1993: Table 3); from around 1990 the relative incomes of university graduates tended to rise moderately for males and more markedly for females.

Together with the accelerated increase in female education, there was an important narrowing of the gender income gap. In 1976, the average hourly wage of men was 30% higher than that of women. By 1992, the differential had dropped to zero (Berry and Tenjo, 1994: Table 9). In terms of monthly labor income, the differential decreased from 62% to around 30% in the same period. About two-thirds of the decline in the differential occurred in the 1970s and early 1980s, with a leveling off toward the latter part of the decade and possibly a new, smaller decline in the early 1990s. The falling earnings differentials during the early 1980s appear to have contributed to the decrease in the level of income inequality during those years in the three cities studied here.

Overall labor-market outcomes reflected the macroeconomic trends of the post-1980 period. Urban unemployment jumped in the early 1980s recession to reach nearly 15% in 1985–1986, and the share of paid workers (excluding domestics) in employment fell by about 2% (López Castaño, 1993: 16).

Labor-Market Reform and Its Effects

Since at least the mid- to late 1980s, there has been an important debate on the need to reform labor legislation and labor practices. The "flexibility" of Colombia's labor market has been a matter of discussion even longer; some trends pointed to a decrease, whereas others suggested the opposite. Thus unionization in large-scale manufacturing had declined from over 60% in the mid-1960s to just 27% in the second half of the 1980s (Ocampo, 1994: 163). Job instability, always high in rural areas, seems to have increased in urban areas since around the end of the 1970s (López Castaño, 1994b: 2). In this sense, the labor market became more flexible, first in fact and then in law (with the reforms of 1990). From about 5–6% of urban employment in 1976–1978, temporary jobs rose to and leveled off at about 13–14% in the late 1980s (Fedesarrollo, 1992: 34). By 1991–1992 the share was on the rise again, reaching a seven-city average of 19.5% in June–September 1992 and averaging 20.8% for males and 21.6% for females in Bogotá from 1990–1992. Some of the views expressed during the prior debate were incorporated in legislation passed in the early 1990s,

Table 6.6 Average Monthly Labor Income of Persons at Selected Levels of Education as a Percentage of the Average Income of Persons with Completed Primary School: Bogotá, Medellín, and Barranquilla, 1976–1993 (March)

Education Level	1976	1980	1984	1989	1990	1991	1992	1993
Men								
No Education	74.7	82.6	79.7	81.1	82.1	86.6	76.0	84.5
Completed Primary	100.0	100.0	100.0	100.0	100.0	100.0	100.0	100.0
Completed Secondary	225.9	168.8	151.0	133.2	132.7	129.6	124.1	123.1
Completed University	586.7	465.7	391.4	367.9	381.1	379.7	376.0	384.1
Average	159.7	148.8	143.1	140.3	141.7	148.9	143.3	140.6
Women								
No Education	95.0	83.3	89.1	80.7	89.0	87.5	82.6	86.7
Completed Primary	100.0	100.0	100.0	100.0	100.0	100.0	100.0	100.0
Completed Secondary	200.4	157.1	154.9	145.4	146.5	154.2	149.5	146.1
Completed University	355.9	311.4	294.6	301.4	295.7	332.4	343.4	358.5
Average	135.6	127.8	133.2	139.7	140.7	150.2	154.1	155.1

Source: Calculations based on DANE household surveys.
Note: Figures refer only to the categories cited; persons with incomplete primary, secondary, or university education are excluded.

Table 6.7 Hourly Labor Income by Levels of Education as a Percentage of Hourly Labor Income of Persons with Completed Primary Education: Bogotá, Medellín, and Barranquilla, 1976–1993

Education Level	1976	1980	1984	1989	1990	1991	1992	1993
Men								
No Education	73.4	73.5	74.5	81.8	90.1	83.8	83.0	84.0
Completed Primary	100.0	100.0	100.0	100.0	100.0	100.0	100.0	100.0
Completed Secondary	244.3	187.7	166.4	139.0	137.5	139.7	138.3	125.5
Completed University	638.7	513.0	436.3	399.6	414.4	431.9	429.5	411.0
Average	169.3	159.7	152.2	146.2	149.9	161.0	157.6	146.6
Women								
No Education	84.9	84.9	83.8	73.9	85.3	88.0	82.7	96.0
Completed Primary	100.0	100.0	100.0	100.0	100.0	100.0	100.0	100.0
Completed Secondary	239.4	190.9	188.7	168.3	169.7	166.5	158.5	169.6
Completed University	485.1	381.2	401.9	361.5	358.8	408.5	392.2	402.5
Average	152.9	144.1	157.0	157.4	159.2	166.9	168.4	171.7

Source: Calculations based on DANE household surveys.

Notes: Figures refer only to the categories cited; persons with incomplete primary, secondary, or university education are excluded. Hourly income is estimated as the ratio of the earnings reported for whatever earning period the respondent identified, divided by hours worked in the last week times a conversion factor based on the relationship between the income reporting period and a week. If the income reporting period was a month, that ratio is 4.3.

which unequivocally eliminated the major legal restrictions on labor mobility. Among the most important reforms were these three:

1. Introduction of the so-called *salario integral* (SI) (complete salary), designed to reduce uncertainty in the prediction of labor costs and to simplify the administration of payrolls. Under this system, the worker has the option to receive a single, simple wage payment but not the fringe benefits that were an important part of total labor costs in the previous system. Some of the fringe benefits were of predictable amount but unpredictable timing; others were unpredictable in both senses.

2. Changes in the severance payment regime (cesantías). Previously, employers were supposed to create a reserve equivalent to one month of salary for each year of work, based on the last salary received by the worker; thus every time the wage/salary of a worker changed (usually upward) the whole reserve had to be reestimated. Further, only the nominal value of earlier withdrawals by the worker from this account were deducted. An annual interest of 12% was paid on the amount owed at date of retirement (Ocampo, 1987). The essence of reform consisted in removing the requirement of readjusting the fund every time the salary changed, in exchange for paying competitive interest rates.

3. Changes removing some job protection and facilitating the use of part-time and temporary workers. Some observers have claimed that changes in the interpretations of the law and the attitude of employers were more important than the actual changes in the legislation in this area.

As López Castaño (1993a, 45) has argued, the previous system of severance payments and firing constraints favored excessive labor rotation initially and made it prohibitive to fire after ten years. With the reform, new workers will operate under the new rules, but workers hired before this date remain under the old system, slightly modified to make it easier to fire after ten years but with payment of a higher indemnity.

It is too early to assess the possible benefits of these reforms on increased labor mobility and firm competitiveness. Some more immediate effects are suggested by available labor-market data. The share of workers in Bogotá, Medellín, and Barranquilla employed in temporary jobs (defined as those who are called to work sporadically, working only in certain times or periods) increased sharply between 1990 and 1992, as did the share working less than forty hours per week and the share of this latter group who wanted to work more (see Table 6.8 and Berry and Tenjo, 1994: Table 13). These shifts are evident in the bottom deciles of the distribution of income but not only there. The 1993 figures, however, show a reversal back to or toward the 1990 levels. This and the fact that these indicators exhibit considerable year-to-year variability mean that several more years of observations will be needed before it can be concluded whether the reforms have brought a lasting change in these dimensions of labor-market functioning.

H. López Castaño (1992), using data from Departamento Administrativo Nacional de Estadistica's (DANE's) household surveys of June 1990 and 1992, concludes that the reform increased employment instability (rate of job separation) for older workers while reducing it for newer workers. Although there is no organized information on the prevalence of fixed term contracts, job contracts, and work on commission, there are indications of rapid increases in the frequency of each (López Castaño, 1993: 40).

How may the loss of job security for some due to the reforms and the expected increase in total labor demand that would benefit others balance out for the lower-income groups? Since the reforms coincided with the sharp increase in inequality, the possibility that on balance they lowered the demand for the labor services of this group must be considered.[15]

The Early 1990s and the
Labor-Market Effects of the Reforms

Between the early and the late 1980s, the previous trend toward greater equality was reversed sharply in urban Colombia, and a significant increase occurred over 1990–1993. Judged by the distribution of income among persons (ranked by per capita household income), the gains of the previous fourteen years were lost in those three.[16] It remains to be seen

Table 6.8   Percentage of People with Temporary Jobs, by Decile of the Distribution of Total Reported Monthly Income Among Employed Persons: Bogotá, Medellín, and Barranquilla, 1976–1993 (March)

Decile	1976	1980	1984	1989	1990	1991	1992	1993
1	36.85	33.55	41.13	34.22	29.80	38.67	35.06	29.65
2	22.05	24.36	29.99	22.87	20.83	22.81	27.29	21.39
3	17.25	11.84	20.79	20.58	14.34	19.01	24.88	18.15
4	14.54	9.01	16.51	19.88	16.67	21.08	23.00	19.83
5	14.21	10.04	16.07	17.30	14.44	15.24	19.14	14.77
6	10.25	12.37	12.72	12.28	9.25	17.23	15.09	14.37
7	10.17	8.58	11.46	10.65	7.21	10.83	14.81	10.42
8	8.61	7.29	9.30	8.92	8.00	9.03	10.28	9.05
9	8.13	5.95	7.98	6.65	6.27	6.86	7.64	6.88
10	4.01	4.04	5.33	4.78	3.97	5.08	4.69	4.58
Average	14.61	12.70	17.13	15.81	13.08	16.58	18.19	14.91

Source: Calculations based on DANE household surveys.

whether this negative distributional shock will prove temporary or lasting; a leveling off of urban inequality from 1993 to 1995 hopefully signals that the upward trend has come to an end. The fact that the increase in inequality coincides temporally with a set of economic reforms instituted in the early 1990s and the fact that comparable reforms in other Latin American and Caribbean (LAC) countries have been systematically associated with marked increases in income concentration suggest a causal relationship with those reforms. At this time, one cannot demonstrate unequivocally what the labor-market impacts of the package of reforms undertaken in Colombia have been and, even less, identify the impact of specific reforms like the apertura and the changes in labor legislation.[17] But it is essential both that the recent trends be better understood and that appropriate countermeasures be taken.

In contrast to the distributional outcome, the liberalization and modernization undertaken since 1990 appear not to have created major short-run employment problems, notwithstanding modest dismissals from the public sector. There is no evidence of a negative trend in unemployment rates over the longer run, and the process of liberalization that began in the early 1990s has coincided with declining unemployment. Though rapid economic growth has not returned, the opening's predicted costs in terms of open unemployment (e.g., Ramírez, 1991) have thus far not emerged. However, as of the early 1990s, open unemployment in Bogotá was, as usual, high for youth aged 16–20 years—19% for males and 27% for females. Female unemployment was relatively high for much of the prime working age range also, only falling below 10% for women over about 35 years.

The interesting question now is what will happen in the medium and longer run. The serious problems that will continue to characterize and be played out in the labor market will be more ones of employment quality, stability, and enhancement of skills than of quantity per se. The demand side will have to adjust further to the gender and educational changes on the supply side. The key question is how these changes in labor-market functioning related to the changes in legislation and in goods markets show up in family incomes, poverty, and instability in family income and welfare.

Whatever the cause of the increased inequality, it creates a set of challenges that will need to be met if the policy reforms are to make the positive impact their architects hope for. One is a much more effective education and training system, in particular one that quickly shrinks that low-skill tail of the labor force, which, if we believe the unfolding patterns in other Latin American countries, may suffer relative income losses from the trade opening. Another is the more effective integration of labor-intensive small and medium-sized firms into successful exporting and import-competing activities. A better understanding of the potential challenges can be provided by a detailed look at the Chilean and Argentine experiences.

Appendix:
Methodology of the Estimates of Income Distribution

The figures on which we base the analysis in this chapter are estimated using DANE's household surveys for Bogotá, Medellín, and Barranquilla that correspond to the month of March.

Income was defined as the sum of labor (including the estimated value of payment in kind when available), business, and "other" income. Several questions provided the basis for our estimates of monthly and hourly labor income: reported income over the normal payment period, hours worked last week, and hours worked in the typical week. For those whose income reporting period was not a month, their monthly income is here estimated as income over the period used, multiplied by 1, 2, 3, or 4.286 according to whether the respondent indicated that payment took place monthly, every two weeks, every ten days, or every week, respectively. In the case of daily payment, the conversion to a monthly basis was done by multiplying the daily earnings by an estimate of the number of days worked in the month, derived from the reported hours actually (rather than typically) worked in the previous week, divided by eight, and multiplied by the number of weeks per month (4.286). This approach is different from that adopted by other studies, which convert daily into monthly payments by multiplying by an estimate of the number of working days in the month (thirty, twenty-five, or some other figure). Note that the different periodicity of income reporting is likely to introduce two types of error in estimates of inequality. First, it overstates inequality among those with short reporting periods; whereas among daily workers there is likely to be some averaging out across the weeks of the month (and year) in amount of work, the procedure used here "assumes" that anyone who worked many hours in the week of the survey did so every week of the month and anyone who worked very little also did so every week of the month. Second, it understates the average difference in monthly income between those with permanent jobs and those without, since some of the latter will go through some weeks in which they do not earn at all.

A possibly major source of distortion that we tried to correct was the truncation in the reporting of incomes produced by the fact that the questionnaires of the household surveys allow only for a maximum of six-figure incomes. Incomes of one million pesos or more are represented by the figure 999,998. This distorts the income of the higher percentiles of the distribution and results in both an underestimate of the Gini coefficient at each point of time and (a bigger problem for the analysis of changes in distribution over time) an increasing underestimate over time because the number of high-income earners whose incomes are excluded rises quickly in a growing, inflationary economy like Colombia's. The correction includes the following steps: (1) it was assumed that the distribution of each income item was log-normal; (2) the mean and standard deviation of the log-normal distribution were estimated using the nonzero values in the sample below $999,998; (3) the conditional mean for values 999,998 or higher were estimated—the conditional mean is given by the unconditional mean plus the unconditional standard deviation times the inverse Mill's ratio defined at the point of truncation; and (4) finally, the truncated values were replaced by the conditional means.

The "trimming" of the sample (exclusion of the highest and lowest two hundred observations) in an attempt to deal with this truncation problem is not, in our judgment, a proper procedure. Unlike the authors of other studies of inequality that we have seen, we did not undertake such a trimming. Though for some purposes this procedure may make sense, it is clearly dangerous when the subject of analysis is income concentration, since the excluded values at the upper end could account for a significant share of total income.

At least two possibly significant methodological problems remain in our basic estimates of inequality presented in Table 6.2. (We are not aware of the full details of the methodologies used in other estimates.) Live-in domestic servants and other nonrelatives of the household head are excluded from the estimation of the distribution of household income per capita, since the normal assumption that household income is fairly evenly spent among household members would not hold for such persons. However, they were included in the distribution of earners' income. Missing values were not estimated.

As a check on the extent to which these problems may have affected our estimates of inequality, we have reestimated the distribution among persons ranked by per capita income by (1) classifying live-in maids (and any children who live with them) as separate families; and (2) estimating missing values based on an earnings equation with education, education squared, experience, and experience squared as the independent variables; and (3) classifying families and hence their members by per adult equivalent family income rather than per capita family income (since the latter creates biases due to the implicit assumption that the welfare meaning of a given level of expenditure or income is the same for an infant as for an adult). In the case of the distribution among earners, only the second adjustment was needed. The impact of these adjustments is shown in Table 6.A1; as noted in Table 6.2, they do not change the trends in any significant way.

Table 6.A1   **Gini Coefficients of Household and Earner Distributions, Unadjusted and Adjusted Data, 1984–1993**

Year	Household Distribution		Earner Distribution	
	Unadjusted	Adjusted	Unadjusted	Adjusted
1984	0.475	0.430	0.442	0.433
1989	0.470	0.413	0.421	0.433
1990	0.459	0.418	0.413	0.406
1991	0.483	0.444	0.451	0.438
1992	0.494	0.455	0.468	0.460
1993	0.507	0.464	0.467	0.471

Notes

Albert Berry is a professor in the Department of Economics, University of Toronto. Jaime Tenjo G. is a professor in the Departamento de Economia, Universidad de Los Andes.

1. The main uncertainty involves the lack of satisfactory and comparable statistics from the rural areas.

2. Although the static Heckscher-Ohlin model has been the construct for consideration of the distributional implications of changes in trading patterns, many other mechanisms could operate differently under a more open, compared to a less open economy, so theory gives little or no overall guidance as to what sort of impacts are most likely. De Melo and Robinson (1980) used a computable general equilibrium (CGE) model to provide evidence that, in light of Colombia's being a primary product exporter, in the medium term outward-oriented policies would be more detrimental to income distribution than would inward-looking ones. Meanwhile, Lora and Steiner (1994) use a static CGE model to test for the effects of elements of the recent trade liberalization policy on Colombia's income distribution. Unfortunately, the model has tracked a declining urban Gini coefficient, when the true shift appears to have been in the other direction.

3. Colombia has yet to confront the challenges associated with a major mineral export boom. Booth (1992: 327) notes that both neoclassical models (highlighting the dichotomy between traded and nontraded goods/services) and broader political economy approaches suggest that the rural sector and the regions from which the traditional export items came will suffer and the urban middle class will be the main beneficiary *during* an oil boom. Whether these effects would still show up in the middle or the long run (with the mineral sector still booming) would depend, among other things, on the responsiveness of migration to earnings differentials and on whether public policy (e.g., spending in the social sectors) was designed to counteract the direct impacts of the boom. The two models have quite different predictions for what will happen *after* the boom ends, the simplest neoclassical versions implying a reversal of the resource flows, though more complete analyses attempt to deal with possible irreversibilities. The political economy models highlight the attempt by the groups enriched by the boom to maintain their new (if it is new) status, income levels, etc.

4. The average nominal tariff level was raised from 32% to 49% between 1982 and 1984, though the average collected tariff did not rise until 1985 and peaked at around 24% between 1986–1988, from the earlier level of around 15% (Ocampo,

1994: 140–141). As of 1991 it was back down to 13.3%, a little below the 1970s level. The tariff equivalent of the quantitative restrictions (QRs) rose quickly from 1982 to 1985 from 11% to 31%, though it fell back quickly in the years to follow.

5. There has been some difference of opinion with respect to how fast Colombia's trade liberalization has taken in comparison with those of other countries of the region. Lora and Steiner (1994) conclude, as does Edwards (1994), that it has been fast. Edwards reports that the Chilean reform took about five years in the 1970s, whereas that of Colombia took just one year after being initiated in 1991. Others, like Sheahan (1994), view the Colombian liberalization as gradual, from back in the mid-1980s. Clearly the issue is partly one of whether one focuses on the tariff and quantitative restrictions or on the size of trade flows.

6. That ratio stood at around 1.5% at the beginning of the decade, fell to 1.1% in 1984, recovered to 1.7–1.9% over 1985–1988 (when a cost, insurance, and freight tax on imports was added to the customs and surtaxes), fell to 1.0% in 1992, but then rose to 1.3% in 1993 as imports surged. The average tax on imports of goods and nonfactor services (excluding the value added taxes applied also to domestic goods) ranged between 10% and 14% over most of the 1980s and fell only in 1992 and 1993 to the neighborhood of 5% (Interamerican Development Bank, 1994: Table 2.A and Table 8).

7. Lasso and Moreno (1993) report a decline between 1978 and 1988 for urban areas, rural areas, and total, the last figure falling from 0.485 to 0.451. Although in other respects quite carefully carried out, their estimates are suspect because of failure to deal with the problem of sample truncation through top-coding (see the discussion in the Appendix). Sarmiento (1995) adjusts for this problem and finds an unchanged level of inequality between these two years, a conclusion that accords with that of Londoño. The proposition that there was an improvement in distribution in Colombia, whether for urban areas only or overall, appears therefore to rest (for the time being at least) mainly on the question of what happened during the earlier 1970s, for which Londoño (especially, 1995) and Reyes Posada (1987) both report declines of the Gini coefficient by about 5 points (see Reyes Posada et al., 1996: 3); consistent with this is the fact that the studies whose data begin in 1976 (including our own) indicate that a decline was ongoing between that date and the early 1980s.

8. Since it is universally the case that capital incomes are less fully reported than labor incomes, we presume that our estimates of inequality understate the actual levels, probably by a few percentage points in the Gini coefficients (see Altimir, 1987, for a discussion). Our assumption and hope is that this and other sources of errors in the estimates will not have changed much over time; in one respect in which we feel this assumption might not hold—related to the introduction of the "salario integral" around 1990—we have undertaken some sensitivity analysis to verify that it does not explain much of the observed increase in inequality since 1990. Another possible bias could result from failure to take account of differences in the cost of living index relevant to different income classes.

9. A careful analysis of the trends in the 1990s for urban areas as a whole by Reyes Posada et al. (1996) shows the same general pattern as do our figures (see Table 6.2, col. 3). Their estimates of earner distribution show less increase in the Gini coefficient from 1990 to 1993 than do ours (0.043 versus 0.056). Theirs levels off in the following two years; we have not yet undertaken estimates for that period. Some authors present data suggesting that the trend in inequality changed direction at some point in the 1980s, e.g., Nuñez and Sánchez Torres (1996: 16), whose figures, which appear to refer only to wage income (of wage earners?), suggest

that the increase occurring in the early 1990s began in 1987. This is consistent with our data and that of the majority of other studies.

One study that includes the early 1990s and is clearly inconsistent with the others for that period (it shows a fall in the Gini coefficient among persons ranked by per capita family income from a peak of 0.50 in 1989 to 0.45 in 1992) is reported as col. 5 of Table 6.2. The most likely explanation for the discrepancy is that this series suffers from several of the methodological flaws mentioned in the Appendix, including the failure to adjust for the truncation problem.

10. Taking the figures literally, the same could be said of "other" income, but as noted earlier, this may be due to a change in reporting procedures. Since it seems safe to assume that some of the reported increase is due to those changes, it would appear that the business component has had a continuous upward trend.

11. Figures presented by Banco de la Republica (1994) suggest little change in inequality between those two years (the respective Gini coefficients being 0.46 and 0.45). But Reyes Posada et al. (1996: 7) conclude that the adjustment for truncation bias in these estimates was incorrectly done. The estimates of Moreno indicate that the 1992 adjustment of the Gini coefficient for that bias was huge—nearly 0.06 (Reyes Posada et al., 1996: 6), and though the adjustment was not made for 1988, it would presumably be considerably smaller; this taken together with the 1988 and 1992 estimates of Lasso and Moreno (1993) would suggest no improvement and perhaps a small worsening over this period.

12. To further confuse the issue, however, the only estimate including the adjustment for truncation bias and covering the whole country in both 1988 and 1992, that of Sarmiento (1995), shows only a small increase in the Gini coefficient (of per capita family income) from 0.488 to 0.502. Sarmiento used a different procedure to estimate the Pareto coefficient to make this adjustment than have the other sources.

13. Another attempt to measure trends in distribution and poverty at the national level, that of Fresneda (1994: Cuadro 5), reports estimated Gini coefficients of 0.481 for 1978 and 0.472 for 1992 (distribution of households ranked by per capita household income). Although he does not present comparable figures for intervening years, if we assume that his figures, like others, show an improvement over the late 1970s and early 1980s, they are consistent with a sharp increase in inequality in the early 1990s for the country as a whole. It is not clear whether his figures include a correction for the truncation bias or not.

14. These figures refer to the average earnings advantage from having one more year of education.

15. There is some possibility that the introduction of the *salario integral* (SI) led to a spurious increase in measured inequality. Workers under the SI system generally receive more money per month than under the previous system but do not get fringe benefits. Since the household surveys estimate only current monthly payments (they do not question workers about their accrued but unpaid fringe benefits), the switch to SI will lead to an increase in some workers' reported monthly income but not (or not in the same degree) in their true income. If earners for whom fringe benefits are important fall disproportionately near the top of the income distribution, the introduction of SI will cause an increase in the reported Gini coefficient, thus creating an apparent (but not real) worsening of the distribution of income. If fringe benefits are most important for low-income workers, the opposite effect would hold. The evidence is inconclusive as to whether the introduction of SI had an effect of this kind (see Berry and Tenjo, 1994).

16. Apart from the data and other uncertainties alluded to previously and in the methodological appendix below, several additional qualifications to this conclusion

that distribution improved markedly, then worsened sharply, should be noted or emphasized. Although in principle all types of personal income are represented in the data, there is no doubt that underreporting is most severe with respect to capital income. We have not attempted a correction for this weakness. When the capital share rises (falls), the estimated trends in inequality are likely to understate (overstate) concentration over time. The fact that the paid labor share, as estimated in the national accounts, has fallen significantly over the period since 1983 (from about 45% to under 40% as of 1990) might suggest an increasing level of concentration.

We have not been able to take account of changes in the relative prices faced by different income groups. It is widely presumed that liberalization lowers the relative price of goods and services purchased by the better-off groups, so we may on this count have understated the increase in inequality since 1990.

The figures presented here refer mainly to primary income and do not reflect most direct taxes and transfers or changes in either the availability or the relative price of publicly provided goods and services. Here it is hard to guess what has been the net effect of changes in tax structure, of the targeted antipoverty programs, and more generally of changes in access to publicly provided goods and services. Since the governments have made significant efforts in this last direction, this is a possibly important omission.

17. Several authors (e.g., Reyes Posada et al., 1996) mention exogenous or possibly exogenous changes on the supply and demand sides of the various labor-market segments as possibly important explanatory factors.

7

Structural Adjustment, Income Distribution, and Employment in Ecuador

Carlos Larrea

Like most Latin American countries, Ecuador was strongly affected by the debt crisis that began in 1982. The impact, however, was particularly severe in Ecuador, as a decade-long phase of rapid oil-induced growth and import-substituting industrialization (ISI) suddenly ended. Economic stagnation and social deterioration then prevailed, as the country slowly adopted structural adjustment policies (SAPs) and shifted to an export promotion strategy.

My main objective in this chapter is to evaluate the social effects of structural adjustment in Ecuador, with emphasis on income distribution, poverty, and employment. I begin with a brief analysis of the Ecuadorean experience in the Latin American context, followed by an overview of SAPs in Ecuador and an analysis of their economic results and social effects. Finally, I present an overall evaluation of the country's performance.

Structural Adjustment, Income Distribution, and Employment in Ecuador

Only five countries—Chile, Colombia, Uruguay, Costa Rica, and Panama—were able to improve both per capita gross domestic product (GDP) and per capita export purchasing power between 1980 and 1993. Chile and Uruguay implemented most of their structural adjustment programs in the 1970s, Colombia was one of the countries least affected by the debt crisis, and Costa Rica has maintained an impressive tradition of social development and human capital formation since the 1948 revolution. Two other main groups can be identified: those with an improvement in export performance and a decline in per capita income, and those with declines in both variables. The largest and most diversified countries in the region, Brazil, Mexico, and Argentina, are among the former group. By contrast, most of the unsuccessful countries are small and less diversified, both in natural endowments and exports.

Ecuador is very close to the regional average on both counts. It outperformed most of the other Andean (Venezuela, Bolivia, and Peru) and Central American or Caribbean countries. As a less extreme case, without the dramatic crises or conflicts of Peru or Guatemala, the Ecuadorean experience may be especially helpful as an example of the economic, social, and political problems of SAPs and export promotion policies in relatively small Latin American countries. Additionally, because Ecuador's social structure is highly inegalitarian, and its social record in the areas of poverty, employment, and basic needs has been weak, it may be an interesting test case of the effects of current development strategies under difficult social conditions (Larrea, 1992). Finally, because Ecuador suddenly moved from an oil export boom in the 1970s to a crisis in the 1980s, the case is also illustrative of Dutch disease problems. Other Latin American oil-exporting countries experienced severe economic setbacks and social tensions as well.

Structural Adjustment Policies in Ecuador: An Overview

Ecuador experienced rapid economic growth during the 1970s, when it became an oil exporter.[1] The domestic reinvestment of export earnings led to a rapid process of ISI and the modernization of some parts of agriculture. Sectoral performance, however, was uneven; manufacturing and construction expanded quickly, but per capita agricultural production stagnated. The growth model was capital- and import-intensive and favored mostly the modern and urban sectors. In spite of rapid urbanization and the expansion of the state apparatus and middle classes, the trickle-down effects of economic growth appeared to be weak. The adoption of capital-intensive technologies led to a disappointing employment performance. In fact, between 1972 and 1980, the percentage of wage earners in the labor force declined in both the urban and rural sectors, and severe structural unemployment persisted.[2] In spite of significant achievements in education and health, poverty and basic needs deprivation continued to be widespread (Larrea, 1992). During the late 1970s, as oil exports stagnated, growth was achieved at the cost of foreign borrowing. As the external situation deteriorated, this growth strategy became unsustainable and the ISI growth model collapsed. To make matters worse, Ecuador was hit by two natural disasters in the 1980s—coastal floods in 1983 and a major earthquake in 1987. Tables 7.1 and 7.2 present basic economic information on Ecuador for the period 1965–1994.

Table 7.1   Basic Economic Data: Ecuador, 1965–1994 (absolute values in 1975 sucres)

Year	Population (thousands)	GDP (10⁹)	GDP Per Capita (1975 sucres)	GDP (1980 U.S.$)	Exports (10⁹)	Imports (10⁹)	Gross Investment (10⁹)	X/GDP (%)	M/GDP (%)	I/GDP (%)	Inflation Rate (%)
1965	4,934.4	50,706	10,276.1	—	8,162	12,443	9,852	16.1	24.5	19.4	—
1966	5,089.7	51,945	10,205.9	—	8,379	13,115	10,057	16.1	25.2	19.4	3.7
1967	5,249.9	55,512	10,573.9	—	8,742	14,905	11,692	15.7	26.9	21.1	4.8
1968	5,415.1	57,749	10,664.4	—	9,233	17,047	12,087	16.0	29.5	20.9	3.1
1969	5,585.6	59,096	10,580.1	—	7,860	16,263	13,033	13.3	27.5	22.1	5.1
1970	5,761.4	62,912	10,919.6	824.0	8,333	17,038	13,576	13.2	27.1	21.6	5.4
1971	5,942.7	66,852	11,249.4	—	9,293	20,555	17,190	13.9	30.7	25.7	9.7
1972	6,129.8	76,493	12,479.0	—	18,294	19,911	14,102	23.9	26.0	18.4	7.4
1973	6,322.7	95,867	15,162.4	—	32,370	20,969	15,952	33.8	21.9	16.6	12.1
1974	6,521.7	102,046	15,647.1	—	30,837	30,189	20,194	30.2	29.6	19.8	23.9
1975	6,686.3	107,740	16,113.5	—	28,242	35,221	24,907	26.2	32.7	23.1	13.2
1976	6,855.1	117,679	17,166.7	—	30,629	34,155	25,268	26.0	29.0	21.5	10.2
1977	7,028.1	125,369	17,838.3	—	29,095	40,175	29,181	23.2	32.0	23.3	12.9
1978	7,205.5	133,632	18,545.9	—	30,032	41,518	33,058	22.5	31.1	24.7	13.1
1979	7,387.3	140,718	19,048.5	—	31,534	41,485	32,955	22.4	29.5	23.4	10.1
1980	7,573.8	147,622	19,491.1	1,443.2	30,792	45,683	34,975	20.9	30.9	23.7	12.8
1981	7,765.0	153,443	19,760.9	—	32,247	41,453	32,442	21.0	27.0	21.1	14.7
1982	7,961.0	155,265	19,503.3	1,442.9	30,647	44,300	32,667	19.7	28.5	21.0	14.7
1983	8,142.0	150,885	18,531.7	—	31,396	33,418	24,127	20.8	22.1	16.0	48.1
1984	8,327.1	157,226	18,881.2	—	35,331	32,613	23,035	22.5	20.7	14.7	30.4
1985	8,516.5	164,054	19,263.1	1,396.4	39,562	35,000	24,564	24.1	21.3	15.0	28.0
1986	8,710.2	169,136	19,418.2	1,401.5	42,944	34,925	25,677	25.4	20.6	15.2	23.0
1987	8,908.2	159,016	17,850.5	1,301.2	36,027	40,286	26,800	22.7	25.3	16.9	30.4
1988	9,110.8	175,742	19,289.4	1,381.7	47,235	36,243	25,465	26.9	20.6	14.5	57.9
1989	9,318.0	176,195	18,909.1	1,351.6	46,440	38,106	25,251	26.4	21.6	14.3	75.4
1990	9,529.9	181,531	19,048.6	1,347.4	51,159	36,692	23,961	28.2	20.2	13.2	48.5
1991	9,746.6	190,384	19,533.4	1,381.4	56,523	42,551	26,295	29.7	22.4	13.8	48.7
1992	9,968.2	197,017	19,764.5	1,396.4	61,940	42,984	28,523	31.4	21.8	14.5	54.6
1993	10,194.9	201,447	19,759.6	1,395.8	64,552	43,309	—	—	—	—	45.0
1994	10,426.7	—	—	1,419.5	—	—	—	—	—	—	27.3

Sources: INEC (1962, 1974, 1982, 1990); Banco Central del Ecuador (several issues); ECLAC (several issues).
Notes: X = Exports; M = Imports; I = Gross Investment.

Table 7.2 Basic External Sector Indicators: Ecuador, 1965–1994 (millions of U.S.$)

Year	GDP	Exports	Imports	Foreign Debt	Terms of Trade[a] (1970=100)	Real Oil Price[b] (1972 U.S.$)	Purchasing Power of Exports (1975 U.S.$)	Import Capacity[c] (1975 U.S.$)	Import Tariffs/ Imports	Real Effective Exchange Rate (for Exports) (1990=100)
1965	1,151	134	170.8	—	90.8	—	274.0	—	—	—
1966	1,255	148	171.9	—	105.4	—	299.3	—	—	—
1967	1,402	166	214.2	—	97.2	—	332.0	—	—	—
1968	1,523	177	255.5	—	92.7	—	354.0	—	—	—
1969	1,675	152	241.8	—	93.4	—	300.7	—	—	—
1970	1,629	190	273.8	242	100.0	—	345.8	466	—	—
1971	1,602	199	340.1	261	93.6	—	344.9	478	—	—
1972	1,874	326	318.6	344	84.3	2.4	520.5	611	—	—
1973	2,489	532	397.3	380	92.4	3.4	728.0	661	—	—
1974	3,711	1,124	678.2	410	192.0	9.4	1,262.8	1,111	—	—
1975	4,310	974	987.0	513	159.0	7.4	974.0	920	17.8	—
1976	5,317	1,258	958.3	693	179.3	7.5	1,251.1	1,222	18.9	—
1977	6,655	1,436	1,188.5	1,264	194.8	7.4	1,317.4	1,357	22.2	—
1978	7,654	1,557	1,505.1	2,975	172.8	6.3	1,245.6	1,368	17.2	47.4
1979	9,359	2,104	1,599.7	3,554	210.5	10.1	1,471.3	1,473	17.0	47.0
1980	11,733	2,481	2,253.3	4,601	236.1	14.0	1,570.3	1,561	15.8	47.0
1981	13,946	2,168	1,920.6	5,868	235.2	14.6	1,459.7	1,391	15.0	47.0
1982	13,354	2,237	2,424.6	6,633	231.1	14.0	1,538.9	1,188	12.7	54.8
1983	11,114	2,226	1,474.6	7,381	191.0	12.4	1,583.0	969	14.7	54.8
1984	11,510	2,620	1,630.0	7,596	216.7	12.6	1,928.2	1,168	14.8	54.8
1985	11,890	2,905	1,766.7	8,111	269.2	11.9	2,137.9	1,221	15.9	54.8
1986	10,515	2,186	1,810.2	9,080	165.0	4.9	1,343.2	866	16.2	68.7
1987	9,450	1,928	2,158.1	10,217	202.3	4.9	1,051.9	1,073	10.5	78.8
1988	9,129	2,193	1,713.5	10,754	178.3	4.0	1,119.3	799	11.9	92.3
1989	9,714	2,354	1,854.8	11,039	194.5	5.2	1,211.3	1,068	10.8	94.6

(continues)

Table 7.2 continued

Year	GDP	Exports	Imports	Foreign Debt	Terms of Trade[a] (1970=100)	Real Oil Price[b] (1972 U.S.$)	Purchasing Power of Exports (1975 U.S.$)	Import Capacity[c] (1975 U.S.$)	Import Tariffs/ Imports	Real Effective Exchange Rate (for Exports) (1990=100)
1990	10,569	2,714	1,861.7	11,700	184.2	5.9	1,263.0	983	11.6	100.0
1991	11,554	2,851	2,398.6	12,271	155.4	4.8	1,336.6	1,111	6.0	95.2
1992	12,483	3,008	2,430.4	12,122	151.3	4.8	1,369.6	933	6.2	94.7
1993	—	3,062	2,562.2	12,806	—	4.2	1,414.6	—	—	83.9
1994	—	3,717	3,642.2	13,664	—	4.0	1,742.6	—	—	77.6

Sources: Banco Central del Ecuador, *Cuentas Nacionales* (several issues); Banco Central del Ecuador, *Boletín Anuario* (several issues); ECLAC, *Statistical Yearbook for Latin America and the Caribbean* (several issues); United Nations, *Monthly Bulletin of Statistics* (several issues); CEPAL (1994); de Janvry, Sadoulet, and Fargeix (1993).

Notes: a. Based on ECLAC estimates, defined as the quotient of the Paasche unit value indices for exports and imports, both referring to the same base.
b. Real oil prices and purchasing power of exports were estimated by deflating oil current prices and current exports, respectively, by the UN price index of manufactures exported by developed countries.
c. The real value (in 1975 U.S. prices) of the imports that the country could buy from the sale of its exports plus any net resource transfer to the country through the capital account.

Ecuador implemented structural adjustment policies from 1981 onward. Generally the process can be characterized as gradual, slow, highly conflictive, selective, and still incomplete.

> The achievements of a decade of stabilization and adjustment are disappointing. In contrast to many other Latin American countries, hyper-inflation, social violence, and a return to authoritarianism have all been avoided, yet neither complete stabilization nor the restoration of growth per capita has been achieved. (de Janvry, Sadoulet, and Fargeix, 1993: 17)

Ecuador has had five presidents since 1981. Their political positions varied from conservative to social democratic. All tried to carry out stabilization programs of varying intensity and priorities, but none was able to enjoy stable support from the legislature, and chronic conflict prevailed.

> The [then] ten year sequence of policy reforms resulted in an overall inadequate performance for stabilization and adjustment for the following reasons: policy initiatives generally were introduced by the executive, only to be atrophied by severe political opposition; the policies introduced were highly unstable; and many of those policies unleashed severe conflicts that led to costly policy enforcement or to equally costly policy reversal. (de Janvry, Sadoulet, and Fargeix, 1993: 18)

In contrast to cases of "shock" adjustment, as in Bolivia in 1985, the process in Ecuador has been slow and lengthy. Social conflict resulted in frequent setbacks, and a stable political consensus on economic policies was never reached. In addition to the expected opposition to SAP policies from popular sectors and the middle classes, interest groups from dominant classes also resisted specific adjustment policies when their interests were threatened, leading to frequent conflicts between the executive and the legislature. As a result, policies such as reduction of state subsidies and import duties became highly conflictual and were implemented slowly.

Opposition to structural adjustment from the poor and left-wing organizations included several national strikes by organized labor, bus and truck driver strikes, frequent riots organized by students and informal sector workers, incipient urban guerrilla activity in the mid-1980s, and the emergence of a powerful indigenous movement that paralyzed the country for one week in 1990. Government repression was violent, particularly during the conservative Febres Cordero administration (1984–1988), when human rights violations, including torture, assassinations, and illegal detentions, became frequent. Under León Febres Cordero, the executive's response to differences with other public bodies included the use of tear gas inside the Congress chamber and a military blockade of the Supreme Court. Political events like the kidnapping of the president by a group of paratroopers in 1987 illustrate the underlying chronic political conflict that has prevailed since 1982.

Measures that did not confront strong opposition from influential dominant-class groups were easily adopted, among them interest and exchange rate liberalization—both judged as either favorable or acceptable by agro-export elites. Conversely, reduction of protection for manufactures and domestic subsidies—particularly in oil derivatives and wheat—generated strong resistance from industrialists and urban middle and subordinate classes. This asymmetry left adjustment policies lacking in consistency, credibility, and stability. Despite the conflict surrounding it, SAP implementation speeded up and became more consistent from 1988 onward, at least partially as a result of deeper and more effective involvement by the international financial institutions (Stallings, 1992).

Exchange rate liberalization had been quickly adopted in the early 1980s. In 1982, the Christian Democratic president, Oswaldo Hurtado, devalued the currency for the first time in more than a decade, and the conservative government of Febres Cordero moved to a market-determined exchange rate in 1984. Interest rates were liberalized as well. Ever since, exchange rates have fluctuated according to market signals, with moderate Central Bank intervention. The anti-export bias that prevailed at times during the 1970s due to overvaluation (the exchange rate remained constant at 25 sucres per dollar between 1971 and 1981, whereas domestic prices nearly quadrupled) was eliminated or greatly reduced. Only from 1992 onward did anti-inflationary policies result in a new trend toward overvaluation. (Real effective exchange rate indices are presented in Table 7.2.) Domestic price liberalization—particularly elimination of oil and food price subsidies—was slowly adopted during the 1980s. Only from 1989 onwards were oil subsidies systematically reduced and eventually eliminated.

Although import barriers were reduced from 1984 on, as late as 1988 tariffs were still both relatively high (on average) and variable (from 0% to 300%), and some quantitative restrictions and prohibitions persisted. The most important step toward trade liberalization was adopted in 1990, when import tariffs were reduced to somewhere within the range of 5% to 80% (most products, except vehicles, were between 5% and 30%), and most import restrictions were lifted. The result was a dramatic expansion of consumer goods imports by a factor of nearly five (from U.S.$179 million to U.S.$585 million) between 1990 and 1994. Since 1994, as the Andean Pact reemerged in the framework of "open regionalism," Ecuador's participation in a free trade area with Colombia and Venezuela has spurred a dramatic jump in intraregional trade: exports to the Andean region rose from U.S.$203.7 million in 1991 to U.S.$385.6 million in 1994, and imports expanded even more.

The foreign debt was renegotiated in 1994 in the framework of the Brady Plan, but its level—U.S.$13.66 billion in December 1994—is still growing and remains higher than GDP, making the ratio of debt to GDP one of the worst in Latin America.

Labor deregulation was pursued continuously during the period; real minimum wages declined and labor legislation was reformed "to increase flexibility and eliminate rigidities unattractive to foreign investors" (de Janvry, Sadoulet, and Fargeix, 1993: 79).

The reduction of the state apparatus was also pursued throughout the 1980s (except for a right-wing "populist experience" between 1986 and 1988) and speeded up in the early 1990s. Between 1982 and 1990, the share of public servants in the national labor force fell from 13.5% to 11.4%. Public expenditure, meanwhile, plunged dramatically from 21.6% of GDP (current prices) in 1981 to 11% in 1992 (see Table 7.3).

Despite these numerous steps, structural adjustment is viewed as incomplete. Privatization of public enterprises is one of the items still on the agenda. Inflation, albeit declining, remains at around 20% per year. Macroeconomic imbalances persist. During the last years, the exchange rate has been used as an anchor to reduce inflation, leading to an overvaluation of the domestic currency. High interest rates and a massive inflow of speculative short-term foreign capital cast doubts on the future stability of economic policies, as Mexico's 1994–1995 crisis has demonstrated. Fiscal reforms have not been successful in strengthening public revenues; in 1993 income taxes still amounted to only 1.2% of GDP. Moreover, debt service will require around 7% of GDP in the near future. Finally, the recent border conflict with Peru has increased fiscal problems and reduced private sector confidence.

Table 7.3   **Public Sector Consumption, Investment, and Expenditure: Ecuador, 1980–1993 (% of GDP at current prices)**

Year	Public Consumption	Public Investment	Total Public Expenditure	Expenditure in:		
				Education	Health	Other
1980	14.5	6.4	20.9	5.3	1.8	13.8
1981	14.3	7.3	21.6	—	—	—
1982	14.0	6.5	20.5	5.1	2.2	13.2
1983	12.5	4.8	17.3	—	—	—
1984	12.3	4.4	16.6	—	—	—
1985	11.5	4.9	16.3	3.7	1.1	11.5
1986	12.1	6.0	18.0	4.0	1.1	12.9
1987	12.8	6.4	19.3	3.9	1.4	14.0
1988	11.5	5.5	16.9	3.3	1.3	12.3
1989	9.4	4.6	14.0	3.0	1.2	9.8
1990	8.6	4.0	12.6	2.7	1.2	8.7
1991	7.7	3.9	11.5	2.9	0.9	7.7
1992	7.2	3.9	11.0	3.1	1.0	6.9
1993	—	—	—	2.7	0.7	—

Sources: ECLAC (1993c); Banco Central del Ecuador, *Cuentas Nacionales* (several issues); Banco Central del Ecuador, *Información Estadística Mensual* (several issues).

Ecuador's Economic Performance: 1982–1994

Ecuador's economic record since 1982 has been weak, in spite of a moderate recovery in the early 1990s. Only in 1992 did per capita income reattain its precrisis (1981) level. Both total and foreign investment rates remain low and flat. Between 1983 and 1992, gross investment (constant 1975 prices) averaged 14.8% of GDP, down from the 21.5% of the 1965–1982 period.[3] There is as yet no sign of a recovery of investment. Foreign investment, in particular, has never reached as much as 1% of GDP after its peak of over 5% of GDP from 1972 to 1974, when the petroleum export sector was established.

Export growth and diversification are central goals of structural adjustment; thus an analysis of export performance is important. Despite the exceptional expansion of 1994, the performance of export revenues has been weak and unstable. Though the export quantum (boosted by oil) grew at a healthy 6.3% per year between 1980 and 1993, a 36% decline in the terms of trade offset much of this growth and was a determining factor in poor overall economic performance, particularly over the late 1980s, when oil, coffee, and cacao prices all plummeted. As a consequence, average export purchasing power for the 1988–1994 period was a little (2.5%) lower in absolute terms than for 1976–1981 (see Table 7.2) and 27% less in per capita terms. The large 1994 recovery is partially explained by soaring coffee prices, the expansion of intraregional trade, and increasing oil export volumes, which cannot be sustained in the medium term.[4] Sustained economic recovery based on a continuous growth of export purchasing power has to date remained elusive.

From 1972 onward, four groups of products have accounted for the bulk of Ecuadorean exports: crude oil and its derivatives, bananas, coffee and cacao beans and derivatives, and fishery products (mostly shrimp). Export diversification has been limited. Despite the rapid growth of the trade in flowers, the most important nontraditional product going to developed countries, they accounted for only 1.5% of total exports in that year. Exports are still overwhelmingly composed of primary or slightly elaborated products—93% as of 1993, according to the Economic Commission for Latin America and the Caribbean (ECLAC, 1993c). The recent opening of the Andean market produced an important increase in intraregional exports, including manufactures, but this may be a one-shot increase.

Social Effects of the Crisis and Structural Adjustment

Available information indicates that social conditions in Ecuador worsened during the post-1982 period. Income distribution became more concentrated, urban poverty increased, underemployment and unemployment rose, real wages declined, and public social services deteriorated. Although some recovery is evident in the last few years, its sustainability is unclear. Labor-market conditions changed also as educational returns declined for low educational levels and wage dispersion increased, both among and within categories defined by education, experience, gender, and sector. Social trends are analyzed in later sections, with emphasis on the urban sector during the 1987–1993 period, for which detailed household survey information is available.

Looking at the post-1982 period as a whole, the most dramatic manifestation of the new economic reality was the sharp drop in public expenditure, whose (current price) share of GDP fell by almost half, from 20.5% in 1982 to just 11% in 1992 (see Table 7.3). Public consumption and social services (education and health) have been particularly hard hit. Reduction of the public bureaucracy has accelerated since 1992. During the Febres Cordero administration (1984–1988), cuts affected mostly social services, but the rest of public expenditure was not severely reduced. By contrast, the social democratic regime of Rodrigo Borja (1988–1992) mainly cut public investment and other components of public expenditure, without affecting social services in the same degree.

In a context of educational budget cuts and shrinking family incomes, gross enrollment rates declined in tertiary education and leveled off in secondary school, reversing their long-term expansion and the remarkable growth during the oil boom period (see Table 7.4).[5] Since the quality of education seems to be declining as well, human capital formation has been seriously impeded, affecting long-term prospects for economic recovery.

Wage policies, mostly wage repression and labor-market deregulation, accompanied a strong decline in real minimum wages during the 1980s. Although information on average wages is only partial, the evolution of

Table 7.4   Gross Enrollment[a] Rates by Education Level: Ecuador, 1970–1990 (percentage)

Educational Level	1970	1975	1980	1982	1985	1986	1987	1988	1989	1990
Secondary	26.1	40.2	52.9	53.5	57.1	57.4	56.0	56.2	53.4	55.7
University	8.1	27.1	37.2	—	—	—	29.4	26.4	20.7	21.1

Source: ECLAC (1993c).

Notes: The 1975 and 1980 figures for tertiary enrollment are probably overestimates, due to overreporting by universities for budgetary reasons. They may also exaggerate the true patterns because of the prevalence of part-time study.

a. The ratio of registered students (including those engaged in part-time studies) to the number of persons in the age group corresponding to the education level in question.

functional income distribution shows a strong decline in the wage share of value added, from about 30% during the 1970s to less than 15% in the early 1990s. During the decade 1982–1992, this dramatic income transfer from labor to capital saw the total wage bill decline by 43.4% in real terms, whereas business income rose by 53% (see Table 7.5).[6] The dramatic wage bill reduction in manufacturing (60.9%), where unions are concentrated, would suggest that organized labor was the most affected social group. Losses among public servants (33.6%) and other urban workers (46.1%) were intermediate. Among capitalist classes, landowners (and farmers) particularly benefited during the 1982–1986 period, when a strong devaluation favored agricultural and fishing exports and real business income from those sectors rose by 46.5% (see Table 7.5). The close links between President Febres Cordero and the nation's agro-export elites help to explain this result. From 1988 to 1992, when the social democrat Rodrigo Borja held office, income transfers primarily benefited the manufacturing elites; their income rose by 7.6% per year, mostly at the expense of labor.

In this context of slow economic growth and falling wages, two especially important changes in labor-force structure took place.[7] The first was a large reduction in wage employment as a share of total employment; between 1982 and 1990 the figure declined from 52.6% to 45.9% at the national level, from 65.7% to 55.7% in the urban sector, and from 38.5% to 33.7% in the countryside. This change indicates an increased relative importance of both the urban informal sector and the peasant subsistence economy.[8] As large labor surpluses exist in both sectors, structural unemployment presumably grew. The second transformation was a marked increase in labor-force participation rates, particularly of females. The global participation rate (the ratio of the economically active population [EAP] to the population of working age) rose from 45.3% to 50.7% and from 18.3% to 26.3% for women. Given the economic stagnation and the income declines that characterized the decade, it is possible that the expansion was a subsistence strategy by poor families in the face of shrinking incomes, that is, that it reflects a backward-bending labor-supply curve of the sort reported by Rocha (1987) in the case of Brazil. Alternatively, it may have simply been a continuation of a long-term positive trend in the female participation rate.

Although information on rural social conditions is fragmentary, the cited national accounts data pointing to a sharp decline in the total agricultural wage bill are complemented by a 1994 Instituto Interamericano de Cooperacion Agricola (IICA) survey in several regions of the country that discloses both a reduction in the share working for a wage (the only exception being new areas of flower production for export) and a shift from permanent to temporary employment (IICA-PRONADER, 1994). Additionally, the crisis in the construction industry reduced employment alternatives for rural seasonal and permanent migrants to the cities.[9]

Table 7.5 Social Income Distribution: Ecuador, 1978–1992

	Millions of 1975 Sucres 1982	Year (Index: 1982 = 100)														
		1978	1979	1980	1981	1982	1983	1984	1985	1986	1987	1988	1989	1990	1991	1992
Wage bill	44,833	84.6	87.4	105.1	103.4	100.0	81.6	77.5	76.5	82.2	79.4	71.4	59.8	55.0	54.4	56.6
Agriculture and fishing	2,747	95.2	113.8	125.6	114.6	100.0	76.4	71.2	68.0	74.4	80.7	75.3	68.2	63.9	66.1	75.4
Manufacturing	6,864	86.1	94.6	107.3	104.5	100.0	77.9	66.5	60.6	66.8	62.6	54.5	46.2	40.4	39.9	39.1
Public sector	13,020	82.3	80.3	102.8	104.7	100.0	86.6	93.9	98.2	106.1	100.8	91.6	71.2	65.7	60.8	66.4
Other urban	22,202	84.2	86.0	103.3	100.8	100.0	80.4	72.0	69.8	74.0	71.9	64.3	56.2	52.2	53.7	53.9
Total urban	42,086	83.9	85.6	103.8	102.6	100.0	81.9	77.9	77.1	82.8	79.3	71.1	59.2	54.4	53.7	55.3
Net business income	97,111	86.7	92.7	90.8	95.5	100.0	104.8	112.6	114.1	116.5	108.7	126.6	129.5	135.7	147.2	152.8
Agriculture and fishing	15,952	106.1	98.1	89.2	93.8	100.0	109.5	120.5	124.8	146.5	138.3	144.0	141.6	140.8	160.7	148.6
Manufacturing	19,074	86.9	92.2	85.6	91.3	100.0	106.2	131.9	126.6	133.2	122.1	156.9	158.4	162.4	186.0	210.9
Other urban	62,085	81.6	91.5	92.9	97.3	100.0	103.2	104.7	107.5	103.7	97.0	112.9	117.5	126.2	131.8	136.1
Total urban	81,160	82.8	91.7	91.2	95.9	100.0	103.9	111.1	112.0	110.6	102.9	123.2	127.1	134.7	144.6	153.7
Total factor income	141,944	86.0	91.0	95.4	98.0	100.0	97.5	101.5	102.2	105.7	99.4	109.2	107.5	110.2	117.9	122.4

Source: Banco Central del Ecuador, *Cuentas Nacionales* (several issues).

In spite of the crisis, not all social indicators deteriorated. Infant mortality rates continued to fall, as they did in all Latin American and Caribbean (LAC) countries generally. Social diffusion of technical progress in medical care, as well as better educational levels, seems to play a role in a general trend toward better health conditions, even under harsh social and economic situations. According to census data, between 1982 and 1990, illiteracy rates declined and the average educational level of the adult population increased by about one year, from 4.6 to 5.6 years (INEC, 1982, 1990). Housing conditions improved as well. These changes were probably a lagged effect of the social investment in education and health undertaken during the oil boom.

Recent Trends in
Urban Income Distribution and Labor Conditions

A series of urban household surveys available since 1987 make it possible to analyze the recent trends in urban socioeconomic structure in some detail and to cover the period of important policy reform in the early 1990s. Although these data suffer from the inaccuracies typical of such household survey information, they nonetheless permit some strong conclusions[10] on patterns and trends of income distribution, poverty, labor-force composition, wages, and returns on education.

Income Distribution

The household survey data point to a sharp increase in income concentration, both among individual income earners and among households, around 1990—coincident with the main phase of import liberalization (see Table 7.6). The Gini coefficient among earners went up from an average of 0.446 in 1988–1990 to an average of 0.498 in 1992–1993.[11] Household income distribution follows a similar, albeit smoother, ascending path. Concentration among households is, as expected, lower than that among earners. Gini coefficients calculated on income figures adjusted upward to correct estimated underreporting, although much higher in absolute terms, show essentially the same trends, that is, a net increase of 5 percentage points, from 0.61 in 1988–1990 to 0.66 in 1992–1993.[12] Although the real value of Gini coefficients is difficult to determine, the corrected figures are likely closer to the truth than the unadjusted ones.

Only two previous estimates from urban household surveys exist, yielding uncorrected Gini coefficients for the employed population of 0.507 in 1968 (Musgrove, 1978) and 0.454 in 1975 (Luzariaga and Zuvekas, 1983). Comparison with the observed inequality of the 1988–1993

Table 7.6   Indicators of Urban Income Distribution: Ecuador, 1988–1993

Panel A: Gini Coefficients of the Urban Income Distribution Among Income Earners and
Among Households in Ecuador, 1988–1993

Category	1988	1989	1990	1991	1992	July 1993	November 1993
Unadjusted Data							
Income earners	0.457	0.427	0.453	0.504	0.491	0.487	0.516
Households	0.440	0.414	0.442	0.488	0.471	0.465	0.500
Wages	0.410	0.386	0.426	0.447	0.424	0.417	0.455
Nonwage income	0.514	0.470	0.476	0.566	0.552	0.549	0.563
Formal sector income	0.394	0.393	0.433	0.452	0.441	0.448	0.484
Nonformal income	0.480	0.432	0.448	0.533	0.510	0.490	0.522
Adjusted Data[a]							
Income earners	0.602	0.602	0.622	0.700	0.657	0.656	0.657

Panel B: Average Personal Income by Main Strata, Urban Areas, 1988–1993 (adjusted data)[a]
(1988 sucres/month)

Poorest 5%	6,900	6,206	5,536	4,405	5,551	4,772	5,085
Next 5%	11,797	10,279	9,544	8,076	8,841	9,129	8,899
Next 10%	20,589	15,419	13,457	11,288	12,850	13,902	13,560
Next 30%	34,390	27,347	25,133	20,495	25,426	26,005	26,980
Next 30%	86,326	79,874	76,864	55,735	70,658	71,652	73,099
Next 10%	192,648	189,681	185,828	150,135	175,891	173,666	175,862
Next 5%	299,823	276,764	284,993	242,272	287,841	286,954	283,286
Richest 5%	756,570	592,706	598,238	800,415	799,786	812,933	842,231
(Richest 1%)	1,751,752	1,103,565	1,188,267	1,934,505	1,971,708	1,881,905	1,926,008
Average income	111,293	96,974	95,443	91,770	102,800	103,743	105,941

Panel C: Average Personal Income by Main Strata, Urban Areas, 1988–1993 (unadjusted data)
(1988 sucres/month)

Poorest 5%	3,310	4,486	4,169	3,479	2,791	3,067	3,326
Next 5%	7,168	8,895	7,341	6,229	6,071	6,703	6,868
Next 10%	11,372	12,809	12,042	9,422	8,757	9,342	10,896
Next 30%	21,534	21,040	18,567	15,731	16,263	17,366	18,524
Next 30%	37,252	37,800	34,009	31,253	30,484	33,718	36,608
Next 10%	58,514	56,842	54,790	52,570	49,390	53,936	57,612
Next 5%	80,701	70,588	75,860	79,347	72,189	78,236	86,242
Richest 5%	172,876	151,171	155,179	196,412	171,295	177,285	224,467
(Richest 1%)	334,868	310,817	295,009	433,221	384,755	371,758	489,797
Average income	37,827	36,405	34,583	34,568	32,456	34,918	39,436

Sources: INEM and INEC, "Encuesta de Hogares" (unpublished database, several years).
Notes: a. Personal income data were adjusted using correction factors to match total wages
and total nonlabor income with the corresponding components of nonprimary GDP. Excluded
primary activities were agriculture, silviculture, fishing, catering, logging, mining, and petroleum extraction and refining. Adjustment factors vary for different kinds of nonlabor income.

period is difficult because of different samples, questionnaires, and methods in household surveys. Such caveats aside, it might be hypothetically in-
ferred from this and other information that urban income inequality was very
high before the oil boom and then went down somewhat during the 1970s,
perhaps mostly as a result of a large expansion of middle classes. Though
the survey data do not suggest that income became more concentrated again

during the crisis of the early 1980s, the national accounts figures point strongly in that direction (see Table 7.5). It may be that the crisis particularly affected the middle classes and popular sectors. However, the clearest change (given that reasonably good data are now available), and possibly also the largest, took place after 1990. Two important factors probably played a role in this recent concentration. Trade liberalization, on the one hand, may have adversely affected small-scale ISI production because of the dramatic expansion of consumer good imports; it may also have induced a wave of technological change. On the other hand, the reduction of public employment, which has accelerated since 1991, strongly affected the middle classes. The combined effect of those various changes was an increase in open unemployment rates from 6.1% in 1990 to 8.9% in 1992 and an expansion of the informal sector from 39.4% to 41.3% of the labor force (see Table 7.10, p. 198).

To probe the factors underlying the increase in inequality at the beginning of the 1990s, I have calculated Gini coefficients for wage and nonwage income and for formal and nonformal activities.[13] Concentration increased within all four groups, albeit in differing degrees. The increment between 1988–1990 and 1992–1993 was 2.5 percentage points for wages, 6.8 percentage points for nonwage income, 5.1 percentage points for the formal sector, and 5.4 percentage points for non-formal activities. This pattern is consistent with the proposition that business income played an important role in the overall increase in concentration, with rising incomes for one subset of business people and falling incomes for another subset producing the increased variance both within the nonwage category and within the formal sector. This change is consistent with a probable negative impact of trade liberalization on small-scale enterprises. Though the increase was less marked, wages became more concentrated as well, a result consistent with empirical evidence of rising wage dispersion in other countries. Coefficients of variation of wage income went up, while regression results show an increased dispersion both among and within groups with similar education, experience, gender, and sector. The increased inequality of nonformal income suggests that some informal activities are a nonregulated appendix of the modern sector. As Alejandro Portes and Richard Schauffler (1992), Oihwa Ong (1991), and others point out, new forms of unregulated and flexible labor relations, such as subcontracting and small-scale sweatshops, are increasingly being adopted in both developed and underdeveloped countries. In this context, technological change and production shifts (e.g., from nontradable to tradable activities) may have important effects on the informal sector as well.

The evolution of real income by income stratum discloses a severe deterioration for the poorest half of the population, exceeding 25% for the bottom quintile, an unstable or slightly declining situation for the next 45%, and a sharp improvement (of 25%) for the richest 5% (see Table 7.6).

In other words, real incomes deteriorated for subordinate and middle classes and increased for the highest echelons of the population; the income of the top decile rose from twenty-four times that of the bottom decile to thirty times, using unadjusted data (see Table 7.7, Panel A), and even more using the adjusted data (see Table 7.7, Panel B). This evolution is consistent with national accounts information on social income distribution, which is presented in Table 7.5.

Poverty

As the previously cited trends in average income and its distribution would suggest, poverty (based on the ECLAC definition[14]) increased markedly between 1988 and 1990; its incidence was as high as 75% of persons, using uncorrected income figures, or 45% using corrected income figures.

Table 7.7 Distribution of Income Among Urban Earners in Ecuador, by Decile, 1988–1993 (percentage)

Decile	1988	1989	1990	1991	1992	July 1993	November 1993
Panel A: Unadjusted Data[a]							
1	1.4	1.8	1.8	1.4	1.4	1.4	1.3
2	3.0	3.6	3.2	2.7	2.7	2.7	2.8
3	4.4	4.6	4.3	3.4	3.8	3.9	3.6
4	6.1	5.3	5.5	4.3	4.9	5.0	4.9
5	6.6	7.0	6.3	5.9	6.3	6.1	5.6
6	8.2	8.3	7.9	6.9	7.5	7.7	7.8
7	9.5	9.9	9.7	8.9	9.1	9.3	8.4
8	11.8	12.2	11.9	11.3	11.6	12.0	11.7
9	15.5	15.3	16.0	15.2	15.2	15.4	14.6
10	33.5	31.9	33.4	39.9	37.5	36.6	39.4
Top 5%	22.9	21.6	22.3	28.4	26.4	25.4	28.5
Top1%	8.9	7.7	8.4	12.5	11.9	10.6	12.4
Average Income	37,827	36,405	34,583	34,568	32,456	34,918	39,436
Panel B: Data Adjusted by National Accounts[a]							
1	0.8	0.9	0.8	0.7	0.7	0.7	0.6
2	1.9	1.6	1.4	1.2	1.3	1.3	1.2
3	2.3	2.0	2.0	1.6	1.8	1.9	1.8
4	3.1	2.8	2.5	2.2	2.4	2.5	2.3
5	3.9	3.7	3.4	2.9	3.2	3.4	2.9
6	5.0	5.0	4.9	4.0	4.3	4.3	4.1
7	7.1	7.4	7.4	5.4	6.2	6.3	6.2
8	11.2	12.3	11.9	8.8	10.1	10.0	9.8
9	17.3	19.6	19.5	16.4	17.1	16.5	16.6
10	47.5	44.8	46.3	56.8	52.9	53.1	54.5
Top 5%	34.0	30.6	31.3	43.6	38.9	39.0	40.8
Top 1%	15.7	11.4	12.5	21.1	19.2	17.2	19.0
Average Income	111,293	96,974	95,443	91,770	102,800	103,743	105,941

Sources: INEM and INEC, "Encuesta de Hogares" (unpublished database, several years).
Note: a. For the difference between unadjusted and adjusted data, see Table 7.6, p. 192.

Average per capita income in food basket units fell significantly for the poor, and the poverty gap index—defined as the fraction of poor population times the relative income gap—rose (see Table 7.8). Trends in the early 1990s vary according to which figures one uses. Since the poverty line in Ecuador falls somewhere in the middle of the income distribution, the fact that the income share of the bottom deciles fell after 1990 does not influence the share of people in poverty since these deciles were already discretely below the poverty line.

Wages

Average real wages have reflected the performance of the Ecuadorean economy fairly closely since 1987; their fall (of 27% in Quito and Guayaquil; see Table 7.9, p. 197) from 1987 to 1989 was probably related both to slow growth (though 1988 was a year of recovery from the output fall in 1987, inflation doubled to 60% that year). Thereafter, as per capita GDP edged up and inflation eased, real wages fell a little more through 1992,[15] then recovered about half of the lost ground in 1993. These survey data corroborate the general wage bill trends reported in the national accounts.

Total wage dispersion has shown no consistent trend since 1987, though the coefficient of variation did jump in the November 1993 survey, suggesting that recovery and increased heterogeneity may be interlinked. Information from 1994 will also be important on this point. The increase of dispersion is concentrated in the formal sector of Guayaquil and Quito and is possibly related to the emergence of new, highly profitable activities in the modern sector. They may be linked to finance, new technology (data processing, communications, biotechnology), or even narcotic smuggling.

Labor-Force Composition

Several significant changes in urban labor-force structure can be identified from 1988 to 1993. First, there was a nonreversed 6%+ reduction in the share of workers defined as adequately employed in the modern sector (see definitions in Table 7.10, p. 198) occurring between 1988 and 1990 but not yet reversed by the end of 1993. The drop is mostly due to the contraction in public employment, coupled with a stagnation in the modern private sector. As modern employment shrank, open unemployment rates went up from 6.1% in 1989 to 9.4% in 1992, leveling off to 8.3% in 1993, and the share of the informal sector increased as well. The trajectory of labor-force composition parallels and presumably underlies, in part, the income trends by strata shown in Table 7.9.

Over the first couple of years, the income declines were general to all strata, reflecting the indifferent performance of the economy. Over the

Table 7.8 Urban Poverty Incidence: Ecuador, 1988–1993

	1988	1989	1990	1991	1992	June 1993	November 1993
Unadjusted Estimates[a]							
Percentage of population that is:							
Nonpoor	33.7	29.3	24.7	26.7	26.2	26.5	31.9
Poor	66.3	70.7	75.3	73.3	73.8	73.5	68.1
Poor nonindigent	31.9	34.6	31.0	28.0	29.1	28.8	27.7
Indigent	34.4	36.1	44.3	45.3	44.7	44.7	40.4
Percentage of households that are:							
Nonpoor	40.0	35.9	30.9	31.6	31.9	35.8	41.3
Poor	60.0	64.1	69.1	68.4	68.1	64.2	58.7
Poor nonindigent	30.6	33.5	30.9	27.9	28.3	27.7	25.7
Indigent	29.4	30.6	38.1	40.5	39.8	36.4	33.0
Per Capita Income (basic consumption baskets)							
Population	1.223	0.942	0.855	0.936	0.904	0.936	1.090
Nonpoor	2.244	1.934	1.986	2.203	2.128	2.217	2.398
Poor	0.529	0.531	0.483	0.476	0.469	0.473	0.474
Poor nonindigent	0.746	0.736	0.732	0.734	0.725	0.732	0.739
Indigent	0.328	0.335	0.309	0.317	0.303	0.307	0.293
Poverty Gap Index (PI)[b]	0.312	0.331	0.389	0.384	0.392	0.387	0.358
Estimates Adjusted by National Accounts[a]							
Percentage of population that is:							
Nonpoor	68.9	61.3	58.0	54.9	61.9	61.2	63.8
Poor	31.1	38.7	42.0	45.1	38.1	38.8	36 2
Poor nonindigent	17.9	18.7	16.5	19.3	17.6	17.1	16.7
Indigent	13.2	19.9	15.5	25.8	20.5	21.7	19.6
Percentage of households that are:							
Nonpoor	71.8	64.1	61.1	58.4	63.4	65.5	68.1
Poor	28.2	35.9	38.9	41.6	35.7	34.5	31.9
Poor nonindigent	16.6	18.3	16.1	18.4	16.8	15.5	14.6
Indigent	11.6	17.6	22.8	23.2	18.9	19.0	17.3

Sources: INEM and INEC, "Encuesta de Hogares" (unpublished database, several years).
Notes: a. For the difference between unadjusted and adjusted data, see Table 7.6, p. 192.
b. PP(1-PY)/100, where PP = percent of population that is poor and PY = ratio of per capita income of the poor to the per capita income that defines the poverty line.

next three years (1990–1993) and with timing that varied according to the group, the top decile more than recovered the lost ground, the middle groups recovered or nearly so, and the bottom quintile lost some more (Larrea, 1996: Table 10), though by late 1993 incomes were on the upswing. In this three-year period the impact of the sharp deterioration in income distribution was felt in the form of the further income losses for the lower groups and income recovery by the upper groups. Declining availability of adequate modern sector employment, including that in the public sector, probably explains a good part of the income losses in the middle part of the distribution. Why the lowest two or three deciles did so badly may more likely be a reflection of the lower-end losses associated with the sharp increase in the variance of nonwage income.

Table 7.9   **Real Wages in Quito and Guayaquil, 1987–1993 (thousands of November 1988 sucres/month)**

Wages	1987	1988	1989	1990	1991	1992	July 1993	November 1993
Mean wages								
All sectors	48.4	42.3	35.2	35.1	34.2	33.0	36.1	40.8
Modern sector	55.3	48.4	39.6	40.1	39.2	37.8	41.4	47.3
Informal sector	31.1	25.2	21.7	20.7	25.9	20.3	19.8	24.4
Agriculture	83.3	57.5	47.5	31.0	35.2	46.9	37.4	46.9
Domestic servants	13.7	11.6	12.5	11.1	10.2	10.3	11.1	10.8
Males	55.2	48.3	39.9	39.5	37.7	36.7	39.6	45.6
Females	36.5	31.5	27.5	27.2	28.0	26.9	29.8	32.4
Private sector	43.1	37.6	31.7	30.2	30.5	29.9	33.0	38.6
Public sector	64.8	55.8	45.0	48.2	46.4	43.7	47.5	49.2
Wages/total income	0.611	0.613	0.553	0.591	0.623	0.578	0.564	0.544
Standard deviation of wages	59.3	45.4	35.4	44.2	41.2	35.3	37.9	57.4
Coefficient of variation of wages	1.226	1.074	1.006	1.258	1.205	1.069	1.049	1.408
Standard deviation of wages in:								
Formal sector	65.0	48.9	37.3	48.6	45.4	37.8	40.7	63.9
Informal sector	21.2	19.2	14.7	13.0	28.8	17.0	15.6	20.4
Coefficient of variation of wages in:								
Formal sector	1.177	1.011	0.941	1.210	1.156	1.000	0.982	1.350
Informal sector	0.680	0.762	0.675	0.629	1.115	0.838	0.789	0.837

Sources: INEM and INEC, "Encuesta de Hogares" (unpublished database, several years).
Note: Domestic service wages include only their monetary component. Additional in-kind remuneration has not been estimated.

A second transformation is an increase in participation rates, particularly among females (see Table 7.10). It has been suggested that this may reflect a subsistence strategy adopted by poor families to face the crisis and may have negative effects on educational enrollment.[16]

The wage recovery in 1993 was coupled neither with a reduction in income concentration (as we saw previously) nor with significant declines in underemployment or unemployment. Such details suggest that the deterioration of distribution is not simply a reversible shift associated with a recession-recovery cycle. Conversely, a new context with higher income concentration, an income transfer from labor to capital, and a different structure in the labor market seems to be emerging as a result of trade liberalization, technological change, and structural adjustment.

Conclusion

Ecuador's economic performance during the post-1982 period has been weak. Structural adjustment policies and export promotion strategies implemented

Table 7.10 Urban Labor-Force Composition in Ecuador by Modern/Nonmodern and by Employment/Unemployment, 1988–1993 (percentage)

	1988	1989	1990	1991	1992	July 1993	November 1993
Properly employed							
modern sector	36.7	32.9	30.0	32.6	30.2	29.9	30.4
Underemployed modern sector							
Invisible							
underemployment	4.0	5.9	9.0	3.7	5.3	5.0	4.4
Visible							
underemployment	2.7	3.6	1.4	1.7	1.3	2.4	2.2
Unemployed							
Former workers	3.6	4.1	2.9	3.0	5.1	5.6	5.1
New workers	2.9	3.8	3.2	2.7	3.8	3.8	3.3
Other modern sector							
(status unknown)	0.4	0.4	2.5	3.5	1.4	1.3	2.0
Subtotal, modern sector	50.3	50.6	48.9	47.2	47.1	48.1	47.4
Informal sector	38.7	38.5	39.4	40.5	41.3	40.8	40.6
Agriculture	5.8	6.4	6.4	7.0	6.0	6.3	6.7
Domestic servants	5.1	4.5	5.3	5.4	5.6	4.8	5.3
Subtotal, nonmodern							
activities	49.7	49.4	51.1	52.8	52.9	51.9	52.6
Labor Force	100.0	100.0	100.0	100.0	100.0	100.0	100.0
Open unemployment rate	6.5	7.9	6.1	5.6	8.9	9.4	8.3
Global participation rate among persons older							
than 12 years	54.9	56.3	55.8	60.4	62.2	61.6	60.6
Female participation in							
labor force	36.0	37.5	36.8	39.3	40.5	38.2	39.7

Sources: INEM and INEC, "Encuesta de Hogares" (unpublished database, several years).
  Note: A worker in the modern sector is considered to be "properly employed" when he/she is not underemployed. Underemployment may be visible when a person works involuntarily less than full time (40 hours/week), or invisible when he/she works at least 40 hours/week but the salary is below the legal minimum wage.

since the early 1980s did coincide with an important expansion in both oil and nonoil export volumes, but because of a sharp decline in the terms of trade export purchasing power remained below its precrisis average. Moreover, export diversification has been weak—nontraditional exports to developed countries account for less than 5% of total exports—and the country has been unable to significantly introduce manufactured products into its export basket.

    From a political viewpoint, policy reforms have been adopted in a painful and conflictive way, without benefit of stable support from the civil society or even from the dominant classes. As a result, for more than a decade the reforms lacked economic coherence and political credibility. Nevertheless, the most important structural adjustment policies have now been implemented, and export promotion has been adopted as a long-term development strategy.

The combination of falling terms of trade and weak export diversification is cause for concern. Export diversification has been limited in all small Latin American economies, with the sole exception of Costa Rica (Buitelaar and Fuentes, 1991). Exports from Ecuador, Bolivia, and most Central American countries are still based on a small group of primary products, with manufactured exports low and limited to traditional activities, such as textiles. The capacity of Latin American countries to diversify their exports and consolidate their insertion in international markets through export promotion strategies depends on both domestic market size and level of development. The largest and most industrialized countries in the region have been able to take advantage of preexisting economies of scale, internal linkages, skilled labor, financial institutions, physical infrastructure, and other positive externalities derived from their import-substitution phase of industrialization. Conversely, small and less-diversified countries usually lack those acquired advantages, as well as scale. The availability of cheap, unskilled labor is not a significant comparative advantage for export diversification, unless it is complemented by a set of features usually derived from a long manufacturing tradition.

Further, as a result of rapid technological change and the massive diffusion of information and communications technology, biotechnology, and other innovations, emerging technologies are less labor-intensive and save both energy and raw materials relative to earlier vintages. The traditional comparative advantages of small Latin American countries—cheap unskilled labor and natural resources—are less important than before. The combined effects of technical change, the internationalization of production, and raw-material substitution have resulted in a declining participation of raw materials, fuels, and foodstuffs in international trade, whereas new comparative advantages are related to the development of human capital and the capacity to integrate and assimilate technological change (Castells, 1993). In this light it is not surprising, though it is worrisome, that the Latin American share in world exports dropped from 12.4% in 1950 to 5.5% in 1970 and 3.9% in 1990 (FAO, 1994).

The simultaneous application of export promotion policies by small Third World economies has led to a frequent oversupply in primary product markets, and technological change has lowered demand. This combination resulted in a severe decline of terms of trade for most primary products; prospects for economic recovery based on such exports seem seriously limited. At the same time, SAPs have reduced public expenditure on education and health and hence human capital formation, further curtailing the potential for dynamic comparative advantages in small countries. Moreover, market-friendly policies discouraged state-induced export promotion policies, which helped successful Southeast Asian countries to move to higher echelons in the international division of labor (Wade, 1990; Deyo, 1988; Gereffi and Wyman, 1990).

Common traits with other small Latin American countries explain only part of Ecuador's recent problems, however. Export diversification has been unusually weak in Ecuador and contrasts sharply to the remarkable diversification achieved in Costa Rica. Several specific hypotheses have been put forward to explain Ecuador's unsatisfactory experience. A. Hofman and R. Buitelaar (1994) postulate that the historical natural resource–based character of Ecuador's economic growth and its high level of instability contributed to a strong rent-seeking behavior among Ecuadorean entrepreneurs. The periodic primary product booms have also had lasting Dutch disease effects, reducing the country's potential for export diversification. Hofman and Builelaar argue that the export promotion strategy, based mostly on market-friendly mechanisms, has been inimical to Ecuador's prospects and that a well-defined regulatory state role is necessary to achieve long-term growth. A. De Janvry et al. (1993) attach some of the blame to an additional set of economic, social, political, and institutional factors, including a deep-rooted regionalism that has prevented the emergence of a national dominant class able to produce consensus or achieve hegemony.

Such arguments suggest that the behavioral patterns of Ecuador's entrepreneurial classes evolved in a historical sequence of easy, albeit short-lived, primary export cycles (Larrea, Espinosa, and Sylva, 1987; Larrea, 1994). The extraction of international rents played an important role in the process of class conformation. During the oil boom period, generous state incentives and subsidies allowed rapid accumulation. Oligopolistic and inefficient market structures prevailed in the economy. Under these circumstances, Ecuadorean entrepreneurs have not developed the skills needed to compete openly and successfully in international markets without state protection, nor have they been able to consolidate a stable and hegemonic political strategy. Both internal fragmentation (with a strong regional component) and weak response capacity of the entrepreneurial classes curtailed the results of adjustment programs. Of course, adequate economic skills, social cohesion, and political capabilities can only be achieved in the medium term.

The social effects of the crisis and adjustment processes have been severe. The redistribution of income from labor to capital/business since 1982 appears to have been extreme, with a sharp increase in inequality occurring between the late 1980s and the early 1990s as liberalization was accelerating. Poverty remains extremely high.

Signs of economic recovery, transfer from nontradable to tradable production, and export-based growth are still weak (through 1995) and may continue to be so for some time. The expansion in labor demand generated by growth in agricultural exports is small and has little positive impact on urban employment and wages. Consequently, short-term social costs of adjustment policies are still dominant.

Although negative short-term social repercussions of adjustment policies are evident, it is difficult to identify direct causal links between specific adjustment measures and their social effects. It is also difficult to differentiate between the effects of the economic crisis, the adjustment programs, and the transformation in the international context because of the simultaneity of economic stagnation, the application of different adjustment components (real devaluations, subsidy reduction, labor deregulation, import liberalization, state reduction, and so on), and the international diffusion of technological change. Despite these problems, some of the social effects of specific adjustment policies and other factors can be hypothesized.

Real devaluation produces an increase in relative prices of tradable goods that may reduce real wages; devaluations generate at least a short-term inflationary effect that tends to lower wages and may increase inequality. Since there may be no alternative to real devaluation, it is hard to judge the extent to which these related phenomena can be said to contribute to greater inequality than would otherwise have occurred. In any case, between 1982 and 1988, repeated devaluations and high fiscal deficits (particularly in 1987) generated a chronic inflationary problem; in the context of slow economic growth, the devaluation-inflation effect was probably the most important specific mechanism of income transfer from labor to capital. After 1988, real devaluations became moderate, and from 1990, a real appreciation in exchange rates reversed the previous trend. Inflation rates declined as well from 75% in 1989 to 27% in 1994, as inflation control became a priority in adjustment policies (Jácome, 1994).

Subsidy reduction or elimination affected mostly middle and urban popular classes. Food subsidies (wheat, imported powdered milk) were reduced in the mid-1980s, and oil subsidies were partially reduced during the 1980s. As inflation repeatedly ate away at oil price hikes, oil subsidy prices became chaotic. Only in the 1990s were oil and energy subsidies eliminated. As a result of the interest rate liberalization adopted in the mid-1980s, credit became more concentrated, and subsidized credit for small producers was drastically reduced, probably increasing income concentration. The regressive effects of real-price policies were thus spread out during the 1980s and became concentrated after 1992.

Trade liberalization, as mentioned, has a negative impact on formerly protected domestic production, particularly small-scale manufacturing activities. Additionally, it encourages luxury consumption among elites, thus reducing savings propensity and future growth. Its negative effect on employment and income distribution is suggested by the coincidence of the large increase in inequality around 1990 with the drastic reduction of trade barriers at that time. Trade liberalization may also accelerate technical change. New technologies are labor saving, have higher skilled labor demand, and tend to displace traditional unskilled labor–intensive activities. Increasing returns on higher levels of education at this time suggest a key role of technical change in the labor-market structure (Larrea, 1995).

Notes

Carlos Larrea is a professor at Facultad Latinoamerica de Ciencias Sociales (FLACSO) in Ecuador. He would like to thank Albert Berry, Gustavo Indart, and Lisa North for comments on earlier drafts of this work. Their suggestions have improved it greatly. He is, of course, responsible for any errors that remain.

1. The main sources on the Ecuadorean structural adjustment experience are Conaghan (1990); de Janvry, Sadoulet, and Fargeix (1991); de Janvry, Sadoulet, and Fargeix (1993); Grindle and Thoumi (1992); and Larrea (1992). Primary information is mostly taken from the Central Bank of Ecuador and ECLAC.

2. According to census information, the percentages of wage earners in the labor force declined in the urban sector from 67.2% in 1974 to 65.7% in 1982 and from 40.1% to 38.5% in the countryside. The figures also reveal a reduced diffusion of wage relations and suggest an important underemployment problem.

3. During the oil boom period, private investment was high not only in the petroleum sector but in manufacturing and finance as well. Public investment was also high, particularly in infrastructure.

4. Proven oil reserves will allow for about twelve more years of exports, with declining volumes and quality and higher extraction costs. Heavy oil prevails in unexploited reserves. See World Bank (1988).

5. The unusual expansion of tertiary enrollment in the 1970s was a result of both the elimination of admission exams in public universities after 1969 and strong financial support during the oil boom. Nevertheless, Table 7.4's 1975 and 1980 figures are probably overestimates because of overreporting by universities for budgetary reasons. They may also exaggerate the true patterns because of the prevalence of part-time study.

6. Since the series in Table 7.5 are based on deflation by the GDP deflator rather than the cost of living index, they do not measure changes in the purchasing power of the wage bill. It appears, however, that the GDP deflator and the cost of living index moved sufficiently close together to allow the former to be a reasonably good proxy for the latter.

7. For a detailed analysis, see Larrea (1992).

8. Among Latin American countries, Ecuador has one of the highest shares of employment in the traditional rural sector and the urban informal sector (62% in 1980). PREALC (1985) identifies employment in those sectors with "underemployment."

9. Construction output declined from 4.7% of GDP in 1982 to 2.8% in 1991 (constant 1975 sucres). See Commander and Peek (1986).

10. Annual employment and income surveys are available since 1988 for the urban sector and since 1987 for the three largest cities (Quito, Guayaquil, and Cuenca). Since 1993, surveys have been taken twice a year.

A common problem in all household surveys is income underreporting. To estimate it, I compared total urban income with the national accounts estimate of income, separately for labor and for nonlabor income and excluding agriculture and petroleum. Judging from this comparison, wage underreporting was relatively small, averaging just 5% over the six years analyzed. Conversely, nonlabor income was underreported by 80%, i.e., only one fifth of non-labor income was reported. Underreporting coefficients remained roughly constant for the 1988–1993 period. Because capital income is the largest component of GDP, the total underreporting factor is thus 65%, a level so high as to cast serious doubt on the reliability of the information. By adjusting capital incomes to equal the national accounts figure, a better estimation can be obtained, although one evidently still open to possibly serious bias because any assumption about how much to adjust each family's capital income is arbitrary. Moreover, an estimation of urban income from published national accounts information is also subject to a wide margin of error. We assumed total urban income in the household survey as equivalent to nonprimary GDP, but since agricultural output does not correspond precisely to rural output, this implies a bias of unknown magnitude.

The second problem is posed by frequent changes in the questionnaire; three different versions have been used. Income questions changed twice, in 1991 and 1992. The 1991 survey in particular seems to be the least reliable in the series. Although the questionnaire applied from 1988 to 1990 is different from that used in 1992 and 1993, the information shows internal consistency for all the variables presented in this chapter and is also reasonably consistent with the national accounts. Other changes in the sampling procedure and the institutional context are less worrisome.

11. Gini coefficients were calculated directly from individual observations. Earners and households with zero income were excluded from their respective distributions. Gini coefficients were estimated for the distributions of earners ranked by own income and of households ranked by total household income. Questionnaires report monthly income for the last month before the survey. For the 1989 and 1990 surveys, in which missing values for nonwage income received in kind by employers and self-employed persons were relatively frequent, these were estimated by a multiple regression. All other cases with missing values were excluded from the calculations for Gini coefficients among earners. As for households, only cases with missing family income were excluded, and missing values for individual household members were not estimated and added to family income. Generally, the frequency of missing values in the surveys is below 2%, except in the case of nonwage in-kind income in 1989 and 1990, in which a regression estimation was used.

12. Our estimates of reporting ratios (defined as the ratio of total survey income to the corresponding national accounts figure) remain roughly unchanged over the period. They are as follows:

Year	Wage	Other Income	Total Income
1988	0.833	0.186	0.340
1989	0.963	0.229	0.375
1990	1.026	0.213	0.362
1991	1.266	0.200	0.377
1992	0.983	0.184	0.316

Because concentration is consistently shown in all the coefficients for specific groups, and samples are large, the reported level of income concentration in the urban sector could not be the result of statistical flaws, changing questionnaires, or random errors. Estimated trends are more subject to error, since there is no easy way of knowing whether the composition of income underreporting (as opposed to the level, which has been relatively constant) may have changed over time. This is a weakness to which all survey-based estimates of inequality trends are subject.

13. Nonformal activities include the informal sector, domestic service, and agricultural workers. The informal sector includes self-employed workers, excluding professionals and technicians with university education; unremunerated family workers; and persons working in establishments with fewer than six workers, excepting activities such as travel, air transport, and exchange agencies or computer centers. Unremunerated family workers were included in all calculations for the informal sector, except the Gini coefficients.

14. Under this definition, a household is defined as poor when its income falls below the cost of a basic consumer basket and indigent when its income is lower than the cost of a normative basic food basket; the cost of the former basket is defined as 1.88 times the cost of the latter. Following previous studies of poverty in Ecuador, an Engel coefficient of 1.88 is used instead of its general value of 2. For 1990 and the following years, the cost of the food basket was estimated from empirical data collected in 1989 and food consumer price indices (Larrea, 1990).

15. The loss was 22% for the total urban sector between 1988 and 1992 and 32% for the two largest metropolitan centers, Guayaquil and Quito, between 1987 and 1992 (see Table 7.9).

16. Since there is no clear negative correlation between average wages and participation rates (compare Tables 7.9 and 7.10), this interpretation is not obvious. The concentration of the participation rate increase in 1991 may suggest data problems. Clearly more research is needed in this area.

8

The Effects of Macroeconomic Adjustment on the Labor Market and on Income Distribution in Brazil

André Urani

During the last fifteen years, the two main goals of Brazilian macroeconomic policy have been avoiding balance-of-payments problems and reducing the rate of inflation, goals pursued through different means and often simultaneously. Although the first objective has almost always been achieved, the anti-inflationary policy has systematically failed. The linkages between these two policy areas have been studied by several authors and will not be explored in this chapter, the purpose of which is to analyze the connections existing between these two policies, the labor market, and income distribution.

If product and labor markets are fully competitive and there is a high level of wage and price flexibility, aggregate demand-management policies like those adopted at the beginning of the period under discussion here should be successful in reducing the rate of inflation without significant loss of output. Allocative flexibility also allows supply shocks (such as an increase in the oil price or a devaluation) to be rapidly absorbed without medium-run efficiency loss.

Flexibility, however, has its own costs, and recent studies suggest that the Brazilian labor market may be *too* flexible, at least in the sense that the weakness and impermanence of worker-employer ties inhibits the accumulation necessary for raising productivity (Amadeo et al., 1993). Nor has such flexibility done much to avoid strong oscillations of incomes, unemployment, and income inequality during the period studied in this chapter (Barros, Cardoso, and Urani, 1993; Barros and Mendonça, 1994a; Bonelli and Ramos, 1993; and Urani, 1993a). A possible explanation of such fluctuations at the macro level may be the aggregation of market segments that are very flexible with others that are rigid. Moreover, each segment can be rigid toward one kind of shock and flexible toward another. Under such conditions, the distributional impacts of policy or external shocks can be quite complicated.

In this chapter I review the main characteristics of the Brazilian labor market; the stylized facts on the Brazilian economy and the evolution of macroeconomic policy from 1981 to 1992; the types of shocks faced by the Brazilian economy during this period and their potential impacts on the labor market and on income distribution; the impacts of those shocks on employment, wages, and relative incomes; and the evolution of income inequality and poverty.

The Main Features of the Brazilian Labor Market

The shares of people living in rural and urban areas of Brazil were inverted between 1950 and 1980; the former share fell from 70% to 30%, whereas the total population of the country more than doubled. Though only some of the swelling urban labor force provoked by this strong industrialization found work in the "modern" urban sectors, the main problem of the Brazilian labor market as of the early 1980s was certainly not that of open unemployment. Though its frequency was very high, both average duration and the unemployment rate itself were quite low in comparison to most other countries (Bivar, 1993). Most of those without modern sector jobs were informally employed (i.e., without a legal contract) or self-employed. In 1981, the participation rate of persons ages 15 and up was estimated at 54.2% (65.2% for men and 34.8% for women).[1] Formal employment covered 42.2% of the labor force, informal employment (excluding self-employment) 28.1%, and self-employment 25.9%, and the rate of unemployment was 6.5%.[2]

The low rate of unemployment and the limited job attachment were due, at least in part, to the lack of an unemployment insurance system and to the existence of several institutional mechanisms that induced a very high rate of turnover, especially for unskilled workers.[3] To have a formal job meant (and still means) to have the right to a minimum wage, paid vacations, a fixed number of hours worked per week, social insurance, and— in most cases—to get a higher income than that attainable in the informal sector.

Wage policy has been an important determinant of the evolution of both nominal and real wages of formal sector workers in Brazil's inflation-prone economy, at least from the mid-1960s on. At first, annual wage adjustments were defined in relation to "expected" inflation, arbitrarily fixed by the military government itself. From the end of the 1960s to the present, however, they have been based on past inflation. The periodicity of one year for indexing was maintained until 1979 when, because of higher inflation and increasing union bargaining power, the index period was cut to six months. The 1979 modification also established that the percent wage adjustment would be a negative function of nominal wages (i.e., larger percentages at lower incomes and smaller at higher), implying a desire to redistribute income within the formal segment of the labor market. Thereafter, the rule for wage adjustment was changed very frequently, the main phases being listed here:

- the distributive (1979–1983) phase, with adjustment exceeding past inflation for lower-wage workers and falling short of it for high-wage workers;[4]
- the regressive (1983–1985) phase, which retained the differential treatment in favor of lower-wage workers but set all adjustments equal to or less than past inflation;[5]
- the trigger-point rule implemented with the Cruzado Plan in 1986;[6]
- the Unidade de Referencia de Preços (URP) (1987–1989), implemented within the Bresser Plan, with monthly adjustments related to the average rate of inflation of the last three months;
- the end of the wage policy at the beginning of the Collor government (1990);
- the adoption in 1992 of wage adjustments every four months.

Although these rules were a powerful determinant of the evolution of nominal wages, the most organized segments of the labor force were often able to negotiate indexation rules more to their liking. In 1985, for instance, though the official rule called for adjustment every six months, a great number of important groups had quarterly adjustments. Still, the influence of the rules described previously is evident in the dynamics of formal sector real wages, which showed a stronger link with the rate of inflation than with the evolution of the gross domestic product (GDP).

Since informal sector work contracts are not covered by legislation, such indexation rules do not affect them directly. The informal sector is a more competitive market in which the contracts are renegotiated more easily. Its informality makes the real wage much more sensitive to the cycle and a little less sensitive to the rate of inflation (Barros and Mendonça, 1994b). The labor of self-employed workers is also sold, albeit not directly, in a highly competitive market; the goods and services they produce are often imperfect substitutes for those produced by the modern sector. Though more able to preserve their real income against inflation than the other participants of the labor force (except perhaps employers), they are, however, more vulnerable to aggregate demand oscillations.

Other important attributes of the Brazilian labor market at the beginning of the 1980s were the low level of human capital and the very high inequality of opportunities. In 1981, the average schooling for the economically active population (EAP) above 25 years old was less than five years; although 7.2% had some university training 21% were illiterate. E. Amadeo et al. (1993) show, further, that the quality of education in Brazil is very low, not only in comparison to countries with a similar level of development but also from a Latin American perspective. The inequality of opportunity to enter and, especially, to remain in the educational system is clearly a major cause—in fact, perhaps the main single cause of income inequality in Brazil, known to be one of the most extreme in the world.[7] Its very high income inequality explains why Brazil's poverty indicators are much higher than those of other countries with similar per capita income. This unsatisfactory record underlies the insistence of most Brazilian policymakers—during the last two decades—on trying to implement nonrecessive adjustment policies when short-run disequilibria appear. For the most part, this strategy has aggravated the disequilibria.

The Post-1980 Period in Historical Perspective

The Brazilian economy entered the 1980s after three decades of strong economic growth, thanks to a successful industrialization process based on import substitution (Bonelli and Malan, 1990). This process was deeper than in other Latin American countries, which for the most part interrupted it after its first stage—the installation of durable and nondurable consumer goods industries. Particularly dependent on imported energy inputs, Brazil chose to adjust to the first oil shock through a deepening of import substitution in capital and intermediary goods, financed by increasing inflows of foreign savings (i.e., external debt accumulation). Thanks to this strategy, GDP growth remained very high, but the rate of inflation practically doubled in annual terms (from 20% to around 40%) and gross external debt grew from less than U.S.$18 billion in 1974 to more than U.S.$43 billion in 1978, as Brazilian external debt became the highest in the Third World. It was also the only one—at least in Latin America—that had as its main counterpart a significant increase in the country's capital stock.[8] At the beginning of the 1980s, then, Brazil had a relatively solid industrial structure but a high degree of vulnerability built into its financial relationships with the rest of the world.

As a result of this vulnerability, the second oil shock and the increase in international interest rates in 1979 had drastic consequences for the trade balance (see Figure 8.1) and the current account of the balance of payments. The deterioration of the terms of trade also had serious repercussions on the rate of inflation (see Figure 8.2) because of the relative price rigidities provoked by the very high degree of concentration among suppliers and by the generalized presence of indexation mechanisms.

The first reaction of the Brazilian government to these new shocks was to attempt another adjustment through growth policy.[9] This time, however,

Figure 8.1 Evolution of the Trade Balance: Brazil, 1974–1992 (billions of U.S.$)

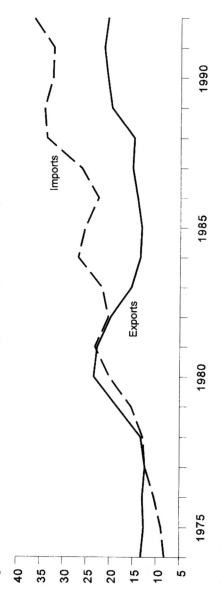

Source: IBGE, unpublished database.

Figure 8.2 Annual Rate of Inflation: Brazil, 1974–1992 (percentage)

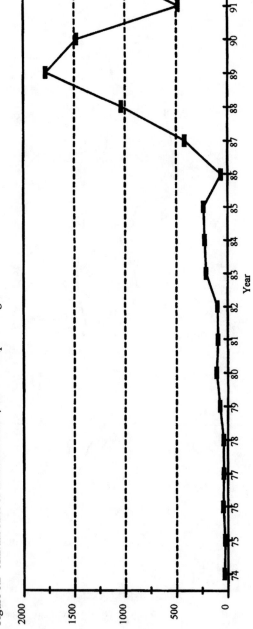

Source: IBGE, unpublished database.

the strategy was ineffective, both against inflation (the annual rate jumped from 40% in 1978 to 100% in 1980) and against the current account deficit (running at U.S.$13 billion in 1980, or about 5.5% of GDP).

At the end of 1980, Brazil's international creditors indicated that they were not inclined to continue financing such large deficits. From 1981, the focus of Brazilian macroeconomic policy shifted from the long to the short run—from growth at any cost to the adjustment of the balance of payments and the reduction of the rate of inflation. It was the beginning of an era of macroeconomic policy experiments of all kinds in an environment of increasing instability, which can usefully be divided into six phases.

1. The "voluntary adjustment" (1981–1982), when the government tried, through a very tight monetary policy and increases in nontariff barriers, to eradicate the trade balance and reduce the rate of inflation. The first objective was accomplished (see Figure 8.1), thanks to a diminution of imports, though this was not enough to reduce the overall demand for foreign currency, given the growing burden of interest on the external debt. Meanwhile, the rate of inflation remained roughly constant (see Figure 8.2). In other words, the monetary cuts affected quantities rather than prices: for the first time in its statistically documented economic history, Brazil suffered, in 1981, a negative growth rate of its GDP.

2. The agreements with the International Monetary Fund (IMF) (1983–1984), during which, to the high degree of protection and to the monetary tightness, were added

- important cuts in government expenditures (Figure 8.3 shows that this was the only time that overall government expenditure decreased during this period);
- the regressive wage policy described in the section on the Brazilian labor market; and
- a substantial devaluation of the domestic currency in real terms (see Figure 8.4).

This shift of relative prices and the reduction of aggregate demand together with the recovery of the world economy allowed exports (especially those of manufactured goods) to grow significantly, while imports continued to fall (see Figure 8.1). The trade surplus became great enough to clear the current account of the balance of payments, but the devaluation also implied a strong acceleration of inflation (see Figure 8.2), which reached 200% annually. GDP at first decreased, but from mid-1984 it started to grow, thanks to the strength of manufacturing exports.

3. The first year of the New Republic (1985), during which the agreements with the IMF were abandoned and the "orthodox" instruments to fight inflation (on the fiscal and monetary sides as well as on the wage

Figure 8.3 Evolution of Government Expenditures as a Percentage of GDP: Brazil, 1981–1992

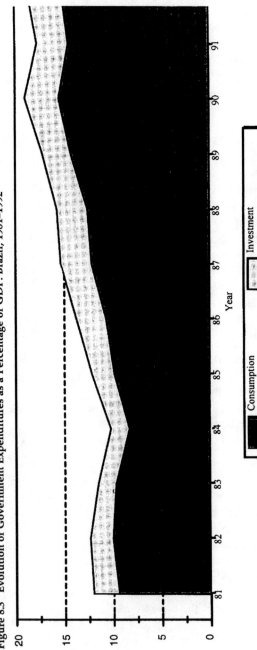

Source: Macrométrica, unpublished database.

Figure 8.4 Evolution of the Real Exchange Rate: Brazil, 1981–1992 (index: 1980 = 100)

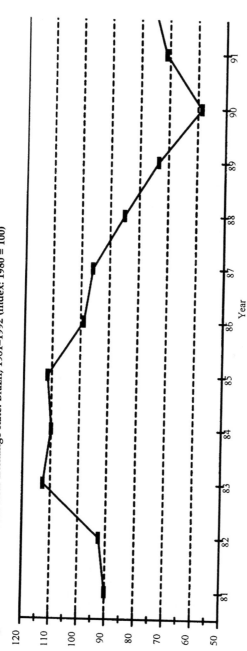

Source: Macrométrica, unpublished database.

one) were abandoned. The emphasis of economic policy swung back to growth issues, and its anti-inflationary component was limited to an ephemeral attempt to delay public price adjustments. Inflation continued at the same level as in the two previous years (see Figure 8.2), and GDP growth recovered to the levels of the 1970s without affecting the trade surplus (see Figure 8.1) or the equilibrium of current account.

4. The Cruzado Plan (1986), which can be seen as an experiment in combining the fight against inflation with the pursuit of GDP growth and income redistribution. This "heterodox" experiment was based on

- a monetary reform;
- the freezing of prices and of the nominal exchange rate; and
- expansive fiscal and monetary policies.

In the short run, the rate of inflation was drastically reduced, and high GDP growth was maintained. But the combination of rising demand and fixed supply led to rationing in the product and currency markets, then to speculative behavior of all kinds, and finally to a progressive erosion of the trade surplus (see Figure 8.1). By the end of 1986, only a few months after the implementation of the monetary reform, the government had to abandon the fixed exchange rate, an act that triggered the chaotic return of inflation (Winograd, 1991).

5. The agony of the New Republic (from 1987 to 1989), during which the basic aspiration of macroeconomic policy was to avoid hyperinflation. Two stabilization plans were adopted (the "Bresser" and the "Summer"), both combining heterodox elements (like temporary price freezes) with orthodox ones (cuts in the money supply), but each was incapable of ending the fiscal voracity of the "new regime." The current account was rapidly cleared, despite the fact that the real exchange rate did not return to pre–Cruzado Plan levels (see Figure 8.4), but the growth rate fell considerably. Given the lack of control on government expenditures (see Figure 8.3) and the lack of political stability that characterized these years,[10] these plans were unable to hold inflation down for more than a few months. This chaotic process culminated with an inflationary explosion at the end of 1989 and the beginning of 1990, with the monthly inflation rate exceeding 80%.

6. The Collor government, when for the first time the stabilization policy was accompanied by significant structural reforms. On the anti-inflationary front the main measures were a new price freeze, the confiscation of 80% (!) of the financial wealth in the hands of the public, and the end of the wage policy; the structural adjustment was—in practice—restricted to a substantial trade reform and a timid attempt at privatization.[11] This policy resulted in a recession as deep as the one recorded a decade earlier (thanks to which the trade liberalization did not produce a new current

account deficit)[12] and, as we see later (in the section on macroeconomic trends in the labor market), in a deep and generalized impoverishment of the population, albeit with a sharp reduction in income inequality.

A Typology of Shocks and Their Labor Market Impacts

Before turning to a detailed look at the labor-market outcomes of the past fifteen years, it is helpful to identify the various types of shocks to which the Brazilian economy has been subjected over that period and to distinguish their likely labor-market impacts.

External Shocks

External shocks are those changes in international relative prices or in international demands and supplies of goods, services, or factors that are independent of domestic economic policy. For Brazil, as for most developing countries, the external shocks par excellence of this period occurred simultaneously at the end of the 1970s—the second oil shock and the increase in international interest rates provoked by the U.S. Federal Reserve's resolution to tighten U.S. monetary policy, complemented by the similar stance of the Thatcher government in the United Kingdom. These shocks put pressure on Brazil to improve its trade balance in order to cope with the increasing burden of external debt in a context of worsened terms of trade. They led to an increase in the current account deficit and a significant acceleration in the rate of inflation, creating the macroeconomic turbulence that characterized the period.

On the labor-market front, adjustment to these shocks is commonly assumed to require (1) a shift of relative wages such as to induce labor to move from the nontradable to the tradable sectors and/or (2) a fall in real wages to help reduce domestic absorption. The latter would, of course, have perverse effects on poverty but not necessarily on wage dispersion. The effects of labor movement between sectors depend on the context; under segmentation or other rigidities, the shift will require relative wages to rise in the receiving sector and fall in the sending sector, which may create or widen income gaps. The effect on distribution would, however, depend on which sector initially had higher wages; it would be expected to differ in the shorter and the longer run. So no generalizations are possible.

Policy Shocks

As noted above, the government tried a great variety of policy experiments in response to the macroeconomic disequilibria caused by the external shocks of the late 1970s. The first policies adopted to deal with accelerating inflation and increasing current account deficits assumed that the problem was an excess *aggregate demand* that could be eliminated by contractionary monetary and fiscal policies. This view was progressively corrected and complemented—but very seldom (only during the Cruzado Plan) completely abandoned.

To the extent that economic agents perceive demand shocks as transitory, firms needing to diminish the size of a heterogeneous labor force will start by firing those workers for whom the costs of selection, training, and dismissal are the lowest, that is, the least skilled. Thus, even if a demand shock is "neutral" in the goods market (in that it hits all the firms in the same way—admittedly a strong hypothesis), it will not be neutral on the labor market. Other labor-market impacts of demand policy depend on the detailed nature of that policy. Abstracting from labor heterogeneity, monetary shocks could be neutral in their labor-market effects if prices and nominal wages were fully flexible. But if prices and nominal wages are somehow rigid, labor demand will fall, leading to either an increase in unemployment or a shift of employment to those segments of the labor market with lower entry barriers and higher wage flexibility or both; such a shock will tend to increase income inequality and poverty.

Overall fiscal restraint was seldom used as a weapon against macroeconomic disequilibria during the period analyzed; total expenditures were reduced only during the agreements with the IMF. Though public investment was very low by historical standards, government consumption increased considerably, particularly during the second half of the 1980s. Any distributional impacts of fiscal policy were thus likely to come from changes in the composition of expenditures.

Supply Shocks

Policy-based supply shocks involved government attempts to interfere in some important relative prices or, in extreme cases, in the overall price level. One of the first government reactions to the debt crisis at the beginning of the 1980s was to increase protectionism by strengthening nontariff barriers. These were maintained at very high levels throughout the decade. (At the beginning of the 1990s, however, they were eliminated, and the average import tariff dropped substantially; see Cordeiro, 1992.) Meanwhile, one of the key elements of the adjustment strategy promoted by the IMF was the devaluation of the real exchange rate.

During the period under discussion, indexation to correct for inflation was the main element of wage policy. Its expected effect on the wage share of GDP and on income and wage inequality is also complex and must be defined against the backdrop of the impacts of the inflation itself and of the causes of the inflation. The more complete the indexation (based on the degree of adjustment and its frequency), the higher will be the wage share, ceteris paribus. But when indirect effects are allowed for, the net impact of an increase in the degree of indexation is ambiguous.[13] The way the degree of indexation varies across groups, when such is the case, must also be taken into account. Where it is inversely related to the wage level, the direct impact on distribution would be positive, but if one effect is to induce firms to fire their less qualified workers, the opposite could be true. Although indexation may decrease wage dispersion within the formal segment, it may also increase the wage gap between the formal and the informal, especially for the less skilled. In practice, however, both the wage gap between these sectors and poverty decreased considerably, thanks to the very expansive fiscal and monetary policies adopted during the Cruzado Plan (Urani and Winograd, 1994).

At first, Collor's government reinstituted the wage policy of the early 1960s: the government ceased mandating wage changes for formal sector workers and limited its intervention to the minimum wage, which was strongly reduced. This withdrawal increased the sensitivity of formal sector real wages to aggregate demand oscillations and diminished the extent of segmentation between the formal and informal segments and the associated wage gap between them.

During the period as a whole, price controls were a key element of the anti-inflationary policy. At first this instrument was applied only to the most oligopolized industries, but as inflation accelerated it became more difficult to maintain firm control over so many sectors, and the government gradually adopted a homogeneous indexation rule, which strengthened the inertial character of the inflation. This rule was abandoned during the first year of the New Republic, when the delay in the public price adjustment became the main instrument of anti-inflationary policy. Since the public sector's demand for labor was not dependent on product price as it would be in the private sector, there was no reason to expect this shift of relative prices to induce an exodus of workers from the public to the private sector. It might even have led to a transitory increase in real wages due to the temporary repression of inflation.

Price controls reached their apex during the Cruzado Plan, when all prices (even those of competitive markets) were frozen for an undefined period.[14] In practice, however, these controls were effective only in the most oligopolized sectors, where they prevented rising aggregate demand from pulling prices up; this rechanneled the excess demand to the more competitive sectors, producing an important increase in their relative and absolute prices. Because the presence of informal workers is higher in the more competitive sectors, this shift in relative prices narrowed the formal/informal wage gap and helped to reduce poverty.

Impacts of Macroeconomic Trends on the Labor Market

The previous section suggests some of the ways in which macroeconomic oscillations caused by external shocks and by erratic economic policy might affect labor-market outcomes and how these outcomes would reflect the degrees of flexibility of the various segments of that market. In this section, I try to relate the observed trends in labor-market outcomes to the shocks suffered by the economy and the macroeconomic policies implemented.

Wage Flexibility

The average real wage has shown much flexibility in the period since 1980. At the same time, wage dynamics have varied considerably across the distinct segments of the labor market. However, the flexibility of the average real wage has not prevented marked oscillations in the unemployment rate and in labor-income inequality.

The real wage volatility that characterized the decade as a whole emerged after 1982. In 1983 the average real wage fell abruptly because of a combination of accelerating inflation (resulting from the devaluation) and reduced wage indexation (see Figure 8.5). During the two first years of the New Republic, the average real wage shot up to a 1986 high 35% above the 1981 level, under the influence of the strengthening of price controls, fiscal and monetary laxness, and increased wage indexation. Accelerating inflation after the collapse of the Cruzado Plan brought real wages back down, over 1987–1989, to the 1985 level of about 10% lower than that of 1981. A further drastic reduction of around 40% occurred in the first three years of the 1990s.[15] Underlying this plunge were the absence of a wage policy, the environment of deep recession and strong trade liberalization, and the decline in the minimum wage to its lowest level in real terms since its creation in 1940.

The sharp oscillations of the average wage have tended to be faithfully reflected in the wages of each educational, sectoral, and occupational category: all suffered severe losses in 1983, achieved big gains in 1985–1986, and lost again in the late 1980s and the early 1990s (Urani, 1993b). For 1981–1992 as a whole, there appears to have been no very clear association between level of education and income change.[16]

Perhaps more revealing are the differences in income trends among formal employees, informal employees, the self-employed, and employers. In 1982, the social cost of the recession appears to have fallen exclusively on the self-employed (see Table 8.1, p. 220). In 1983–1984, however, the cost of the adjustment of the current account fell predominantly on wage earners, both formal and informal, but especially the former. With accelerating inflation, formal sector workers had to accept a reduced indexation,

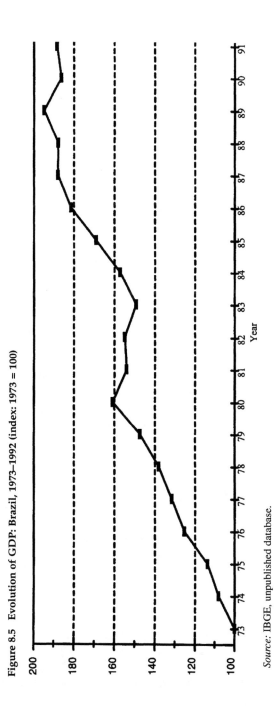

Figure 8.5 Evolution of GDP: Brazil, 1973–1992 (index: 1973 = 100)

Year

Source: IBGE, unpublished database.

Table 8.1   Evolution of Labor Real Income by Occupation: Brazil, 1981–1990
(index: 1981 = 100)

Occupation	Formal Employee	Informal Employee	Self-employed	Employer
1981	100.00	100.00	100.00	100.00
1982	102.52	106.96	95.32	102.09
1983	81.51	81.34	85.90	92.24
1984	79.21	83.07	84.46	91.24
1985	90.26	96.76	98.51	107.07
1986	109.31	138.75	153.75	166.11
1987	92.29	103.10	107.49	111.20
1988	96.10	98.00	98.52	106.70
1989	102.39	114.10	128.87	142.02
1990	81.07	109.92	100.15	101.52
Average 1981–1982	101.26	103.45	97.66	101.04
Average 1983–1984	80.36	82.20	85.18	91.74
Average 1985–1986	99.78	117.75	128.20	136.59
Average 1987–1990	92.96	106.28	108.77	130.36
Variable coefficient	0.10	0.10	0.15	0.18

Source: IBGE, PNAD, 1981–1990.

which reflected their loss of bargaining power in the recession. Their income fell by more than that of the self-employed. These latter also benefited the most from the generalized excess demand during the Cruzado Plan. Average real income rose more for informal employees than for formal sector workers, in spite of the increased indexation of formal labor contracts. Though the self-employed also suffered relatively large losses at the end of the 1980s and the beginning of the 1990s, when GDP growth rates fell considerably (see Tables 8.1 and 8.2), over the whole period from 1981 to 1992 they seem to have done as well as the other groups, whereas the formal employees appear to have done least well.

The data seem to suggest that wage earners, and particularly those in the formal sector, were better able to preserve their real income during recessions (if they were able to keep their jobs), presumably because they sell labor through relatively organized and formal contracts. However, the self-employed demonstrated a larger capability to protect their real incomes against the accelerating inflation but were (indirectly) more vulnerable to cyclical fluctuations in labor demand because they sell goods and services in competitive markets (Urani and Winograd, 1994). Finally, because the formal labor market operates in conditions of excess supply, an increase in demand does not necessarily mean an increase in wages; since the informal segment acts as a buffer, its supply is diminished (and its average wage increased) when labor demand increases in the formal sector. Overall, as Table 8.1 shows, wage earners suffered somewhat fewer income fluctuations than did the self-employed and employers. In summary, it appears that when adjustment is undertaken through recession, the burden

Table 8.2   Real Income by Occupation During the Last Three Months of the Collor Government[a], Six Metropolitan Regions (index: last three months of Sarney government[b] = 100)

Occupation	Porto Alegre	São Paulo	Rio de Janeiro	Belo Horizonte	Salvador	Recife
Employer	69.3	53.3	51.8	63.4	56.8	51.3
Formal employment	68.6	59.2	61.7	74.9	64.3	61.7
Informal employment	68.0	60.2	73.1	74.5	66.3	62.6
Self-employed	63.4	50.4	58.2	64.4	60.7	52.8

Source: IBGE, PME, 1989 (fourth quarter) and 1992 (third quarter).
Notes: a. 1993, third quarter.
   b. 1989, last quarter.

falls more on the informal segments of the labor force (and particularly on the self-employed), and when it is done through an acceleration of inflation, the opposite is the case.

Wage data by economic sector are available only for the 1980s, from Pesquisa Nacional por Amostra de Domicilios (PNAD) (see Table 8.3). Agriculture, whose wages are among the more volatile, seems to have been the main victim of the contractionary policy of 1982. In 1983–1984, by contrast, agricultural workers suffered smaller losses than others; two possible interpretations suggest themselves.

- The effects in the agricultural sector are somehow similar to those described above for the self-employed, in the sense that, like the trade and other private services sectors in urban areas, agriculture is characterized by generally informal labor relations, and income is determined competitively and is, as a result, very sensitive to cyclical fluctuations; or
- A great proportion of agriculture's output (coffee, soya, cocoa, oranges, etc.) being tradable, the sector may have benefited from the relative price changes promoted by the devaluation of 1983.

The explosion of aggregate demand during the Cruzado Plan resulted in significant gains for all sectors, but particularly—as expected—for the most competitive and less formalized ones: trade, building, agriculture, and other private services. Workers in the two sectors with the most highly formalized labor relations (manufacturing and public administration) had the smallest real income increases in 1986. With the stagflation of the late 1980s, finally, the only sector that had an increase in average real income was (not surprisingly) the financial one. All the others, and especially agriculture, lost significantly.

Taking the decade as a whole, the manufacturing sector, usually thought of as the modern sector par excellence, saw the largest real income

Table 8.3 Evolution of Labor Real Income by Economic Sector: Brazil, 1981–1990
(index: 1981 = 100)

	Agriculture	Manufacturing	Building	Trade	Public Admin.	Private Services	Financial
1981	100	100	100	100	100	100	100
1982	92	99	111	105	106	100	102
1983	88	80	63	85	84	80	82
1984	88	79	83	84	79	78	77
1985	99	88	94	99	97	88	89
1986	144	112	144	148	115	132	103
1987	99	90	104	102	97	100	96
1988	86	96	97	99	95	98	106
1989	113	101	125	135	102	122	119
1990	85	80	105	100	97	98	85
Average 1981–1982	91	99	105	102.25	103	100	101
Average 1983–1984	88	79.50	73	84.5	81.5	79	79.5
Average 1985–1986	121	100	119	123.5	106	110	96
Average 1987–1909	95.75	91.75	107.75	109	97.75	104.5	101.5
Variable coeffient	0.17	0.11	0.20	0.18	0.10	0.16	0.13

Source: IBGE, PNAD, 1981–1990.

declines. Workers in the building industry, trade, and other private services were most successful in preserving the purchasing power of their earnings against the macroeconomic turbulence of the 1980s, an unexpected result since these sectors are often seen as *buffers,* whose relative income should decrease in periods of economic stagnation like this one. (These were, however, the sectors of highest wage flexibility, and given the fluctuations in relative wages from year to year, any conclusion may be sensitive to the end year chosen.)

Overall, then, real wages were very flexible over the 1981–1992 period; the degree of flexibility differed somewhat by educational level and significantly by sector and by occupation. The record suggests that macroeconomic instability can force flexibility of real wages in either of two ways.

- Through fluctuations of aggregate demand, usually leading to corresponding oscillations in the unemployment rate and affecting principally the income of the most competitive segments of the labor force. Such macroeconomic adjustments tend to be more painful for informal than for formal workers and for those who work in agriculture, trade, or private services than for those in public administration or manufacturing; or

- Through accelerating inflation (caused, for instance, by an attempt to devalue the domestic currency in real terms), which especially affects the more organized segments of the labor force that have greater difficulty in indexing their income.

In the various adjustment phases, the workers in the most competitive markets lost the most under the "voluntary adjustment" of the early 1980s, benefited the most from the loss of control of aggregate demand during the heterodox attempts at stabilization and devaluation in the mid-1980s; and had the highest losses with the new recessive adjustments of the late 1980s and early 1990s. By contrast, during the agreements with the IMF, the burden of adjustment fell on the overall labor force, but especially on workers in the most organized segments. No single segment of the labor force showed strong wage rigidity.[17]

Allocative Flexibility

E. Amadeo and J. M. Camargo (1994) define allocative flexibility of the labor market in terms of its capability to continuously allocate the labor force so that the marginal productivity of a given type of labor is equal in all the activities in which it is used. Attainment of this goal depends both on real wage flexibility and on the absence of barriers to labor mobility. Symptoms of a lack of such flexibility include

> a high unemployment rate or sharp increases in that rate; increases of the degree of informality not caused by a reduction of the formal/informal wage differential; and changes in the sectorial composition of employment unrelated to an improvement of the relative wages in the sectors whose share of total employment is rising. (Amadeo and Camargo, 1994)

In spite of the low average growth rate and the high instability that characterized the 1980s, open unemployment did not worsen dramatically. Average unemployment in the main metropolitan areas never exceeded 7.5%, though it did record strong oscillations (see Table 8.4). It reached its maximum during the 1981–1983 recession, diminished considerably with the recovery starting in mid-1984—particularly during the Cruzado Plan— and finally increased again after the collapse of this plan, though it never returned, even during the deep recession of the early 1990s, to that earlier peak. If the range of this variable is measured in terms of percentage of the labor force, one might conclude that the adjustment of the labor market was effected about equally through unemployment (range of 4.4%) and through buffer-type informal sector employment (5.1%).

The unemployment rate shows qualitatively similar fluctuations over time for all educational categories. The rate for males oscillated more than

Table 8.4   Unemployment Rates (%) and Participation of the Informal Segments in the Overall Labor Force: Brazil, 1981–1990

	Unemployment Rate (%)	Informal Employment/ Labor Force (%)	Self-employed/ Labor Force (%)	Formal Employment/ Labor Force (%)
1981	6.63	28.12	25.95	39.30
1982	5.82	28.52	26.71	38.95
1983	7.55	32.94	26.66	32.85
1984	6.73	29.98	24.98	38.31
1985	5.10	29.17	26.09	39.64
1986	3.89	28.57	25.59	41.95
1987	5.06	28.36	25.19	41.39
1988	4.98	28.32	25.64	41.06
1989	4.13	27.97	24.40	43.50
1990	5.30	27.81	25.32	41.57
Average 1981–1982	6.23	28.32	26.33	39.12
Average 1983–1984	7.14	31.46	25.80	35.60
Average 1985–1986	4.50	28.87	25.84	40.79
Average 1987–1990	4.88	28.12	25.14	41.86
Variable coefficient	0.20	0.05	0.03	—

Source: IBGE, PNAD, 1981–1990.

that for females and exceeded the latter when overall unemployment was highest (1983); further examination reveals that male unemployment was generally higher than female for unskilled workers, whereas for the more skilled the opposite was the case.

The available data for the beginning of the 1990s (PME, for the six main metropolitan areas and for the years 1990–1993) reveal an unemployment rate both lower and less sensitive to the recession (in the sense of rising less) than that of the early 1980s; average duration had diminished (Bivar, 1993) in contrast to what happened during the 1981–1983 recession. This change of pattern seems strange given that the two recessions were of similar magnitude; that the reduction in demand for formal employees was stronger in the early 1990s than in the early 1980s; and that whereas in the 1980s no unemployment insurance system was in place, by the 1990s the one set up during the Cruzado Plan was present and starting to become rather expensive.[18] One possible explanation is that over the course of the intervening decade there was an important change in workers' expectations. One can imagine that in the early 1980s, because of both the previous history of sustained growth and the nature of the adjustment policies implemented, the workers interpreted the fall in output and in formal sector demand for labor as transitory phenomena and accordingly maintained the supply of labor to that segment of the labor market. By the early 1990s, in contrast, after an entire decade of low GDP growth and facing a genuine structural adjustment package, the workers may have quickly understood that the fall in labor demand was not necessarily transitory and therefore moved without delay to other segments of the labor market. This different response may indicate an increase in the allocative flexibility of labor (Amadeo and Camargo, 1994).

Informalization

The relative insensitivity of the unemployment rate to GDP fluctuations during this period could be a result of the capability of the informal segments of the labor market to absorb an excess supply in the formal sector caused by its wage rigidity. Participation in the informal sectors did vary countercyclically throughout the 1980s. Most striking is its dramatic increase from 28.5% of total employment in October 1982 to 32.9% in October 1983; while unemployment rose by just 1.7% of the labor force in the face of the decline in formal sector employment from 39.0% to 32.9%, informal employment rose by over 4% (see Table 8.4). A year later, however, the shares had nearly returned to their 1981–1982 levels. Thereafter there was a more or less continuous slow growth in the formal sector share at the expense of unemployment and of the informal sector.

Pesquisa Mensal de Emprego (PME) data, from four cities, show the same general pattern over the 1980s, though with rather stronger formal sector oscillations and differences of timing. After 1990 there was a drastic reduction in formal sector participation, by an average of about 8 percentage points. This sharp fall was reflected mainly in an increase in self-employment, with informal paid work easing up more modestly. As of the end of 1992, according to these data, both formal and paid informal shares were lower than in 1982, but self-employment had nevertheless risen in all of the cities.

These figures suggest a contrasting role of informal sector employment in the two recessions. During the first half of the 1980s, the informal segments of the labor market worked only partially as buffers, in the sense that their absorption of workers did not greatly exceed the increase in the number of persons unemployed. In the early 1990s, however, the buffer role was more important. On the one hand, the probability that a formal sector employee who lost her job would move to an informal job increased; on the other, the income losses caused by this transition diminished. In other words, this greater allocative flexibility of the labor market may have helped to attenuate the social impacts of macroeconomic adjustment during this period.

The 1980s as a whole saw a diminution of the relative importance of the primary and secondary sectors in overall employment and, consequently, an increasing participation of the tertiary sector. Although more slowly than in the previous decade—when the reduction in its share of employment was from 44% to about 25% (Cacciamali, 1992), agriculture's share decreased by another 6% to 19% (see Table 8.5). The building sector's employment share fell from 9% to 7%, whereas that of manufacturing was nearly constant. Tertiary employment was swelled by the increasing relative weight of public administration, trade, and particularly private services (by 1990, almost 30% of the total). In spite of an increasing participation in GDP, the financial sector's employment share showed no net advance over the decade. Average real income in each of these tertiary sectors was practically the same in 1990 as in 1981, whereas that of the other sectors was, in most cases, lower.[19] These sectors acted as good buffers, absorbing large amounts of labor without decreasing average income of the workers.

Macroeconomic Adjustment and Allocative Flexibility

There are at least three reasons for believing that the Brazilian labor market's allocative flexibility was high during the period studied in this chapter. First, the unemployment rate was maintained at relatively low levels, and its pattern became less and less related to that of GDP. Furthermore, the duration of unemployment increased during the 1980s but decreased in the early 1990s; it was, in any case, always very low when compared to that of most countries with this kind of data. Second, the informal segments of

Table 8.5   Evolution of Employment by Sectors: Brazil: 1981–1990

	Agriculture	Manufacturing	Building	Trade	Public Admin.	Private Services	Financial
1981	24.89	13.99	9.67	11.79	10.88	25.98	2.81
1982	25.08	13.88	8.58	11.69	11.05	26.80	2.92
1983	22.58	12.99	11.41	11.95	11.16	26.81	3.11
1984	25.78	13.28	6.93	12.09	11.33	27.42	3.17
1985	24.40	13.85	6.90	12.36	11.54	27.67	3.28
1986	22.63	14.90	7.56	12.77	11.80	27.54	2.79
1987	21.03	14.60	7.77	13.06	11.88	28.83	2.84
1988	20.79	14.34	7.41	13.05	12.40	29.24	2.77
1989	19.79	14.75	7.28	13.72	12.22	29.33	2.91
1990	19.27	14.19	7.20	14.31	12.37	29.90	2.76
Average 1981–1982	22.99	13.94	9.13	11.74	10.97	26.39	2.87
Average 1983–1984	24.18	13.14	9.17	12.02	11.25	27.12	3.14
Average 1985–1986	23.52	14.38	7.23	12.57	11.67	27.61	3.04
Average 1987–1990	20.22	14.47	7.42	13.54	12.22	29.33	2.82

Source: IBGE, PNAD, 1981–1990.

the labor market became progressively bigger and better buffers, in the sense that their share of the overall labor force became, more and more, the main counterpart to the formal sector labor demand and that formal/informal wage differentials were decreasing. Finally, the evolution of the sectoral composition of employment was such that the sectors with increases in relative wages were, with the exception of construction, those whose participation in overall employment increased the most.

Distributive Effects of Macroeconomic Adjustment

By the 1970s, Brazil had become famous as a country whose fast growth had not led to a low level of poverty because of the high and at times (the 1960s) rising inequality. During the 1980s, GDP growth fell abruptly; per capita GDP in 1990 was still a bit lower than in 1981. What were the consequences of the relative stagnation and the associated macroeconomic turbulence of this period for income inequality and poverty?

Labor income inequality increased during the 1980s as a whole (see Figure 8.6). One can deduce that as the average income decreased over this period, the incidence of poverty increased. In fact, all the deciles suffered a net decline in real income (see Table 8.6). Between the last quarter of 1989 and the third quarter of 1992 (the last year of Fernando Collor de Mello's government), the level of inequality was sharply reduced even as incomes fell dramatically (from 27% to 45% across the six metropolitan areas for which data are available). The average Gini coefficient for these six areas fell from 0.60 to 0.54, the sharpest such reduction ever recorded for the Brazilian economy. The income share of the richest decile diminished considerably in all of these metropolitan areas, but in most cases the

Figure 8.6 Personal Labor Income Inequality and Lorenz Curves: Brazil, 1981 and 1990

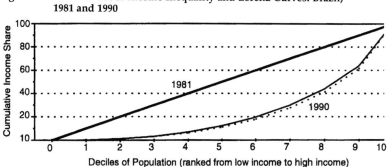

Source: Barros and Mendonça (1995), based on special tabulations of IBGE, PNAD, 1981 and 1990.

Table 8.6   Evolution of Average Real Income by Decile of the Personal Income Distribution: Brazil, 1981–1990 (index: 1981 average income = 100)

	1	2	3	4	5	6	7	8	9	10
1981	3.32	10.40	21.13	34.97	52.23	74.11	102.48	140.99	199.10	361.28
1982	3.16	10.18	20.76	34.59	51.90	73.65	101.73	140.08	199.48	366.37
1983	2.90	8.34	16.77	27.35	40.39	57.47	79.93	111.25	161.24	302.17
1984	2.61	8.10	16.73	27.29	40.15	57.32	79.93	111.34	160.35	299.93
1985	2.65	8.68	18.32	29.81	44.37	63.53	89.07	124.88	182.07	347.49
1986	4.87	15.34	29.10	46.05	68.38	97.35	135.06	187.13	267.64	507.78
1987	2.94	9.80	19.58	31.82	47.94	69.13	97.04	135.83	196.67	370.13
1988	2.23	7.61	16.36	27.02	40.96	59.02	83.06	117.31	172.19	342.53
1989	2.57	8.81	18.01	28.72	43.16	62.50	88.67	125.99	188.02	387.79
1990	2.85	9.23	17.11	27.77	42.13	61.52	87.57	124.19	181.53	349.55

Source: Barros and Mendonça (1995), based on special tabulations of PNAD/IBGE.
Note: a. Each figure refers to the average income of a given decile in a given year as a percentage of average 1981 income. Thus the average income of persons in decile 1 in 1990 was 2.85 percentage of the overall 1981 average income.

Figure 8.7   Percentage of Persons Living in Families with Average Income Below the Poverty Line: Brazil, Selected Years, 1981–1990

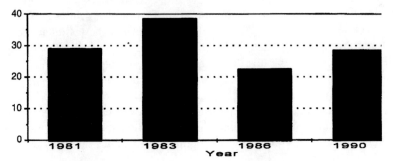

Source: Barros and Mendonça (1995), based on special tabulations of IBGE, 1981, 1983, 1986, and 1990.

share of the bottom deciles increased. The reduction of inequality in the early 1990s accompanied a recessive adjustment that, in contrast to that of a decade earlier, hurt the richest more than the poorest (see Figure 8.7).

Conclusion

Since the early 1980s, the Brazilian economy has had to confront severe adjustment challenges in the form of short-run imbalances caused by the external shocks that hit it in the late 1970s. The adjustment of the balance of payments was fast and extremely successful: from 1984 through the first half of the 1990s Brazil produced a trade surplus big enough to balance its current account. The adjustment was, however, extremely costly in terms of inflation and of real wage volatility and decline. On the one hand, the attempts at real devaluation of the domestic currency were at the root of the exponential acceleration of inflation during the first half of the 1980s. On the other hand, as the devaluation was accompanied by a strong reduction in aggregate demand, unemployment increased and real wages fell. As a consequence, income inequality and poverty rose considerably.

The inability of the orthodox stabilization therapies to combat inflation led the first civilian government (after more than two decades of military rule) to adopt heterodox anti-inflationary strategies that were strongly focused on price controls and with no attention to the pattern of aggregate demand. These strategies, and particularly the Cruzado Plan, were very successful in the short run, reducing the rate of inflation abruptly in a context of strong GDP growth and decreasing inequality (and thus, also of poverty alleviation). But the gains were ephemeral, since the combination of supply rigidities and demand explosion quickly produced an excess demand that had negative repercussions on the balance-of-payments equilibrium. The need to devalue again in an environment of rapid demand expansion brought renewed, severe inflation. The end of the 1980s, therefore, was dominated by consecutive attempts to avoid hyperinflation that combined orthodox and heterodox instruments. As a consequence, the trajectory of the economy became even more erratic than in the previous period, and average GDP growth fell significantly. Nonetheless, the unemployment rate did not return to the levels of the first half of the decade, since the informal segments of the labor market—and particularly self-employment—began to act more effectively as buffers. By the end of the decade, all deciles of the personal income distribution were poorer (in real terms) than in 1981—and inequality was higher.

In the early 1990s, a new democratically elected government tried shock therapy against inflation; its key elements were a very strong reduction in the money supply and a set of structural reforms including trade liberalization, privatization, and the attempt to eliminate wage indexation. The initial results on the anti-inflationary front were modest, and the policy generated a deep recession but not a very significant rise in the unemployment rate, despite the increasing importance of the unemployment insurance system. The main counterpart of the diminution of the formal sector's share in overall employment during this period was the growth of informal employment. These movements were accompanied by a fall of formal/informal wage differentials that implied a considerable diminution of income inequality. This was not enough, however, to avoid a strong increase in poverty. At the beginning of the 1990s, consequently, the Brazilian economy was in a situation opposite to that of two decades before, when during the *economic miracle* both the distance between rich and poor and the total income were rising per capita.

Notes

André Urani works at the Instituto de Economia da Universidade do Rio de Janeiro (IE-UFRJ) and the Directoria de Pesquisa do Instituto de Pesquisa Econômica Aplicada. He thanks Albert Berry, Gustavo Indart, José Marcio Camargo, Martin Rama, and José Carlos dos Reis Carvalho for their useful comments on a preliminary version of this chapter and Mariana Ramalho for efficient research assistance. Any remaining errors are his.

1. As measured by IBGE's Pesquisa Nacional por Amostra de Domicílios (PNAD).

2. Note that 1981 was a year of deep recession, with the result that both the unemployment rate and the share of the informal segments (informal employment plus self-employment) in the labor force were unusually high. It is, however, the first year of the 1980s for which there are PNAD data because in 1980 the demographic census substituted for this survey.

3. Amadeo et al. (1993) show that this is typically the case of the Fundo de Garantia por Tempo de Serviço (FGTS).

4. Under Law 6708 of November 1979, the twice-yearly adjustment of nominal wages was set at 110% of past inflation for workers earning less than three minimum wages (MW), 100% for those earning between three and ten MWs and 80% for those earning more than ten MWs. In January 1991, Law 6886 increased the progressivity of the rules.

5. No fewer than five different wage policies were implemented during the agreements with the IMF, from the beginning of 1983 to 1985. Law 2012 (February 1983) set the adjustment at 100% of past inflation for workers earning less than three MWs, 95% for those between three and seven MWs, and 80% for those between seven and fifteen MWs. By August of that year Law 2045 set the adjustments at 80% of past inflation for all workers. Further changes occurred over the next year.

6. Under this rule, nominal wages were to be fully adjusted each time that the accumulated rate of inflation reached 20%.

7. Note, though, that as we see in this chapter, the path of income inequality during this period was not related in any simple way to the evolution of the educational profile of the labor force (see also Barros, Cardoso, and Urani [1993]).

8. In most Latin American countries (Argentina, Mexico, Venezuela, etc.), the sharp increase in external debt was triggered by capital flight.

9. Mario Henrique Simonsen, the planning minister at the time, recommended a decrease in the rate of growth of GDP as a means of reducing the current account deficit and avoiding an acceleration of the rate of inflation. This therapy was judged inconsistent with the government's political aim of restoring democracy. As a consequence, Simonsen was rapidly replaced by Antonio Delfim Netto, who had been finance minister during the "economic miracle" of 1968–1973.

10. The new constitution (in force since 1988) and the uncertainty about the length of the government mandate and hence of the proximity of the first free presidential elections since the beginning of the 1960s contributed to this lack of political stability.

11. The nontariff barriers were abruptly abolished and "tariffied," and the average tariff was progressively reduced. For more details on the timing and depth of the trade reform, see Cordeiro (1992).

12. In contrast to what occurred in Mexico and Argentina, for instance. This fact has at least two possible explanations: (1) the reforms in Brazil were done in

a recessionary environment, and (2) the nominal exchange rate was not used—until the implementation of the Real Plan in mid-1994—as the "anchor" of the new monetary standard.

13. If, however, the result of the indexation rules is a real wage level inconsistent with the demand and supply of labor, too successful indexation can produce a disequilibrium wage rate with the distributional effects noted in the discussion of fiscal restraint. Or if firms have the power to determine their prices through, for instance, a fixed mark-up rule, use of this rule could produce an acceleration of the rate of inflation that would eliminate the initial effect on the real wage. (The trigger-point rule, implemented during the Cruzado Plan, applied to all the formal wages and represented a strong increase in the degree of indexation; it became explosive when, from the beginning of 1987, inflationary pressures reappeared as a consequence of the rationing provoked by the price and nominal exchange rate freezing.) Finally, if in spite of the inflationary process there is a lack of demand for certain goods, an increase in the real wage could raise that demand. It is clear, in the light of these various considerations, that the net effect of an increase in the degree of indexation on the labor market is ambiguous.

14. In spite of the failure of this measure, it would be adopted three more times, in the Bresser, Summer, and Collor plans respectively, but for shorter periods than on this first occasion.

15. The last available PNAD is that of 1990. Pesquisa Mensal de Emprego (PME) is a monthly household survey taken in the six main Brazilian metropolitan regions: Porto Alegre (PA), São Paulo (SP), Rio de Janeiro (RJ), Belo Horizonte (BH), Salvador (SA), and Recife (RE). There are some important differences between PNAD and PME: PNAD, in fact, is an *annual* survey that covers the *entire Brazilian territory* (except the rural zones of the North region, i.e., the Amazon), not only the main metropolitan areas.

16. Barros, Cardoso, and Urani (1993) and Bonelli and Ramos (1993) have shown that the evolution of Brazilian income inequality was not related to that of the educational profile of the labor force since the beginning of the 1980s.

17. Barros and Mendonça (1994b) show, through a very detailed analysis of PME data, that formal employees' real wage flexibility during the 1980s was low relative to other segments of Brazil's labor market but very high by international standards.

18. Almost four million people accessed these benefits in 1993. For more details on the recent developments of the Brazilian unemployment-insurance program, see Azeredo and Chahad (1992) and Machado (1994).

19. Average real income in public administration fell slightly, as noted earlier. This was due to increasing participation of unskilled workers and the diminution of their average wage.

Part 3

Conclusion

9

Conclusion

Albert Berry

Income distribution has been highly unequal in most countries of Latin America as far back as the record extends. Accordingly, poverty has been more prevalent than would be suggested by the average incomes of these countries, most of which fall in the upper- to middle-income range for developing nations; as of 1993, the regional average was about U.S.$3,000, yet something like a third of the population was below the poverty line. Depressing as this current situation may be, it is clear that the incidence of poverty was declining at a fairly brisk clip over most of the postwar period until the region was racked by the regional crisis of the 1980s, associated mainly with the international debt crisis. Over the period 1950–1980, the region's per capita income rose by about 3% per year, and the incidence of poverty (defined as in Altimir, 1982) probably fell from a level of about 65% in 1950 to around 25% by 1980. Had per capita income growth continued at the earlier rate, poverty incidence would probably have fallen to about 10–15% by the end of the century, and it would have been realistic to think that no more than a few percent would have been critically poor.

But the crisis erupted and pushed poverty rates back up again. By the early 1990s, growth had returned to the region, but it has not, from 1990 to 1995 at least, been able to regain the momentum of the precrisis years. In particular, with gross domestic product (GDP) growth still less than half its 1950–1980 average of over 5.5% per year, the per capita gain of about 1% per year was only a third of what it had been in that earlier period. With economic growth—a key determinant of poverty incidence—sputtering, it is especially important that positive rather than negative impacts on poverty levels come from the other factors: changes in the distribution of income, in particular changes that involve the shares of the groups below and near the poverty line; and poverty redressal policies (social spending that affects poverty, the various types of transfers forming the social safety net, etc.). The great concern at this time, together with the mediocre growth of the region so far in the 1990s, is the fact that income distribution has shifted toward greater inequality, thus raising the rate of poverty associated with any given level of per capita income and lowering the poverty reduction associated with any given rate of economic growth. Meanwhile, more conservative monetary and fiscal policies have been implemented as part of the economic reforms, in order to help close an external imbalance or stabilize domestic prices (both of which may be considered important to making the country a more acceptable partner in today's international markets). These policies have impact on the poor: fiscal tightness affects them through social spending and monetary tightness through a reduction of financial flows specifically directed toward the poor.

It is too early to judge the lasting effects of the economic crisis, the need to adjust (including the curtailing of total public expenditures and perhaps those in the social areas as well), and the impact of attempts to improve the efficiency of social spending. As N. Lustig (1995: 31–32) notes in her recent review of the regions's experience with poverty in the 1980s, none of the countries was ready to adequately protect the poor from the impact of the crisis and adjustment. Social investment funds, for example, were usually implemented several years or even a decade after the crisis had erupted. As the fiscal noose tightened in the 1980s, it was inevitable that the provision of social services in many countries would be curtailed: either growth of the quantity of services provided had to slow, quality had to decline, or efficiency of provision had to improve. The threat that the cuts would be prejudicial to the poor was evident. One dangerous potential effect of fiscal tightening is an increase in the share of spending going to wages (e.g., Peru) and sometimes to administration as well (e.g., Venezuela)[1] because of the resistance against and hence the difficulty of cutting this component of government costs. As a result, too little is spent on complementary materials, equipment, and investment, and effectiveness is curtailed. Where this effect is in evidence, and when the need to reduce spending is not short-lived, major rather than minor institutional adjustments are likely to be necessary to avoid a lasting decline in quality. Falling morale, better workers leaving and poorer ones staying, and other negative fallouts from the fiscal tightening also frequently contribute to quality erosion beyond that implicit in the expenditure cuts per se.

Judging by the evidence presented in Lustig (1995), there seems to have been no very general pattern with respect to whether spending on the social sectors fell faster or slower than other public spending. In Argentina, social spending was actually higher in the 1980s than in the previous decade, both as a share of total public expenditures and in real per capita terms (Beccaria and Carciofi, 1995: 202); the health, education, and other social systems limped along with their accumulated weaknesses, and one main effect of the squeeze was declining standards in education (Beccaria and Carciofi, 1995). In the case of Mexico, the government drastically reduced total expenditures during the adjustment of 1983–1988, with spending on social development hit harder than that on nonsocial categories (Friedmann, Lustig, and Legovini, 1995: 348–349). Though cuts in education and health were less than for other social areas, basic (primary and junior high) education was cut more than other education, and programs targeted to the poor were subject to sharp cuts.

Social spending tended to either fall in absolute terms or to suffer a slowing of its rate of growth during the crisis and adjustment years. But the social indicators other than household income—life expectancy, infant mortality, average years of schooling, enrollment rates, and so on—tended to continue to improve even during the crisis years. This outcome is variously interpreted as a reflection of the lag between investment in and the benefits from spending on education and health, for example; of the fact that the quanta of some services do not fall as much in times of recession as does spending on them (since real wages of service workers tend to fall sharply, reducing costs of provision); and of the fact that technological improvements have permitted health improvements even where expenditures have fallen. D. Raczynski and P. Romaguera (1995: 323) argue, with reference to the Chilean case, that in a country with a broad preexisting system of educational and health services, it is possible to sustain improvements in welfare indicators despite deteriorating income distribution and increases in absolute poverty. Existing services and long-standing national programs with social legitimacy facilitated the implementation of programs that targeted the very poor. Wage declines and other strains did, however, lead to loss of quality of some services (see Table 9.1).

That inequality has risen in most countries of the region is generally accepted (see Chapters 1 and 2 and Morley, 1995). The increases, in many cases dramatic, have prevented a return to the relatively successful attack on poverty that characterized the precrisis years. For each of the three countries with the largest absolute levels of poverty in the region—Brazil, Mexico, and Peru—it will be necessary to wait a little longer before it is possible to judge whether there is a lasting increase in inequality and how severe it may be. In Brazil, the reforms that in many other countries have coincided with increasing inequality are too recent for the effects to be clear; in Mexico the observed changes from 1989–1992 include anomalies not yet understood; and in Peru, although first indications are that the reforms undertaken in the 1990s have not produced greater inequality, prudence suggests waiting and monitoring for a while before drawing firm conclusions.

With neither the growth nor the distribution records looking good thus far in the 1990s, it is of obvious importance to look for ways to improve performance on both counts. Although the focus of the previous chapters

Table 9.1   Summary Economic Statistics for Latin America and the Caribbean, 1950–1995

Indicator	1950	1950–1980	1980	1980–1990	1990	1990–1995	1995
Per capita GNP (1993 dollars)	1,270	3.0	3,086	−1.7	2,660	0.8	2,769
GDP growth rate	—	5.7	—	1.2	—	2.9	—
GDP per capita growth rate	—	3.0	—	−0.8	—	1.0	—
Incidence of poverty	65%	—	25%	—	31%	—	26%
Life expectancy	—	—	—	—	68	—	69
Population growth rate	—	2.7	—	2.1	—	1.8	—

Sources: Per capita GNP figures based on the 1993 figure of 2,950 from World Bank (1995: 163), and forward and backward extrapolations using estimated growth rates from CEPAL (1995) and ECLAC, *Economic Survey of Latin America and the Caribbean*, various issues.

Notes: For incidence of poverty, see Berry (Chapter 1) for 1950 and 1980; the 1990 figure is based on Morley (1994: 20), whose figures for 1980 and 1989 are 26.5% and 31% respectively. His figure for 1980 is a little above ours, but we assume the percent change would be about the same as his over 1980–1989; since regional per capita GDP fell in 1990, we assume there was a poverty increase in that year. The 1995 figure is based on the 5.1% increase in per capita income between 1990 and 1995 that brings the per capita figure within about 2.5% of that for 1980, with growth in two of the three countries with the largest absolute amount of poverty in the region (Brazil and Peru) and decline in the third (Mexico). Figures for 1980, 1990 in ECLAC 1995a: 146, show a higher poverty incidence for each year, but the trend is similar.

is not the process of growth per se, it is important to assess each aspect of economic and social policy from that perspective simultaneously with the distribution perspective. The fact that the success stories of East Asia have outperformed the Latin American countries on both grounds is of interest, since it suggests that there may be more complementarity than conflict between the two goals when policy is well designed. Policymaking in the region needs henceforth to reflect an understanding of the sources of the observed increases in inequality. What must be hoped for is that those components of policy that contribute most to growth (including elements of the new market-friendly economic model)[2] are not also the ones contributing most to inequality. The East Asian experience suggests clear grounds for optimism in this regard, but the issues must be thought through carefully in the Latin American context, and such thinking is still incipient at this point.

One main concern of the chapters that make up this book has been to assess the distributional trends in the countries reviewed and to advance the discussion of the sources of those generally negative trends. The conclusions may be summarized as follows:

1. There has been a preponderance of negative shifts in income distribution over the last two decades in Latin America, including most of the

countries studied here—Chile, Argentina, Uruguay, Mexico, Colombia, Ecuador, and the Dominican Republic.[3]

2. In most cases, the timing of increases in inequality has coincided clearly with that of the implementation of economic reforms on the trade, labor market, and often other fronts. In a number of cases, other events were also occurring that might have played a significant role, in particular economic downturn or crisis and inflation. But those countries that have recovered reasonably normal growth rates and relative price stability have, with few exceptions, higher levels of inequality than before they entered their downturns, so it seems clear that those events do not bear sole responsibility for the worsening. The reforms are implicated by the timing of the shifts and by the apparent presence of some mechanisms that might be expected to increase inequality. Costa Rica, Peru, and Jamaica may have avoided such negative shifts, however. If further analysis demonstrates this to have been the case, their experiences may provide valuable positive lessons for other countries.

3. Since the reforms with the greatest apparent impacts in most of the countries seem to have been those in the areas of labor and of trade/foreign investment, the possibility that they have contributed to the shift must be taken seriously. It seems likely that technological change has also played a role. It may be that the factors at work have differed considerably across the countries. A great deal more detailed research will be necessary before the central processes have been adequately identified. Still, it is very important to advance understanding on some of the major fronts, certainly including the impacts of trade/foreign investment policy and of labor-market policy.

4. Meanwhile, however, it is clearly necessary to attack the distribution problem with as many useful instruments as possible, regardless of the origins of the deterioration. This includes, on the one hand, a reconsideration of some of the reform policies themselves and, on the other, a somewhat independent search for any instruments that are likely to have a positive effect on the generation of productive employment for lower-income people and hence on distribution. Direct poverty redressal instruments are among these.

Policy Implications

Both the recent and longer-run experience of growth and equity in Latin America and the varying experiences of other parts of the world are relevant to the specification of some of the main priority policy areas for the coming years. In this specification, it is helpful to think both in terms of the sectors that are most likely to contribute to growth with equity and in terms of main policy areas likely to contribute to such a process. In terms of sectors, particular importance attaches to small-scale agriculture and to small and medium-sized enterprise outside the agricultural sector. Their importance should not preclude the search for policies that may raise the labor intensity of large farms and large nonagricultural enterprises or at least prevent their labor intensity from falling. But only very limited optimism would seem called for in this aspect of policy, so the main attention is appropriately focused, one way or another, on the small-scale sector.

1. One priority is *healthy rural development,* in which income is relatively well distributed among the population and incentives for savings, investment, innovation, and growth are good. Such a healthy rural sector has been a hallmark of the most successful development experiences around the world, including those of Japan, Taiwan, Indonesia, Costa Rica, and others; it has been the normal precursor to healthy overall development both in the postwar period and in the historical experience of the now-developed countries. Achieving it involves continued attention to raising productivity in small-scale agriculture, especially in countries where this remains the dominant sector of the economy and in low-income regions where agriculture is the main source of income. It also involves the design and implementation of policies to facilitate and strengthen rural nonagricultural activities, especially in countries where the rural share of population remains high and the potential for such linkages appears to be good. Support for rural microenterprise is one aspect of such policy, as is investment in rural infrastructure, education, and health systems. Most countries of Latin America have been strikingly deficient in these areas, for reasons that hark back to the highly unequal distribution of land that they suffer and the absence of land reform to correct it. It will thus be a major challenge for them to approximate the success stories cited above. The danger that future agricultural growth within the outward-oriented model will have major negative impacts on income distribution is well demonstrated by the recent experience of Paraguay (see Chapter 1). But there are enough positive experiences in the region, albeit mostly on a small scale thus far, to provide some grounds for optimism. Small agriculture advanced relatively well in Colombia from the mid-1970s through much of the 1980s, partly, it would appear, on the basis of the sort of support provided within the integrated rural development programs. The at-least-temporary success of vegetable exporting based on small farm production in Guatemala was noted in Chapter 1. Attempts to assist small-scale producers outside agriculture are more widespread than before. And rural educational levels, although still very low in most countries, are on the rise.

It will be important to take advantage of each of these conditions or openings but also to be realistic in any assessment of how fast the rural sector is likely to change for the better in most of Latin America. Whether reasonably inclusionary policies are possible without major structural reform (e.g., significant land redistribution) remains a big unknown. Although some pessimism is no doubt warranted, policymakers must nonetheless confront the challenges in the hope that some useful policy adjustments are possible.

2. General *support for small and medium-sized enterprise* (SME, including microenterprise), in the form of improved credit institutions, marketing assistance (fairs, etc.), and technological and training assistance, is another priority that overlaps with the previous one because some of the enterprises in question are found in rural areas. The SME sector will continue to provide the bulk of new jobs for some time. For that part of the sector that has export potential, special support will be needed since otherwise the export basket, being dominated by large enterprise, may not create much employment. Although many SMEs face serious problems in breaking into export markets, these problems are now somewhat better understood, and it is not unreasonable to believe that well-designed policies could appear in some Latin American and Caribbean (LAC) countries over the course of the next decade. And for that part of the sector that is import-competing, it will be important that it not suffer from unstable exchange rates, import surges, or other challenges to its existence and health that have nothing to do with its fundamental efficiency.

Though policymakers now recognitize the sector's importance, the quality of policymaking in the SME area remains low in almost all countries of the region, especially with respect to the size range above microenterprises. Though many SMEs can be significantly affected by macroeconomic, trade, and exchange rate policy, in most countries the sector has virtually no voice in the making of such policy, and policymakers typically know almost nothing about the sector and its needs. The increasing dominance of policy by macro specialists unfamiliar with the economics of major sectors of the economy (agriculture and SME come immediately to mind) may make the criteria for policymaking unduly simplistic.

The experience of many counties, including Japan and some of its Asian neighbors, illustrates the potential importance of linkages between efficient modern industry and smaller firms (Kaneda, 1980; Cho, 1995). Though the evidence is scanty from Latin America, it suggests that such mutually beneficial synergies are significantly less frequent, a situation attributed by some to the history of excessive protection under import-substituting policies, the lack of competition in local markets, and the daunting initial gap between the large and the small in productivity, technology, and even culture. The contribution of effective linkages of this sort is likely to be more important in the open economy than in the closed one; in countries where the larger firms do most of the exporting (as in Brazil, for example), export success may bring little productive employment in its wake unless smaller subcontractors are hooked into the process. Policies to foster productive small-small and small-large linkages may thus have a good payoff at this time; although not too much is known about what interventions may assist the process, some useful experiments are under way in the region (Berry, 1997).

3. A central priority is the *strengthening of the human capital* of persons toward the lower end of the earnings profile, through improved coverage and quality of primary education, better and more applicable vocational education, and support for on-the-job training for lower-skilled persons. There are both positive and negative reasons to put weight on improving the distribution of education and human capital.[4] On the positive side, it appears that the character and rapidity of technological change has raised the payoff to skills, or perhaps better put, it has changed the set of skills on which the economic payoff is high and increased the advantages of training-for-flexibility and general training. On the negative side, there is evidence from several LAC countries (e.g., Mexico and at times Chile) that earnings differentials by level of education have widened in recent years, often in the wake of changed economic policies or greater outward orientation. Since unequal distribution of human capital is now perhaps the main single source of inequality in LAC countries, it is obviously important to avoid outcomes in which either earnings differentials by level of human capital become even wider or the distribution of that capital becomes even more unequal. The most straightforward way to avoid such outcomes is to diminish the concentration of such capital. In the context of most of the poorer LAC countries, this means ensuring that as few people as possible are stuck with low levels of education or poor-quality education. In some countries, making sure that everyone completes primary school may be the highest-priority aspect of this response; in others, the quality of primary school, especially in rural and poorer urban areas, is central. Adult education may also be very important in some cases, as may a more flexible and effective vocational training system. The objective of such policy is to diminish the size of the lower tail of the income distribution when the factor underlying the low incomes of the people found there is their lack of human capital.

4. Maintenance or increase in the *level of social spending* (on education, health, etc.) and improvements in the quality of and payoff on that spending is necessary. The importance of raising the human capital of those toward the bottom of the income profile highlights the importance of raising the level of "effective social spending." Whether this necessarily requires an increase in total social spending remains to be ascertained in each country, but the reality or threat of shrinking spending (depending on the country) obviously creates a challenge to dramatically raise the effectiveness of or

to redirect such expenditures toward poorer people. The experience with targeting social expenditures toward the poor is growing, and it is hoped that it will be a useful tool in raising the payoff, though overall success cannot be judged with any precision at this time. There is evidence that maintaining such spending has apparently enabled a few countries to avoid increasing levels of inequality (Puerto Rico and perhaps Costa Rica). Absence of an adequate safety net can have strongly counterproductive effects on the level of social stress, crime, and insecurity, of which there has been all too much evidence in the countries of Latin America. Major increases in the levels of crime in countries have occurred in developed countries like England during the period of increasing inequality and shrinkage of the safety net since the early 1980s.

5. *Careful management of the new freer trade system* so that it does not lead to instability and to long-run loss of productive capacity, especially in the activities and types of firms that create many of the lower-paying jobs, is essential. In part this involves developing the instruments now in widespread use in industrial countries to prevent the effects of "dumping" and other "unfair practices," import surges, and so on. These instruments are not yet in place in most developing countries as they lower their trade barriers but will be needed quickly.

To the extent that the infant-industry argument for protection comes back into favor, as it will if the effects of the now freer trade system on growth and distribution are ultimately judged to fall well short of the optimal, ways will be needed to impose such protection more carefully and selectively than in the past.

6. Great care in the *management of the capital account* is required so as to avoid overvaluation and instability of the real exchange rate, since both of these outcomes tend to discourage exports, lower growth, and increase unemployment. Although there remains a considerable weight of opinion in the international financial institutions and elsewhere that favors totally free movement of capital, the absence of serious theoretical support for such a preference together with the obvious evidence of its costs will hopefully move opinion toward a more prudent middle ground fairly soon. Since greater freedom of capital movement than in the past will no doubt remain the norm, developing countries like those of Latin America will have to make decisions on how much freedom of movement to allow and what instruments of control to use. The fact that the two countries with the most successful growth performances over recent years, Chile and Colombia, both use controls is probably indicative of things to come. Avoiding exchange rate fluctuations appears especially important to small and medium-sized exporters, on whose employment-creating capacity so much depends in the future.

7. *Strong regulatory regimes* must be developed to complement the process of privatization, which can otherwise easily lead to a concentration

of wealth and income as favored groups reap the benefits of underpriced assets. In the case of Chile, as noted in Chapter 1, extensive privatization led to an acute concentration of ownership and the formation of large conglomerates. Another sizable share of national income was transferred to private banks and other debtors via bailouts with public funds. Both of these programs probably contributed to the dramatic increase in inequality in Chile between 1973 and the mid-1980s.

8. Policymakers must carefully consider *changes in labor-market institutions*. The conceptual and empirical underpinnings of some ongoing reforms appear to be weak, and potential negative effects need to be duly taken into account. Among the labor-market institutions under serious debate (and frequent attack) in the current reform programs are the level of job security built into the labor codes, the high level of nonwage costs, the mobility-reducing nontransferability of some pension plans and systems, and the management of the minimum wage (including the way it is indexed for inflation). The appropriate role and structure of the unions is a more general question that lies behind these more specific concerns.

Given the inequalities so manifestly present in most LAC countries, the important potential role of unions as a defense of the worker is obvious, and their contribution along these lines may have been considerable. As in many other developing countries, however, the unions and much of the legislation have been criticized as protecting the interests of a labor elite at the expense of both the capitalist class and the rest of workers; contributing to microeconomic inefficiency and macroeconomic instability; and, of particular relevance to poverty and income distribution questions, pushing down the earnings of the poorer, unprotected workers by reducing labor demand in the formal sector of the economy. It is noteworthy that some of the more egalitarian countries of the developing world are found in East Asia, where unions and labor legislation are less powerful than in LAC. Within Latin America, however, there appears to have been a positive association between equality and the strength of labor legislation and unions; Argentina had both the lowest level of inequality (prior to the late 1970s) and the strongest legislation and unions.

Though many of the criticisms leveled at the previous set of institutions and policies that held sway until the recent wave of reforms are likely to be valid, at least up to a point,[5] research has not gone far in clarifying the details of a really good system or of how to proceed from an inferior to a better one. There is little persuasive empirical evidence to help guide the policymaker as to how the reforms undertaken to date have affected or will affect performance. It is hard to sort out any growth effects of the reform packages from those of other factors at work at the same time, and it has not been possible to demonstrate convincingly that they have led to an increase in "productive mobility" of labor, reduced firms' reluctance to hire, or raised human capital accumulation. If labor-market reforms have had an impact on distribution, they have almost certainly been negative. Chile has had the most complete reform; there the question is whether or how much the changes adopted contributed to the long and costly adjustment, whether they continue to have a negative impact on income distribution, and whether they have contributed to the strong growth since the mid-1980s. S. Horton, R. Kanbur, and D. Mazumdar (1991: 42) deduce from the comparison of the experiences of Bolivia and Costa Rica that the wholesale dismantling of labor institutions is neither necessary nor sufficient to economic success.

The impact of minimum wages on employment, wages, and income distribution remains controversial in the LAC countries, partly because enforcement is variable and not always well known and partly because the effects are neither easily predictable nor detectable even when enforcement is systematic. But S. A. Morley (1995) strongly argues that avoiding too great a decrease in the minimum wage was helpful in avoiding increases in inequality and poverty in Latin American countries in the 1980s.

Given the major dislocations in the labor market due to the crises and structural adjustment programs, the value of effective labor-adjustment support programs has not been lost on the LAC governments. Some have initiated new schemes, some of them adaptations of systems in use in developed countries. They have shown reasonable promise and deserve to be retained as one instrument in the tool kit.[6]

The reform of labor institutions may well be an important task at this time; but it is not clear what the reformed system should look like. It should no doubt avoid some of the extremes of labor protection that have contributed to immobility, lack of worker incentive, and inefficiency. It should shift some of the onus of protection against unemployment from the firm to an unemployment insurance system of some sort; many countries have moved in this direction. Perhaps most of all, it needs to be thought through with the needs of small and medium-sized enterprise in mind together with those of the workers. In the past much legislation has de facto not been applied to firms in this size range. Some continuing de facto difference between the regulations applicable to smaller and to larger firms is probably desirable, but the existing reforms do not appear to have been based on much understanding of the modus operandi of small firms.

9. *Technological change* may have been a significant factor in the recent increases in inequality in LAC countries. It is probable that the speed and character of technological change will directly and indirectly be a major and perhaps a dominant determinant of the evolution of productive employment and income distribution in the LAC countries, as elsewhere, over the coming decades. While bringing benefits in the form of growth, such change also holds the threat of increased income inequality, given

current human capital patterns. At present, governments tend to have little understanding and even less access to policy instruments that could give them some direct control over the process and the effects of technological change. Support for small farms, for microenterprise, and for small and medium-sized enterprise can influence these outcomes indirectly, since such units tend to choose less capital-intensive technologies than do larger ones. One of the issues in the assessment of the relative merits of alternative trade policies is the way they affect the evolution of technology.

Technological change has long been suspect as a key factor in the inability of Latin America's growth to generate enough increased demand for labor to improve income distribution. The main argument was that technology developed in industrial countries was not suited to the factor proportions of the region and that it tended to be transferred with little adaptation. V. E. Tokman (1989) suggests that the prevalence of foreign technology may have played a role in falling real wages of unskilled workers in a number of LAC countries, though others feel that this view is too pessimistic. The "appropriate technology" question is an especially tricky one for LAC, since the region is less labor-abundant than the Asian countries; its comparative advantage in labor is less obvious. Technological change is essential, but if it is either too fast[7] or of the wrong type, its distributional effects are likely to be negative and even its growth effects uncertain. It is this "double-edged sword" aspect of technology that makes the policy decisions about it so tricky. We are still searching for adequate inducement mechanisms to generate the "right" rate of change. When well complemented by a high investment rate, a strong human capital formation policy, and a strong SME technology policy, the risks associated with fast technological adoption are reduced. It is likely that exchange rate and trade policies have impacts on the pattern (as well as the rate) of technology change, but these have not been well identified thus far. Logic dictates that industrialized-country technology will sometimes be inappropriate, but empirically about all that can be said so far is that, if the extensive technological contact with the developed world over the postwar period as a whole has had negative effects on employment and distribution, these were not strong enough to produce a generalized worsening of distribution in the region prior to the crisis. It is possible that the transfer occurring after the crisis has played a role in the observed worsening of distribution in many developed countries of the region since the more liberalized trade and investment arrangements permit a freer flow of technology and a faster process of catching up. Concern with the appropriateness of technology needs to be kept very much alive, and a major research effort directed at both better understanding the distributional impacts of technological change and assessing the potential of various policy instruments needs to be undertaken.

10. It is evident that there will be a period of continuing or recurring poverty and distribution crises in the countries of the region. Accordingly, effective *poverty redressal policies* will be important over at least the medium run. The Puerto Rican experience, in which the rise in transfer payments prevented an increase in inequality and a possible increase in poverty over parts of the 1970s and 1980s, is interesting in this regard (see Chapter 1), although the fact that the transfers in question came from the United States means that their level would be hard to replicate elsewhere.

A number of LAC countries, including Brazil, Bolivia, Chile, and Peru, introduced emergency employment policies in response to the labor-market crises of the 1970s and 1980s. They appear to have been effective for these emergency situations, can be implemented quickly and at low cost, and can be quite selective and hence help the poorest. They tend to raise the income of lower-income families rather than lower unemployment; 70–90% of the beneficiaries were women (Tokman, 1989: 168). To avoid mismatches, it is important to spell out the characteristics of the persons to be helped and take these into account in the sort of jobs provided.

11. It is urgent to *increase the capacity for planning and monitoring* in key areas, including SME and human capital policy. Most LAC countries have given less serious attention to policy in the social areas (health, education, and labor) or to SMEs than to macroeconomic policy, trade policy, and so on. Yet it is clear that the quality of policymaking in the former areas will be pivotal to the rate of poverty alleviation in the coming years. In most countries, some appropriate and needed policy changes or foci have been identified, but there are a number of important policy questions to which the answer is not clear at this time. Further, the best feasible means to achieving such agreed-upon goals as quality improvement in primary education or technical transfers to small enterprises are not clear and will certainly require not only solid, up-front analysis but, probably even more important, a system with the monitoring capacity to allow for the early correction of mistakes. As countries consider significant policy changes in areas like these, it is distressing to see how little clear evidence is brought to bear on what works best.

The analysis and monitoring system needed to help guide countries toward an effective and efficient education and training system or a well-designed and well-performing support system for SMEs will not be easy to attain, since it involves several features that are almost completely the opposite of past practices. It needs to produce solid analyses on the key controversial issues, to greatly improve administrative and implementation capacity, and to mount a solid information/monitoring/analysis system to keep track of progress in those areas in which experimental policies are undertaken.

Many LAC countries suffer a grave shortage of top-notch personnel in their social sector ministries and a correspondingly inadequate planning/

analysis/monitoring capacity in these areas. In the SME area, the problem is partly that no clear institutional base acts as the focus of policy considerations. There is no organized and up-to-date compilation of information that could be effectively used by policymakers. In both these areas and others like them, there must be high quality, adequate quantity, and good continuity of personnel, together with reliable data. None of these conditions is close to being met at present, though with human capital accumulation targeted to improving bureaucracy (along with higher pay), significant improvements are not out of the question.

Notes

1. As reported in Marquez (1995: 413).

2. Emphasized, for example, in World Bank (1993a).

3. Several other countries show apparent negative trends. ECLAC (1995a) reports for urban areas that between about 1980 and a year in the early 1990s Panama and Venezuela also fit this category, as did Brazil. They report the opposite trend for Uruguay since 1986.

4. Endogenous growth models like those of Romer (1986) and Lucas (1988) support this thrust, as does World Bank (1993a).

5. Riveros (1992: 19) concludes that Latin America got into a vicious circle of policies and pressures around labor issues and ended up with a highly inefficient and, in many ways, counterproductive labor-market system.

6. Experience in Mexico and Chile indicates that training courses of two to three months' duration and costing about $600 per trainee can contribute to worker reemployment; greater success is expected when the program is closely tied to the private sector, with intermittent periods of on-the-job training (Cline, 1992: 17). Mexico's Labor Retraining Program began in 1984, with enrollment peaking at 546,000 in 1984.

7. There is some danger of inducing overly capital-intensive technologies by allowing either (or both) low (or negative) interest rates or an overvalued exchange rate. Large firms have been the usual beneficiaries of low interest rates and of cheap, rationed foreign exchange when the exchange rate is overvalued. The continuing very high level of income inequality in Brazil and other LAC countries—although it does not demonstrate that these phenomena have played a significant role—is consistent with that conclusion.

References

Abugattas, J., and D. R. Lee (1991). "The Economic Crisis, Policy Reforms and the Poor in Peru During the 1970's and the 1980's." Paper presented at the Seminar on Macroeconomic Crises, Policy Reforms and the Poor in Latin America, Cali, Colombia, 1–4 October.

Ahamed, L., and S. Edwards (eds.) (1986). *Economic Adjustment and Exchange Rates in Developing Countries.* Chicago: University of Chicago Press.

Alarcón, D. (1993). *Changes in the Distribution of Income in Mexico During the Period of Trade Liberalization.* Ph.D. diss., University of California at Riverside.

——— (1994). *Changes in the Distribution of Income in Mexico and Trade Liberalization.* Tijuana, Mexico: El Colegio de la Frontera Norte.

Alarcón, D., and T. McKinley (1994a). "Gender Differences in Wages and Human Capital: Case Study of Female and Male Urban Workers in Mexico from 1984 to 1992." *Frontera Norte* 6, no. 12, Tijuana, Mexico: El Colegio de la Frontera Norte, July–December.

——— (1994b). "Wage Differentials in Mexico from 1984 to 1992: A Profile of Human Capital and Earnings." Paper presented at the symposium "El Impacto del Ajuste Estructural en los Mercados de Trabajo y en la Distribución del Ingreso en America Latina," San José, Costa Rica, September 1994.

——— (1994c). "Widening Wage Dispersion Under Structural Adjustment in Mexico." Paper presented at the symposium "El Impacto del Ajuste Estructural en los Mercados de Trabajo y en la Distribucion del Ingreso en America Latina," San José, Costa Rica, September 1994.

Allen, S. G., and G. J. Labadie (1994). *Labor Market Flexibility and Economic Performance in Uruguay and Chile.* Report to the Tinker Foundation, New York.

Almeida Reis, J. G., and R. Barros (1990). "Desigualdade Salarial: Resultados de Pesquisas Recentes." In J. M. Camargo and F. Giambiagi (eds.), *Distribuição de Renda no Brasil.* São Paulo: Paz e Terra.

Altimir, O. (1979). "La dimensión de la pobreza en América Latina." Santiago: ECLAC, *Cuadernos de la CEPAL* series no. 27, UN publication S.81.II.G.48.

——— (1982). "The Extent of Poverty in Latin America." World Bank Staff Working Paper no. 522, Washington D.C.: World Bank.

——— (1986). "Estimaciones de la distribución del ingreso en la Argentina, 1953–80." *Desarrollo Económico* 25, no. 100, Buenos Aires, Instituto de Desarrollo Económico y Social.

———— (1987). "Income Distribution Statistics in Latin America and Their Reliability." *The Review of Income and Wealth* 33, no. 2, New Haven, Conn., International Association for Research on Income and Wealth.

———— (1991). "Latin American Poverty in the Last Two Decades." Paper presented at the Seminar on Macroeconomic Crises, Policy Reforms and the Poor
in Latin America, Cali, Colombia, 1–4 October.

———— (1992). "Cambios en las desigualdades de ingreso y en la pobreza en
América Latina." Paper presented at the fifth Interamerican Seminar on Eco-
nomics organized by the National Bureau of Economic Research, the Catholic
University of Rio de Janeiro, and the Instituto Torcuato Di Tella, Buenos
Aires, 8–9 May.

Amadeo, E., and J. M. Camargo (1989a). "The Brazilian Labor Market in an Era of
Adjustment." Texto para discussão no. 225, PUC-RJ.

———— (1989b). "Market Structure, Relative Prices and Income Distribution."
Texto para discussão no. 213, PUC-RJ.

———— (1994). "Institutions and the Labor Market in Brazil." Texto para discussão
no. 315, PUC-RJ.

Amadeo, E., R. Barros, J. M. Camargo, R. Mendonça, V. Pero, and A. Urani
(1993). "Human Resources in the Adjustment Process." Texto para discussão
no. 317, IPEA, Rio de Janeiro.

Arida, P. (ed.) (1982). *Dívida Externa, Recessão e Ajuste Estrutural: O Brasil di-
ante da Crise,* Rio de Janeiro: Paz e Terra.

Arida, P., and A. Lara Rezende (eds.) (1986). *Brasil, Argentina e Israel: Inflação
Zero.* Rio de Janeiro: Paz e Terra.

Azeredo, B., and J. P. Chahad (1992). "O Programa Brasileiro de Seguro-Desemprego: Diagnóstico e Sugestões para o seu Aperfeiçoamento." Série Seminários em Estudos Sociais e do Trabalho no. 2/92, IPEA, Rio de Janeiro.

Bacha, E. (1979). "The Kuznets Curve and Beyond: Growth and Change in Inequalities." In E. Malinvaud (ed.), *Economic Growth and Resources.* New
York: St. Martin's Press.

———— (1981). *Macroeconomia: Um Texto Intermediário.* Rio de Janeiro: IPEA.

Bacha, E., and H. S. Klein (eds.) (1986). *A Transição Incompleta: Brasil desde
1945.* Rio de Janeiro: Paz e Terra.

Bacha, E., and L. Taylor (1978). "Brazilian Income Distribution in the Sixties:
Facts, Model Results and Controversy." *Journal of Development Economics*
3:271–297.

Baer, W., and L. Breuer (1986). "From Inward to Outward-oriented Growth:
Paraguay in the 1980s." *Journal of Interamerican Studies and World Affairs*
28, no. 3 (fall).

Banco Central de Chile (1994). *Boletin Mensual 796.*

———— (1987). *Indicadores Economicos y Sociales, 1960–85.*

Banco Central del Ecuador (several issues). *Boletín Anuario.* Quito: Banco Central
del Ecuador.

———— (several issues). *Cuentas Nacionales.* Quito: Banco Central del Ecuador.

———— (several issues). *Información Estadística Mensual.* Quito: Banco Central
del Ecuador.

Banco de la Republica (1994). "Distribucion del Ingreso en Colombia; Una Nueva
Estimacion." In "Notas Editoriales," *Revista del Banco de la Republica,* enero.

Barros, R., and R. Mendonça (1994a). "The Evolution of Welfare, Poverty and Inequality in Brazil During the Last Three Decades: 1960–1990." *Série Seminários Estudos Sociais e do Trabalho,* no. 08/94. Rio de Janeiro: IPEA.

———— (1994b). "Flexibilidade do Mercado de Trabalho Brasileiro: uma Análise Empírica." Mimeo.

———— (1995). "Mensuração da Pobreza e da Desigualdade." Rio de Janeiro: IPEA, mimeo.

Barros, R., E. Cardoso, and A. Urani (1993). "Inflation and Unemployment as Determinants of Inequality in Brazil: The 1980's." In R. Dornbusch and S. Edwards, *Reform, Recovery and Growth: Latin America and the Middle East.* Chicago: University of Chicago Press.

Barros de Castro, A., and F. E. Pires de Souza (1986). *A Economia Brasileira em Marcha Forçada.* Rio de Janeiro: Paz e Terra.

Baumol, W. J., and E. N. Wolff (1996). "Catching Up in the Postwar Period: Puerto Rico as the Fifth 'Tiger'?" *World Development* 24, no. 5 (May):869–886.

Beccaria, L. A. (1991). "Distribución del ingreso en la Argentina: Explorando lo sucedido desde mediados de los setenta." *Desarrollo Económico* 31, no. 123, Buenos Aires, Instituto de Desarrollo Económico y Social.

Beccaria, L., and R. Carciofi (1995). "Argentina: Social Policy and Adjustment During the 1980s." In N. Lustig (ed.) (1995), *Coping with Austerity: Poverty and Inequality in Latin America.* Washington, D.C.: Brookings Institution.

Beccaria, L., and A. Minujin (1991). "Sobre la medición de la pobreza: Enseñanzas a partir de la experiencia argentina." Buenos Aires: UNICEF Working Paper no. 8.

Becerra, B., M. Francisco, J. Vivas Reyna, L. F. Medina S., and I. Hernandez R. (1993). *Colombia: Estado, Crecimiento Económico y Equidad.* Bogotá: Contraloria General de la República.

Berger, S. (1995). *Mujeres en sus Puestos.* Buenos Aires: FLACSO Programa Argentina.

Berry, A. (1983). "Income Distribution Trends in Neoclassical and Labor Surplus Economies." In G. Ranis, R. West, C. Morris, and M. Leiserson (eds.), *Comparative Development Perspectives.* New York: Praeger.

———— (1990). "The Effects of Stabilization and Adjustment on Poverty and Income Distribution: Aspects of the Latin American Experience." Mimeo prepared for the World Bank.

———— (1993). "The Effects of Stabilization and Adjustment on Poverty and Income Distribution: Aspects of the Latin-American Experience." Mimeo.

———— (1995). "The Social Challenge of the New Economic Era in Latin America." Mimeo.

———— (1997). "SME's Competitiveness: The Power of Networking and Subcontracting." Washington, D.C.: Inter-American Development Bank discussion paper.

Berry, A., and J. Escandón (1994). *Colombia's Small and Medium-Size Exporters and Their Support Systems.* Washington, D.C.: World Bank, Policy Research Department Working Paper 1401. December.

Berry, A., and F. Stewart (1997). "Market Liberalization and Income Distribution: The Experience of the 1980s." In Roy Culpeper, Albert Berry, and Frances Stewart (eds.), *Bretton-Woods: 50 Years Later.* New York: Macmillan.

Berry, A., and J. Tenjo (1994). "Guessing the Income Distribution Effects of Trade Liberalization and Labour Reform in Colombia." Paper presented at the Conference on the Colombian Economy, Lehigh University, October.

———— (1995). "Guessing the Income Distribution Effects of Trade Liberalization and Labour Reform in Colombia." Mimeo.

Berry, A., M. T. Mendez, and J. Tenjo (1994a). *Growth, Macroeconomic Stability and Employment Expansion in Latin America.* Paper prepared under the ILO/UNDP project "Economic Policy and Employment." Paper no. 6. Geneva: ILO.

———— (1994b). "Growth, Macroeconomic Stability and the Generation of Productive Employment in Latin America." In A. R. Khan (ed.), *Growth, Macroeconomic Stability and the Expansion of Productive Employment: A Global Strategy.* New York: Macmillan.

Bianchi, A., R. Devlin, and J. Ramos (1985). *External Debt in Latin America: Adjustment Policies and Renegotiation.* Boulder, CO: Lynne Rienner Publishers/ECLAC, United Nations.

———— (1987). "El proceso de ajuste en la América Latina, 1981–86." *El Trimestre Económico* LIV (4), no. 216, Mexico City, Fondo de Cultura Economica.

BINEGI (Instituto Nacional de Estadistica, Geografia, e Informatica). Electronic database. Mexico.

Bivar, W. S. B. (1993). "Estimativas da Duração Média do Desemprego no Brasil." *Pesquisa e Planejamento Econômico* 23, no. 2, Rio de Janeiro.

Bonelli, R., and P. S. Malan (1990). "Brazil, 1950–1980: Three Decades of Growth-Oriented Economic Policies." Texto para discussão no. 187, IPEA, Rio de Janeiro.

Bonelli, R., and L. Ramos (1993). "Distribuição de Renda no Brasil: Avaliação das Tendências de Longo Prazo e Mudanças na Desigualdade desde Meados dos Anos 70." Texto para discussão no. 288, IPEA, Rio de Janeiro.

Booth, A. (1992). "Income Distribution and Poverty." In Anne Booth (ed.), *The Oil Boom and After: Indonesian Economic Policy and Performance in the Soeharto Era.* Singapore: Oxford University Press.

Bourguinon, F., and C. Morrisson (1989). *External Trade and Income Distribution.* Paris, OECD Development Centre.

Buitelaar, R., and J. Fuentes (1991). "The Competitiveness of the Small Economies of the Region," *CEPAL Review* 43.

Cacciamali, M. C. (1989). "Emprego no Brasil durante a Primeira Metade dos Anos 80." In R. Barros, and G. Sedlacek (eds.), *Mercado de Trabalho e Distribuição de Renda: uma Coletânea.* Série Monográfica IPEA no. 35, Rio de Janeiro.

Camargo, J. M. (1980). "A Nova Política Salarial, Distribuição de Rendas e Inflação." *Pesquisa e Planejamento Econômico* 10, no. 3.

———— (1989). "Informalização e Renda no Mercado de Trabalho." In R. Barros and G. Sedlacek (eds.), *Mercado de Trabalho e Distribuição de Renda: uma Coletânea.* Série Monográfica IPEA no. 35, Rio de Janeiro.

Camargo, J. M., and C. A. Ramos (1988). *A Revolução Indesejada: Conflito Distributivo e Mercado de Trabalho.* Rio de Janeiro: Campus.

Canitrot, A. (1981). "Teoría y práctica del liberalismo: Politica antiinflacionaria y apertura economica en la Argentina, 1976–1981." *Desarrollo Económico* 21, no. 82, Buenos Aires, Instituto de Desarrollo Económico y Social.

———— (1992). "La macroeconomía de la inestabilidad." Mimeograph.

Canitrot, A., and S. Junco (1992). "Apertura y condiciónes macroeconómicas: el caso argentino." Washington D.C.: Inter-American Development Bank (IDB) Working Papers series no. 108.

Carciofi, R. (1990). "La desarticulación del pacto fiscal: Una interpretación sobre la evolución del sector público argentino en las dos últimas décadas." Buenos Aires: CEPAL, documento de trabajo 36.

Carneiro, D. D. (1985). "Stabilization Policies and Adjustment: The Brazilian Economy During the 1980's." Texto para discussão no. 138, PUC-RJ.

Carter, M. R., B. L. Barham, and D. Mesbah (1996). "Agricultural Export Booms and the Rural Poor in Chile, Guatemala, and Paraguay." *Latin American Research Review* 31, no. 1.

Castells, M. (1993). "The Informational Economy and the New International Division of Labor." In Martin Carnoy, Manuel Castells, Stephen Cohen, and Fernando Henrique Cardoso (eds.), *The New Global Economy in the Information Age*. University Park: Pennsylvania State University Press.

CEB (Centro de Estudios Bonaerenses) (1994). "Distribución del ingreso y tributación: Las consecuencias de gravar al consumo." *Informe de Coyuntura* 4, no. 37 (September).

CEPAL (1991). "Indicatodes macroeconómicos de la Argentina." Buenos Aires: CEPAL, October.

——— (1995). "Indicatodes macroeconómicos de la Argentina." Buenos Aires: CEPAL, January–March.

Cho, M. (1995). "Interfirm Networks: The Foundation of the New Globalization Economy of South Korea." Paper prepared for the UNCTAD workshop on "Poverty Alleviation Through International Trade," Santiago.

Cline, W. (1992). *Facilitating Labor Adjustment in Latin America*. Washington, D.C.: IDB, Economic and Social Development Department working paper, October.

Comision Economica para America Latina y el Caribe (CEPALC). (1987a). *Antecendentes de la distribucion del ingreso en Costa Rica, 1958–1982*. Santiago: CEPAL.

——— (1987b). *Antecedentes Estadisticos de la Distribucion del Ingreso: Chile, 1940–1982*. Santiago: Naciones Unidas.

——— (1994). *Estudio Economico de America Latina y el Caribe 1993*. Vol. 1. Santiago: CEPALC.

——— (1994). *Preliminary Overview of the Latin American and Caribbean Economy*.

——— (1995). *Balance Preliminar de la Economía de América Latina y el Caribe: 1995*. Santiago: CEPALC.

Commander, Simon, and Peter Peek (1986). "Oil Exports, Agrarian Change and the Rural Labor Process: The Ecuadorean Sierra in the 1970s." *World Development* 14 (November 1).

Conaghan, C. (1990). "Business and the 'Boys': The Politics of Neoliberalism in the Central Andes." *Latin American Research Review* 15, no. 2.

Contraloría General de la República (1994). *Economía Colombiana*, no. 247, Marzo–Abril.

Corbo, V. (1985a). "Reforms and Macroeconomic Adjustment in Chile During 1974–1984." *World Development* 13, no. 8, Washington, D.C.

——— (1985b). "The Role of the Real Exchange Rate in Macro-Economic Adjustment: The Case of Chile 1973–82." Washington, D.C.: World Bank discussion paper DRD145.

——— (1986). "Problems, Development Theory and Strategies of Latin America." Washington, D.C: World Bank discussion paper DRD190, September.

——— (1988). "Problems, Development Theory and Strategies of Latin America." In Gustav Ranis and T. Paul Schultz (eds.), *The State of Development Economics: Progress and Perspectives*. Oxford: Basil Blackwell.

Corbo, V., and P. Meller (1984). "Trade and Employment in Chile in the 60s." *American Economic Review* 69, no. 2.

Corbo, V., and F. Sturzenegger (1988). "Stylized Facts of the Macroeconomic Adjustment in the Indebted Countries." Washington, D.C.: World Bank, CECMG, mimeo.

Cordeiro, M. (1992). "Liberalização comercial brasilera nos anos 80 e 90; uma analição preliminar," *Texto para discussão interna*, no. 87.

Correia do Lago, L. (1990). "Uma Revisão do Período do Milagre—Política Econômica e Crescimento, 1967–1973." Texto para discussão no. 225, PUC-RJ.

Corseuil, C. H. L. (1994). "Desemprego: Aspectos Teóricos e o Caso Brasileiro." *Série Seminários Estudos Sociais e do Trabalho*, no. 4/94, IPEA, Rio de Janeiro.

Cortazar R., and J. Marshall (1989). "Indice de Precios al Consumidor en Chile during 1970–1978." Coleccion Estudios, CIEPLAN, Santiago.

Cortés, R. (1985). "Cambios en el mercado de trabajo urbano argentino, 1974–1983." Buenos Aires: FLACSO, *Documentos e Informes de Investigación* 13.

———— (1994). "Regulación institucional y relación asalariada en el mercado urbano de trabajo, Argentina 1980–1990." *Realidad Económica* 121.

Cortés, R., and A. Marshall (1993). "State Social Intervention and Labour Regulation: The Case of the Argentine." *Cambridge Journal of Economics* 17, no. 4.

Culpeper, R. (1993). *Resurgence of Private Capital Flows to Latin America: The Role of American Investors*. Ottawa: North-South Institute.

Cumby, L., and R. Levich (1987). "On the Definition and Magnitude of Recent Capital Flight." In D. Lessard and J. Williamson (eds.), *Capital Flight and Third World Debt*. Washington, D.C.: Institute for International Economics (IIE).

de Janvry, A., E. Sadoulet, and A. Fargeix (1991). *Adjustment and Equity in Ecuador*. Paris: OECD.

de Janvry, A., et al. (1993). *The Political Feasibility of Adjustment in Ecuador and Venezuela*. Paris: OECD.

de Melo, J., and S. Robinson (1980). "The Impact of Trade Policies on Income Distribution in a Planning Model for Colombia." *Journal of Policy Modelling* 2, no. 1.

Deyo, F. (1988). *The Political Economy of the New Asian Industrialism*. New York: Cornell University Press.

Diaz-Alejandro, C. F. (1963). "A Note on the Impact of Devaluation and the Redistributive Effect." *Journal of Political Economy* 71:577–580.

Diaz-Alejandro, C. F. (1976). *Foreign Trade Regimes and Economic Development: Colombia*. New York: National Bureau of Economic Research.

———— (1985). "Goodbye Financial Repression, Hello Financial Crash." *Journal of Development Economics* (September–October).

Echevarría, J. J., and G. Perry (1981). "Aranceles y Subsidios a las Exportaciones: Análisis de su Estructura Sectorial y de su Impacto sobre la Industria Colombiana." *Coyuntura Económica* (July).

ECLAC (Economic Commission for Latin America and the Caribbean). *Panorama Económico*.

———— (several issues). *Econommic Survey of Latin America and the Caribbean*. Santiago: ECLAC.

———— (several issues). *Statistical Yearbook for Latin America and the Caribbean*. Santiago: ECLAC.

———— (1979). "América Latina en el umbral de los anõs 80." Santiago: ECLAC, November, E/CEPAL/G.1106.

———— (1986). "The Economic Crisis: Policies for Adjustment, Stabilization and Growth." Santiago: ECLAC, *Cuadernos de la CEPAL* series no. 54, UN publication E.86.II.G.12.

—— (1988). "Antecedentes estadísticos de la distribución del ingreso: México, 1950–1977." Santiago: ECLAC, *Distribución del Ingreso* series no. 7, LC/G.I445.

—— (1990). *Changing Production Patterns with Social Equity, Santiago, Chile.* Santiago: ECLAC, UN publication E.90.II.G.6, March.

—— (1991a). "Estabilización y equidad en América Latina en los ochenta" Santiago: ECLAC, LC/L.1132.

—— (1991b). "La equidad en el panorama social de América Latina durante los anõs ochenta." Santiago: ECLAC, LC/G.1686.

—— (1991c). "Magnitud de la pobreza en América Latina en los anõs ochenta." Santiago: ECLAC, *Estudios e Informes de la CEPAL* series no. 81, UN publication S.91.II.G.10.

—— (1991d). "Una estimación de la magnitud de la pobreza en Chile 1990." Santiago: ECLAC, LC/R.1069.

—— (1992a). "El perfil de la pobreza en América Latina a comienzos de los anõs 90." Santiago: ECLAC, LC/L.716 (Conf.82/6).

—— (1992b). "Equity and changing production patterns: An integrated approach." Santiago: ECLAC, LG/G.1701/Rev.1–P, UN publication E.92.II.G.5.

—— (1992c). *Preliminary Overview of the Economy of Latin America and the Caribbean 1992.* Santiago: ECLAC.

—— (1993a). "Panorama Social de America Latina: Edición 1993." Santiago: ECLAC, LC/G.1768.

—— (1993b). *Preliminary Overview of the Economy of Latin America and the Caribbean, 1993.* Santiago: ECLAC.

—— (1993c). *Statistical Yearbook for Latin America and the Caribbean.* Santiago: ECLAC.

—— (1994). *Preliminary Overview of the Economy of Latin America and the Caribbean, 1994.* Santiago: ECLAC.

—— (1995a). *Social Panorama of Latin America: 1995.* Santiago: ECLAC.

—— (1995b). *Statistical Yearbook for Latin America and the Caribbean: 1995 Edition,* Santiago: ECLAC.

Edwards, S. (1985). "Economic Policy and the Record of Economic Growth in Chile 1973–1982." In Gary M. Walton (ed.), *The National Economic Policies in Chile: Contemporary Studies in Economic and Financial Analysis* 51, New York.

—— (1994). "Trade and Industrial Policy Reform in Latin America." Paper presented at the seminar on Macroeconomic, Structural and Social Policies for Growth, Rio de Janeiro, March.

Edwards, S., and A. Edwards (1987). *Monetarism and Liberalization, The Chilean Experiment.* Cambridge, Mass.: Ballinger Publishing.

Fanelli, J. M., R. Frenkel, and G. Rozenwurcel (1990). *Growth and Structural Reform in Latin America. Where We Stand.* Buenos Aires: Centro de Estudios de Estado y Sociedad (CEDES).

FAO (Food and Agriculture Organization) (1994). *La Política Agrícola en el Nuevo Estilo de Desarrollo Latinoamericano.* Santiago: FAO.

Favaro, E., and A. Bension (1993). "Uruguay." In Simon Rottenberg (ed.), *The Political Economy of Poverty, Equity and Growth: Costa Rica and Uruguay.* Baltimore: Johns Hopkins University Press, for the World Bank.

Fedesarrollo (1992). *Coyuntura Social,* no. 7.

Feliciano, Z. (1993). "Workers and Trade Liberalization: The Impact of Trade Reforms in Mexico on Wages and Employment." Harvard University, mimeo.

Ferraro, R. and L. Riveros. (1994). *Historia Económica de Chile: Una Visión Económica, Vol. 1.* Santiago: Facultad de Ciencias Económicas, Universidad de Chile.

Ffrench-Davis, R. (1992). "Economic Development and Equity in Chile: Legacies and Challenges in the Return to Democracy." Paper presented at the conference "The New Europe and the New World: Latin America and Europe 1992," Oxford University, September.

Ffrench-Davis, R., and D. Raczynski (1987). "The Impact of Global Recession and National Policies on Living Standards: Chile, 1973–1989." Santiago: Corporación de Investigaciónes Económicas para Latinoamérica (CIEPLAN), Notas Técnicas CIEPLAN no. 97.

FIDE (1989). *Coyuntura y Desarrollo*. (Fundacion de Investigaciones para el Desarrollo).

———— (1993). *Coyuntura y Desarrollo*. January–February, no. 173/174. Buenos Aires.

FIEL (Fundacion de Investigaciones Economicas Latinoamericanas) (1993). *Indicadores de Coyuntura*, no. 12. Buenos Aires.

Fields, G. (1984). "Employment, Income Distribution, and Economic Growth in Several Small Open Economies." *Economic Journal* 94 (March).

Figueroa, A. (1992). "Social Policy and Economic Adjustment in Peru." Paper presented at the Conference on Poverty and Inequality in Latin America, Brookings Institution/Inter-American Dialogue, Washington, D.C., July.

Fiorencio, A., and A. Urani (1990). "Restrição Cambial e os Limites da Política Econômica." *Pesquisa e Planejamento Econômico* 20, no. 3.

Fischer, S. (1988). "Devaluation and Inflation." In R. Dornbusch and L. Helmers (eds). *The Open Economy: Tools for Policy Makers in Developing Countries*. Oxford: Oxford University Press.

Fishlow, A. (1972). "Brazilian Size Distribution of Income." *American Economic Review* 62, no. 2.

Franco, G., and W. Fritsch (1989). "Trade Policy, MNCs and the Evolving Pattern of Brazilian Trade: 1970–1985." Texto para discussão no. 230, PUC-RJ.

Frenkel, R. (1986). "Salários e Inflação na América Latina: Resultados de Pesquisas Recentes na Argentina, Brasil, Chile, Colombia e Costa Rica." *Pesquisa e Planejamento Econômico* 16, no. 1.

Fresneda, O. (1994). "Evolucion de la Pobreza en Colombia: Un Balance de dos Decadas." Mimeo. Bogotá.

Friedmann, S., N. Lustig, and A. Legovini (1995). "Mexico: Social Spending and Food Subsidies During Adjustment in the 1980s." In N. Lustig (ed.), *Coping with Austerity: Poverty and Inequality in Latin America*. Washington, D.C.: Brookings Institution.

Frisch, W., and G. H. B. Franco (1994). "Import Compression, Productivity Slowdown, and Manufactured Export Dynamism, 1975–90." In G. K. Helleiner (ed.), *Trade and Industrialization in Turbulent Times*. New York: Routledge.

Garcia, N. E. (1991). "Restructuración, ahorro y mercado de trabajo." Geneva: International Labour Office (ILO)/Regional Employment Programme for Latin America and the Caribbean (PREALC), Employment Studies no. 34.

Gelbard, E. A. (1990). "Changes in Industrial Structure and Performance Under Trade Liberalization: The Case of Argentina." Ph.D. diss., University of Toronto.

Gereffi, G., and D. Wyman (1990). *Manufacturing Miracles: Paths of Industrialization in Latin America and East Asia*. Princeton: Princeton University Press.

Gindling, T. H., and A. Berry (1992). "The Performance of the Labor Market During Recession and Structural Adjustment: Costa Rica in the 1980s." *World Development* 20, no. 11, November.

Gregory, P. (1986). *The Myth of Market Failure: Employment and the Labor Market in Mexico.* Baltimore: Johns Hopkins University Press.

Grindle, M., and F. Thoumi (1992). "Muddling Towards Adjustment: The Political Economy of Policy Change in Ecuador." In Anne Krueger and Robert Bates (eds.), *The Political Economy of Structural Adjustment.* London: Basil Blackwell.

Hachette, D., and R. Luders (1987). "Aspects of the Privatization Process: The Case of Chile, 1974–85." Washington, D.C.: World Bank, April, mimeo.

Handa, A. (1995). "Structural Adjustment and Income Distribution in Jamaica: 1989–93." Mimeo.

Hanson, G., and R. C. Feenstra (1994). "Foreign Investment, Outsourcing and Relative Wages." Paper prepared for the conference "Political Economy of Trade Policy," Columbia University, November.

Harvey, D. (1989). *The Condition of Postmodernity.* New York: Blackwell.

Helleiner, G. K. (ed.) (1994). *Trade and Industrialization in Turbulent Times.* New York: Routledge.

Hernandez-Laos, E., and J. Cordoba (1982). *La distribucion del ingreso en Mexico.* Mexico: Centro de Investigacion para la Integracion Social.

Heskia, I. (1980). "Distribución del ingreso en el Gran Santiago 1957–1979." Santiago: University of Chile, Department of Economics, documento serie investigación no. 53, October.

Hoffmann, R. (1989a). "Evolucao da Distribucao da Renda no Brasil, entre pessaos e entre familias, 1978–86." In Gulherme Luis Sedlacek and Ricardo Paes de Barros (eds.), *Mercado de Trabalhoe e Distribução da Renda.* Vina Coletanea.

—— (1989b). "A distribução da renda no Brasil em 1985, 1986 e 1987." *Revista de Economia Politica* 9, no. 2 (Abril–Junho):122–126.

—— (1992). "Crise económica e pobreza no Brasil no periodo 1979–90." Working paper, Universidade de Sao Paulo/Escola Superior de Agricultura. "Luiz de Queiroz"/Deparmento de Economia e Sociologia Rural, July.

Hofman, A., and R. Buitelaar (1994). "Ventajas Comparativas Extraordinarias y Crecimiento a Largo Plazo: El Caso del Ecuador." *Revista de la CEPAL no. 54.*

Horta, M. H. T. (1989). "Políticas de Ajustamento aos Choques Externos nos Anos 80." In IPEA, *Perspectivas da Economia Brasileira—1990.* Rio de Janeiro: IPEA.

Horton, S., R. Kanbur, and D. Mazumdar (1991). *Labor Markets in an Era of Adjustment: An Overview.* Washington, D.C.: World Bank, Economic Development Institute.

IBGE (Instituto Brasileiro de Geographia e Estadistica). (various issues). Pesquisa Nacional por Amostra de Domicilios (PNAD). Rio de Janeiro: IBGE.

—— (various issues). Pesquisa Mensal de Emprego. Rio de Janeiro: IBGE.

IBRD (International Bank for Reconstruction and Development) (1979). *Chile: An Economy in Transition.* Washington, D.C.: World Bank Country Study.

—— (1990). Chile's Country Economic Memorandum. Washington, D.C.: World Bank.

IDB (Inter-American Development Bank) (1994). *Colombia: Socioeconomic Report.* Washington, D.C.: IDB, Economic and Social Development Department, Country Economics Division.

—— (1994) *Progreso Económico y Social en América Latina 1994.* Washington, D.C.: Inter-American Development Bank.

IICA-PRONADER (1994). *Encuesta de Base en 12 Areas de Desarrollo Rural.* (IICA stands for Instituto Interamericano de Cooperación Agropecuaria.) San José, Costa Rica.

IMF (International Monetary Fund) (various issues). *International Financial Statistics.* Washington, D.C.: International Monetary Fund.

—— (1994). *Comentarios sobre la situación económica 1994.* Washington, D.C.: International Monetary Fund.

Indart, G. (1996). "Trade Liberalization and Structural Adjustment in Uruguay." University of Toronto, Centre for International Studies, working paper.

INDEC (Instituto Nacional de Estadística y Censos). *Encuestra Industrial* (several years, unpublished).

—— (1965). *Censo Nacional de Población y Vivienda—1960.* Buenos Aires: INDEC.

—— (1970). *Censo Nacional de Población y Vivienda—1970.* Buenos Aires: INDEC.

—— (1980). *Censo Nacional Economico—1974.* Buenos Aires: INDEC.

—— (1981). *Censo Nacional de Población y Vivienda—1980.* Buenos Aires: INDEC.

—— (1989). *Censo Nacional Economico—1985.* Buenos Aires: INDEC.

—— (1993a). *Información de Prensa.* Buenos Aires: INDEC. May and October.

—— (1993b). *Censo Nacional de Población y Vivienda—1991.* Buenos Aires: INDEC.

—— (1994). *Información de Prensa.* May and October.

INDEC-EPH (various years, 1970–1994). *Encuesta Permanente de Hogares (EPH).* October.

INE (Instituto Nacional de Estadísticas) (1995). *Ingresos 1990–1993 de Hogares y Personas: Encuesta Suplementaria de Ingresos.* Santiago: INE.

INEM and INEC. "Encuesta de Hogares." Unpublished database, several years.

INEC (Instituto National de Estadistica y Censos) (1962). *Censos de población.* Quito: INEC.

—— (1974). *Censos de población.*

—— (1982). *Censos de población.*

—— (1990). *Censos de población.*

Instituto Nacional de Estadistica, Geograia e Informatica (INEGI) (1989). *Encuesta Nacional de Ingresos y Gastos de los Hogares, 1984.* Mexico: INEGI.

—— (1992). *Encuesta Nacional de Ingresos y Gastos de los Hogares, 1989.* Mexico: INEGI.

—— (1993). *Encuesta Nacional de Ingresos y Gastos de los Hogares, 1992.* Mexico: INEGI.

Jácome, L. (1994). "De la Inflación Crónica a la Inflación Moderada en el Ecuador." *Revista de la CEPAL* 52.

Kaneda, H. (1980). "Development of Small and Medium Enterprises and Policy Responses in Japan: An Analytical Survey." *Studies in Employment and Rural Development* 32. World Bank, Economics Department, Washington, D.C.

Kosacoff, B. (1989). "Desarrollo industrial e inestabilidad macroeconómica: La experiencia argentina reciente." In B. Kosacoff and D. Azpiazu, *La Industria Argentina: Desarrollo y Cambios Estructurales.* Buenos Aires: CEAL-CEPAL.

—— (1993). "La industria argentina: Un proceso de reestructuración desarticulada." In B. Kosacoff (ed.), *El desafío de la competitividad: La industria argentina en transformación.* Buenos Aires: CEPAL/Alianza Editorial.

Krueger, A. O. (1988). "The Relationship Between Trade, Employment and Development." In Gustav Ranis and T. Paul Schultz (eds.), *The State of Development Economics: Progress and Perspectives.* Oxford: Basil Blackwell.

Kuznets, S. (1955). "Economic Growth and Income Inequality." *American Economic Review* 45, no. 1.

Langoni, J. G. (1973). *Distribuição de Renda e Desenvolvimento Econômico no Brasil.* Rio de Janeiro: Expressão e Cultura.

Lara Rezende, A., and F. L. Lopes (1981). "Sobre as Causas da Recente Aceleração Inflacionária." *Pesquisa e Planejamento Econômico* 11, no. 3.

Larrain, F. (1988). "Public Sector Behavior in a Highly Indebted Country: The Contrasting Chilean Experience 1970–1985." Washington, D.C.: World Bank, LAC, mimeo.

Larrain, F., and P. Meller (1990). "The Socialist-Populist Chilean Experience: 1970–73." Santiago, mimeo.

Larrea, C. (1990). *Pobreza, Necesidades Básicas y Desempleo: Area Urbana del Ecuador.* Quito: ILDIS-INEM.

—— (1992). "The Mirage of Development: Oil, Employment and Poverty in Ecuador (1972–1990)." Ph.D. diss., York University.

—— (1994). "Proyectos Democráticos y Estrategias de Desarrollo para el Ecuador: Una Visión Retrospectiva." Paper prepared for the seminar "Democracia, Desarrollo y Descentralización," Universidad de Cuenca, October.

—— (1996). "Structural Adjustment, Income Distribution and Employment in Ecuador." University of Toronto, Centre for International Studies, working paper.

Larrea, C., M. Espinosa, and P. Sylva (1987). *El Banano en el Ecuador.* Quito: Corporación Editora Nacional.

Lasso, F. J., and H. Moreno (1993). "Perfil de pobreza para Colombia—años 1978, 1988, 1991 y 1992: Metodología de ajuste de ingresos de las encuestas de hogares a Cuentas Nacionales y obtención de los índices de pobreza." *Estudio de Incidencia del Gasto Público Social.* Mision de Decentralizaión y Focalización de los Servicios Sociales, DNP, Bogotá, Septiembre.

Lattes, A., and M. Sana (1992). "Los nuevos patrones de la redistribución de la población en la Argentina." Buenos Aires: Primer Congreso Nacional de Estudios del Trabajo, 1992, mimeo.

Loehr, W., and J. P. Powelson (1981). *The Economics of Development and Distribution.* New York: Harcourt Brace Jovanovitch.

Londoño, J. L. (1986). "Ciclo de vida, relaciones contractuales y la inserción de los jovenes en el mercado de trabajo." *Coyuntura Económica* 16, no. 3, Bogotá, Octubre.

—— (1987). "La dinamica laboral y el ritmo de actividad economica: Un repaso empirico de la ultima decada." In José Antonio Ocampo and Manuel Ramírez (eds.), *El Problema Laboral Colombiano: Informes a la Mision Chenery.* Bogotá: Contraloría General de la República, Departamento Nacional de Planeación and Servicio Nacional de Aprendizaje-SENA, Tomo 1.

—— (1989). *Income Distribution in Colombia 1971–88: Basic Estimation.* Washington, D.C.: Report to the World Bank.

—— (1990). *Income Distribution During the Structural Transformation: Colombia 1938–1988.* Ph.D. diss., Harvard University.

—— (1995). *Distribución del Ingreso y Desarrollo Economico: Colombia en el Siglo XX.* Bogotá: TM Editores, Banco de la Republica y Fedesarrollo.

—— (1996). "The Social Impact of the Colombian Economic Model." Document prepared for the conference "The Colombian Economic Model: Institutions, Performance and Prospects," University of London, Institute of Latin American Studies, April.

Lopes, F. L. (1986). *O Choque Heterodoxo.* Rio de Janeiro: Campus.

López Castaño, H. (1992). "Cuánto Ganan las Empresas con la Reforma a las Cesantías? Hay un Buen Margen para una Mayor Cotización Patronal a la Seguridad Social." Medellín: Universidad de Antioquia, documento Universidad de Antioquia/ISS no. 1.

—— (1993). "Contexto Macroeconómico Colombiano, Mercado Laboral Urbano y Retos Para una Política de Empleo." Medellín: Fundación Friedrich Ebert de Colombia (FESCOL), Documentos de Trahajo.

—— (1994a). *Mercado Laboral, Papel del SENA y Sistema de Informacion Para el Empleo.* Medellín: Informe de Consultoria para el SENA, Junio.

—— (1994b). "Mercado laboral urbano y desempleo friccional y estructural en Colombia: El papel del SENA." *Planeación y Desarrollo* 25, Edicion Especial, "Lecciones de Indonesia: Formacion para un nuevo mercado laboral." Mayo.

Lora, E., and A. M. Herrera (1994). "Ingresos rurales y evolucion macroeconomica." In C. Gonzalez and C. F. Jaramillo, *Competitividad sin Pobreza.* Departamento Nacional de Planeación-Fonade-TM editores.

Lora, E., and R. Steiner (1994). "Structural Reforms and Income Distribution in Colombia." Paper presented at the Interamerican Seminar on Economics, sponsored by the National Bureau of Economic Research, Mexico City, November.

Lucas, R. (1988). "On the Mechanics of Economic Development." *Journal of Monetary Economics* 22.

Lustig, N. (1992). *Mexico: The Remaking of an Economy.* Washington, D.C.: Brookings Institution.

—— (ed.) (1995). *Coping with Austerity: Poverty and Inequality in Latin America.* Washington, D.C.: Brookings Institution.

Luzuriaga, C., and C. Zuvekas (1983). *Income Distribution and Poverty in Rural Ecuador, 1950–1979.* Tempe: Arizona State University, 1983.

Machado, D. C. (1994). "O Impacto do Seguro-Desemprego no Mercado de Trabalho: o Caso Brasileiro." Rio de Janeiro: IPEA, *Série Seminários em Estudos Sociais e do Trabalho* no. 3/94.

Marquez, G. (1992). "Poverty and Social Policies in Venezuela." Paper presented at the Conference on Poverty and Inequality in Latin America, Washington, D.C., Brookings Institution/Inter-American Dialogue/Caracas, Instituto de Estudios Superiores de Administración, mimeo.

—— (1995). "Venezuela: Poverty and Social Policies in the 1980s." In N. Lustig, *Coping with Austerity: Poverty and Inequality in Latin America.* Washington, D.C.: Brookings Institution.

Marquez, G., and J. Mukherjee (1991). "Distribución del ingreso y pobreza en Venezuela." Caracas: Instituto de Estudios Superiores de Administración, November.

Marshall, A. (1980). "Labour Markets and Wage Growth: The Case of Argentina." *Cambridge Journal of Economics* 4, no. 1.

—— (1985). "La estructura de los salarios en la Argentina, 1976–1982." Buenos Aires: FLACSO, *Documentos e Informes de Investigación* 24.

—— (1988a). *Políticas Sociales: El Modelo Neoliberal.* Buenos Aires: Legasa.

—— (1988b). "Emigration of Argentines to the United States." In P. Pessar (ed.), *When Borders Don't Divide.* New York: Center for Migration Studies.

—— (1989). "The Fall of Labor's Share in Income and Consumption: A New 'Growth Model' for Argentina?" In W. Canak (ed.), *Lost Promises: Debt, Austerity, and Development in Latin America.* Boulder, Colo.: Westview Press.

—— (1993). "El retroceso del consumo de los asalariados en la Argentina: ¿Una restricción al crecimiento? *Economía y Trabajo* 1, no. 1.

—— (1994). "Estabilidad y cambio en la estructura de los salarios, 1976–1993." Buenos Aires: Segundo Congreso Nacional de Estudios del Trabajo, August, mimeo.

Marshall, A., and D. Orlansky (1983). "Inmigración de países limítrofes y demanda de mano de obra en la Argentina, 1940–1980." *Desarrollo Económico* 23, no. 89.

Melgar, A. (1981). "Distribución del ingreso en el Uruguay." Montevideo: Centro Latinoamericano de Economia Humana (CLAEH), Serie Investigaciónes no. 18.

——— (1988). "El Mercado de Trabajo en la Coyuntura." *SUMA*, no. 4 (April).

——— (1995). "Pobreza y Distribución del Ingreso: La Evolución Reciente." *Salario, Pobreza y Desarrollo Humano en el Uruguay.* Montevideo: CLAEH-PNUD.

Melgar, A., and F. Villalobos (1986). "La Desigualdad como Estrategia." Montevideo: CLAEH and Ediciones de la Banda Oriental.

Meller, P. (1991). "Adjustment and Social Costs in Chile During the 1980's." *World Development* 19, no. 11 (special issue).

——— (1992a). *Adjustment and Equity in Chile.* Paris: OECD Development Centre.

——— (1992b). "Latin American Adjustment and Economic Reforms: Issues and Recent Experience." *United Nations Conference on Trade and Development, Discussion Paper* no. 53. Geneva: UNCTAD.

Ministerio de Agricultura y Departamento Nacional de Planeación (1990). *El Desarrollo Agropecuario en Colombia, Informe Final: Mision de Estudios del Sector Agropecuario.* Bogotá: Editorial Presencia.

Ministero de Economía y Obras y Servicios Públicos, Secretaria de Programmacíon Económica (nd). *Argentina en Crecimiento.* Buenos Aires: Ministerio de Economía y Obras y Servicios Públicos.

Ministerio de Finanzas (Chile) (1993). *Estado de la Hacienda Pública.* Santiago de Chile: Ministerio de Finanzas.

Ministerio de Salud Publico (1982). *Encuesta de Utilizacion de Servicios y Gasto en Atencion Medica.* Buenos Aires.

Ministerio de Trabajo y Seguridad Social (1991). "La recaudación por impuestos al trabajo 1950–1990." Buenos Aires: Proyecto Gobierno Argentino/PNUD/OIT, Informe 6.

Misión de Empleo (1986). *Informe Final de la Misión de Empleo: El Problema Laboral Colombiano: Diagnóstico, Perspectivas y Políticas.* Published as Separata no. 10 (Agosto–Septiembre de 1986) of *Economía Colombiana.* Bogotá: Revista de la Contraloría General de la República.

Modiano, E. (1985). "Salários, Preços e Câmbio: os Multiplicadores do Choque em uma Economia Indexada." *Pesquisa e Planejamento Econômico* 15, no. 1.

Montenegro, A. (1991). *Bases del Plan de Desarrollo.* Ponencia presentado en el Foro Programas Socio-laborales y Modernización Económica. Bogotá, Marzo.

Morley, S. A. (1993). "Poverty and the Distribution of Income During Latin American Adjustment in the 1980's." Mimeo.

——— (1994). *Poverty and Inequality in Latin America: Past Evidence, Future Prospects.* Washington, D.C.: Overseas Development Council.

——— (1995). *Poverty and Inequality in Latin America: The Impact of Adjustment and Recovery in the 1980s.* Baltimore: Johns Hopkins University Press.

Morley, S. A., and C. Alvarez (1992). "Poverty and Adjustment in Costa Rica." Washington, D.C.: IDB, Department of Economics, January, mimeo.

Mujica, P., and M. Basch (1994). "Capitulo Macroecomico." In Universidad de Chile, *Analisis Economico.* Santiago de Chile: Universidad de Chile.

Musgrove, P. (1978). *Consumer Behaviour in Latin America: Income and Spending of Families in Ten Andean Cities.* Washington, D.C.: Brookings Institution.

Nacional Financiera (1994). *La Economia Mexicana en Cifras*. Mexico: Nacional Financiera.

Nugent, Jeffrey (1989). "Variations in the Size Distribution of Korean Manufacturing Establishments Across Sectors and Over Time." Seoul: Korea Development Institute Working Paper 8932.

Nuñez M. J., and F. Sánchez Torres (1996). "Educacion y Dispersion Salarial en Colombia, 1976–1995." Departamento Nacional de Planeación, Republica de Colombia. Bogotá: Departmento Nacional de Planeación.

OIT (Oficina Internacional del Trabajo) (1994). *OIT Informa, Panoramo Laboral '94*. Buenos Aires: OIT.

Ocampo, J. A. (1987). "El Régimen Prestacional del Sector Privado." In José Antonio Ocampo and Manuel Ramírez (eds.), *El Problema Laboral Colombiano: Informes a la Mision Chenery*. Bogotá: Contraloría General de la República, Departamento Nacional de Planeación and Servicio Nacional de Aprendizaje–SENA, Tomo 2.

——— (1994). "Trade Policy and Industrialization in Colombia, 1967–91." In Gerald K. Helleiner (ed.), *Trade Policy, Industrialization and Development: New Perspectives*. Oxford: Clarendon Press.

Ong, Oihwa (1991). "The Gender and Labor Politics of Postmodernity." *Annual Review of Anthropology* 20.

Orlansky, D. (1990). "Empleo público y condiciones de trabajo. Argentina 1960–86." In A. Marshall, ed., *El Empleo Público Frente a la Crisis: Estudios sobre América Latina*. Geneva: International Institute for Labour Studies.

——— (1993). "Reforma del estado e inflación política: Su impacto en el empleo público." Seminario IIEL/PREALC Instituciones Laborales frente a los Cambios en América Latina, Santiago, mimeo.

Pack, H. (1992). "Learning and Productivity Change in Developing Countries." In Gerald K. Helleiner (ed.), *Trade Policy, Industrialization and Development: New Perspectives*. Oxford: Clarendon Press.

Página 12 (1994). Economic Supplement. January.

Pardo, L. (1993). "El Sector Social: Politica Social, Pobrezà y Equidad." In Universidad de Chile, *Analisis Economico*. Santiago de Chile: Universidad de Chile.

Pardo, L., F. Balmaceda, and I. Irarrazaval (1993) "Pobreza, Crecimiento y Politicas Sociales." Documento de Trabajo 16, Department de Economía, Universidad de Chile.

Paredes, R. (1987). "Stylized Facts on Adjustment and Labor Market Trends in Chile." Universidad de Chile, mimeo.

Paredes, R., and L. Riveros (1993). "El rol de las regulaciones en el mercado laboral: el caso de Chile." *Estudios de Economía* 20, no. 1:41–68.

Pastor, M. (1987). "The Effects of IMF Programs in the Third World: Debate and Evidence for Latin America." *World Development* 15, no. 2.

Pero, V., and A. Urani (1993). "Determinantes do Excesso de Mão-de-Obra do Setor Formal do Mercado de Trabalho Metropolitano." In IPEA, *Perspectivas da Economia Brasileira—1994*. Rio de Janeiro: IPEA.

Petrei, A. Humberto (1984). "El presupuesto nacional de 1984." *Estudios* 7, no. 31.

Pfeffermann, G. (1985). "The Social Costs of Recession in Brazil." Washington, D.C.: World Bank, mimeo.

Pfeffermann, G., and R. Webb (1983). "Poverty and Income Distribution in Brazil." *Review of Income and Wealth* 29, no. 2.

Pollack, M., and A. Uthoff (1987). "Pobreza y mercado de trabajo en el Gran Santiago: 1969–1985." Santiago: ILO/PREALC, documentos de trabajo no. 299.

Portes, Alejandro, and Richard Schauffler (1992). "The Informal Economy in Latin America: Definition, Measurement, and Policies." PCID Working Paper Series No. 5 (Baltimore: Johns Hopkins University).

PREALC (Programa Regional de America Latina) (1985). *Beyond the Crisis.* Santiago: ILO.

Presidencia de la Republica (1994). *Quinto Informe de Gobierno, 1993.* Mexico: Presidencia de la Republica.

Programa Nacional de Asistencia Técnica para la Administración de los Servicios Sociales en la República Argentina (PRONATASS) (n.d.). "El gasto público social." Buenos Aires: Gobierno Argentino/BIRF/PNUD/ARG.88/005.

Psacharopoulos, G., S. Morley, A. Fiszbein, H. Lee, and B. Wood (1993). *Poverty and Income Distribution in Latin America: The Story of the 1980s.* Washington D.C.: World Bank, LATHR Report no. 27.

Raczynski, D., and P. Romaguera (1995). "Chile: Poverty, Adjustment and Social Policies in the 1980s." In N. Lustig, *Coping with Austerity: Poverty and Inequality in Latin America.* Washington, D.C.: Brookings Institution.

Ram, R. (1989). "Can Educational Expansion Reduce Income Inequality in Less Developed Countries?" *Economics of Education Review* 8, no. 2.

Ramírez, M. (1991). "Efectos de las Medidas de Apertura Sobre Produccion y Empleo." Bogotá: Ministerio de Trabajo y Seguridad Social.

Ramos, L. (1990). "The Distribution of Earnings in Brazil; 1976–1985." Ph.D. diss., University of California at Berkeley.

República de Colombia (1991). Presidencia y Departamento Nacional de Planeación. *La Revolución Pacifica: Modernización y Apertura de la Economía.* Bogotá: Departamento Nacional de Planeacion.

Revenga, A. (1994). "Employment and Wage Effects of Trade Liberalization: The Case of Mexican Manufacturing." Paper prepared for Labor Markets Workshop, World Bank, July.

Reyes Posada, A. (1987). "Tendencias del Empleo y la Distribución del Ingreso." In José Antonio Ocampo and Manuel Ramírez (eds.), *El Problema Laboral Colombiano: Informes a la Misión Chenery.* Bogotá: Contraloría General de la República, Departamento Nacional de Planeación and Servicio Nacional de Aprendizaje-SENA, Tomo 1.

Reyes Posada, A., S. Farné, J. Perdomo, and L. Angel Rodriguez (1996) "Distribucion de los Ingresos Urbanos en Colombia en la Decada del Noventa." Facultad de Economia, Universidad Externado de Colombia, Abril.

Ritter, A. R. M. (1992). *Development Strategy and Structural Adjustment in Chile: From the Unidiad Popular to the Concertación, 1970–92.* Ottawa: North-South Institute.

Riveros, L. A. (1985). "Desempleo, distribución del ingreso y política social." *Revista del Centro de Estudios Públicos,* no. 20. Santiago, Centro de Estudios Publicos (CEP).

——— (1986). "Labor Market Maladjustment in Chile: Economic Reforms and Friction Among Sub-Markets." *Analisis Economico* 1, no. 1 (November).

——— (1988). "International Comparisons of Wage and Non-Wage Costs of Labor." Washington, D.C.: World Bank research paper, CECMG, October.

——— (1992). "Labor Markets, Economic Restructuring and Human Resource Development in Latin America." Washington, D.C.: IDB, working paper.

―――― (1994). "Labor Markets in an Era of Adjustment: Chile." In Susan Horton, Ravi Kanbur, and Dipak Mazumdar (eds.), *Labor Markets in an Era of Adjustment.* Washington, D.C.: World Bank, EDI Development Studies.

Riveros, L., and R. Paredes (1990). "Factores Estructurales y Ciclicos y la Composición del Desempleo en Chile." *Revista de Análisis Económico* 5:47–60.

Riveros, L., and C. Weber (1987). "Structural Economic Reforms, Financial Stress and Targeting the Poor: Trends in Income Distribution and Social Expenditures in Chile, 1974–1981." Washington, D.C.: World Bank, CECDA, mimeo.

Robbins, D. J. (1994). "Relative Wage Structure in Chile, 1957–1992: Changes in the Structure of Demand for Schooling." Harvard University, draft.

Rocha, C. (1987). "The Market for Unskilled Labour in Brazil." Ph.D. diss., York University.

Rodriguez G., Jorge (1985). *La distribución del ingreso y el gasto social en Chile, 1983.* Santiago: ILADES.

Romer, P. (1986). "Increasing Returns and Long-run Growth." *Journal of Political Economy* 94.

Ros, J. (1994). "Mexico's Trade and Industrialization Experience Since 1960: A Reconsideration of Past Policies and Assessment of Current Reforms." In G. K. Helleiner, *Trade and Industrialization in Turbulent Times.* New York: Routledge.

Sabóia, J. M. (1986). "Transformações no Mercado de Trabalho no Brasil durante a Crise 1981–1983." *Revista de Economia Política* 6, no. 1.

Sanatan, I., and M. Rather (1993). "The Distributive Impact of Fiscal Policy in the Dominican Republic." In Ricardo Hausmann and Roberto Rigobón (eds.), *Government Spending and Income Distribution in Venezuela.* Washington, D.C., and Venezuela: IDB and IESA.

Santiago, C. (1992). *Labor in the Puerto Rican Economy: Postwar Development and Stagnation.* New York: Praeger.

Santiere, J. J. (1989). "Distribución de la carga tributaria por niveles de ingreso." Buenos Aires: Banco Mundial-Secretaría de Hacienda, documento de investigación, mimeo.

Sarmiento A., Libardo (1993). "Política Social y Gasto Público en los Noventa: Qué Tan Significativos Son los Cambios?" *Coyuntura Social,* no. 8, Agosto.

Sarmiento, E. (1995). "Se hizo el milagro de la distribucion del ingreso?" *Coyuntura Social* 12, Fedesarrollo, Bogotá, Mayo.

Sedlacek, G. (1989). "A Evolução da Distribuição de Renda entre 1984 e 1987." In IPEA, *Perspectivas da Economia Brasileira—1990.* Rio de Janeiro: IPEA.

Sheahan, J. (1994). "Experiencias en America Latina." Paper presented at the conference on "Retos y Perspectivos de la Economia Peruana," organized by the Consorcio de Investigacion Economica, Lima, 22–23 November.

Sotomayor, O. J. (1996). "Poverty and Income Inequality in Puerto Rico, 1969–89: Trends and Sources." *Review of Income and Wealth* 42, no. 1.

Stallings, B. (1992). "International Influence on Economic Policy: Debt, Stabilization and Structural Reform." In Stephan Haggard and Robert Kaufman (eds.), *The Politics of Economic Adjustment.* Princeton: Princeton University Press.

Taylor, L. (1981). "IS-LM in the Tropics: Diagrammatics of the New Structuralist Macro-Critique." In W. Cline and S. Weintraub (eds.), *Economic Stabilization in Developing Countries.* Washinton, D.C.: Brookings Institution.

Tenjo, J. (1993). "Evolucion de los Retornos a la Inversion en Educacion 1976–89." In *Educacion, Mercado de Trabajo y Desarrollo en Colombia,* special issue of *Planeación y Desarrollo.* Bogotá: Departamento Nacional de Planeación.

Thoumi, F. E. (1979). "La Utilización del Capital Fijo en la Industria Manufacturera Colombiana." *Revista de Planeación y Desarrollo* (Septiembre–Diciembre).

Tokman, V. E. (1989). "Urban Employment Problems: Research and Policy in Latin America." In Bernard Salome (ed.), *Fighting Urban Unemployment in Developing Countries*. Paris: OECD Development Centre.

———— (1990). "Le Secteur Informel en Amérique Latine: Quinze Ans Après." In B. Salomé, A. Schwarz, and D. Turnham (eds.), *Nouvelles Approches du Secteur Informel*. Paris: Séminaires du Centre de Développement de l'OCDE.

Torche, A. (1985). "Pobreza y Politica Fiscal." Documento de Trabajo. Santiago de Chile: Universidad Catolica.

Torres, C. (1982). "Evolución de la Política Arancelaria: Período 1973–1981." Santiago: Central Bank, Report no. 16.

Trejos, J. D. (1991). "Crisis, ajuste y pobreza: La experiencia de Costa Rica en los ochenta." Paper presented at the Seminar on Macroeconomic Crises, Policy Reforms and the Poor in Latin America, Cali, Colombia, 1–4 October.

Trejos, J. D., and M. L. Elizalde E. (1986). "Ingresos, Desigualdad y Empleo: Evidencias Recientes Sobre Las Caracteristicas y Evolucion del Perfil Distributivo en Costa Rica." *Revista Ciencias Economicas* 6, no. 2.

Trejos, J. D., and P. Sauma (1994). "Pobreza y distribucion del ingreso en el era del ajuste: Costa Rica 1980–1992." Paper presented at the symposium "El Impacto del Ajuste Estructural en los Mercados de Trabajo y en la Distribucion del Ingreso en America Latina." San José, Costa Rica, September.

UNCTAD (1992). *Trade Liberalization in Chile*. New York: United Nations, Trade Policy series no. 1.

United Nations (several issues). *Monthly Bulletin of Statistics*.

Urani, A. (1993a). "Políticas de Estabilização e Equidade no Brasil: Uma Análise Contra-Factual 1981–1983." *Pesquisa e Planejamento Econômico* 23, no. 1.

———— (1993b). "Mercado de Trabalho e Distribuição de Renda durante o Governo Collor." In IPEA, *Perspectivas da Economia Brasileira—1994*. Rio de Janeiro: IPEA.

———— (1994). "A Evolução da Ocupação na Indústria de Transformação." Rio de Janeiro: Banco Nacional de Desenvolvimento Economico e Social (BNDES), mimeo.

———— (1995a). "Tendências Recentes da Evolução da Ocupação." In H. Zylberztaijn (ed.), *O Trabalho no Brasil no Limiar do Século XXI*. São Paulo: USP/OIT.

———— (1995b). "Ajuste Macroeconômico e Flexibilidade do Mercado de Trabalho no Brasil." In J. M. Camargo (ed.), *A Flexibilidade Perversa*. Rio de Janeiro: Contraponto.

Urani, A., and C. Winograd (1994). "Distributional Effects of Stabilization Policies in a Dual Economy: The Case of Brazil 1981–1988." *Revista Brasileira de Economia* 48, no. 1.

Vargas de Flood, M. Cristina, and M. M. Harriague (1993). "El gasto público consolidado." Buenos Aires: Secretaría de Programación Económica, documento de trabajo GP/02.

Villar, L. (1983). "Las Exportaciones Menores en Colombia: Determinantes de su Evolución y su Composición." M.A. thesis, Universidad de los Andes, Bogotá.

Wade, R. (1990). *Governing the Market: Economic Theory and the Role of Government in East Asian Industrialization*. Princeton: Princeton University Press.

Walton, G. M. (ed.) (1985). *The National Economic Policies in Chile, Contemporary Studies in Economic and Financial Analysis* 51. New York: Jai Press.

Weisskoff, R. (1992a). "The Paraguayan Agro-Export Model of Development." *World Development* 20, no. 10.

———— (1992b). "Income Distribution and Economic Change in Paraguay, 1972–88." *The Review of Income and Wealth* 38, no. 2 (June).

Williamson, J. (1990). "The Progress of Policy Reform in Latin America." Washington, D.C.: Institute for International Economics (IIE), Policy Analyses in International Economics, no. 28, January.

———— (ed.) (1990). *Latin American Adjustment: How Much Has Happened?* Washington, D.C.: IIE.

Winograd, C. (1991). "Inflation Chronique Elevée, Indéxation et Stabillization Héterodoxe: Le Plan Cruzado au Brésil." Mimeo.

World Bank (1980). *World Tables: The Second Edition.* Baltimore, Md.: Johns Hopkins University Press for the World Bank.

———— (1988). "Ecuador—Country Economic Memorandum." Washington, D.C.: World Bank.

———— (1991). *World Development Report 1991. A Challenge of Development.* Washington, D.C.: Oxford University Press.

———— (1993a). *The East Asian Miracle: Economic Growth and Public Policy.* New York: Oxford University Press.

———— (1993b). *World Development Report 1993.* Washington, D.C.: World Bank.

———— (1995). *World Development Report 1995.* Washington, D.C.: World Bank.

Yañez, J. (1979). "Una Corrección del Indice de Precios al Consumidor Durante el Período 1971–1973." Universidad de Chile, Santiago, Departmento de Economía, Documento Serie Investigación no 34.

————. (1993). "Capitulo Politica Fiscal." In Universidad de Chile, *Analisis Economico.* Santiago de Chile: Universidad de Chile.

Index

About the Book

The recent worsening of income distribution in Latin America and the implications of that worsening for the alleviation of poverty are the focus of this collection of two comparative chapters and six country studies. The authors conclude that economic reforms have contributed significantly to the increase in inequality; and that the economic crisis of the 1980s, while clearly playing a part, has not been the sole, and perhaps not even the major, factor in this trend.

Albert Berry is a professor of economics at the University of Toronto. His many publications include *Global Development Half a Century After Bretton-Woods* (coedited with Roy Culpeper and Frances Stewart) and *Success in Small and Medium-Scale Enterprises: The Evidence from Colombia* (coauthored with M. Cortes and A. Ishaq).